Copyright for Schools:
A Practical Guide
4th Edition

Carol Simpson

Linworth
Books

Professional Development Resources for
K-12 Library Media and Technology Specialists

Library of Congress Cataloging-in-Publication Data

Simpson, Carol, 1949-
   Copyright for schools : a practical guide / Carol Simpson.—4th ed.
      p. cm.
   Includes bibliographical references and index.
   ISBN 1-58683-192-5 (pbk.)
      1. Fair use (Copyright)—United States—Popular works. 2.
Copyright—United States—Popular works. I. Title.
KF3020.Z9S57 2005
346.7304'82—dc22

                                                    2005005430

Published by Linworth Publishing, Inc.
480 East Wilson Bridge road, Suite L
Worthington, Ohio 43085

ISBN 1-58683-192-5

5 4 3 2 1

Table of Contents

Table of Figures

Acknowledgements

The creation and revision of a book of this sort requires the background assistance of many, many people. I am assisted daily by teaching assistants, colleagues, editorial assistants and editors, attorneys, librarians (of all types), friends, and family. Remove even one of those of my support network and this book never sees print.

I have special words of appreciation for three people who reviewed this manuscript in development: Steve Gillen, Esq., of Cincinnati, OH; Dr. Sara Wolf, Auburn University; and Dr. Judi Repman, Georgia Southern University. Their comments were always helpful. I also thank the many, many people who email copyright questions, from whom the sample questions in this book are drawn.

My interest in copyright is leading me on a new path, and I can count the many friends I have made on this adventure for that epiphany. To the librarians and teachers and administrators who have invited me to share my thoughts on copyright and schools, I humbly thank you for your confidence. To my publisher, Marlene Woo-Lun, who puts up with an author who refuses to sign a contract because she doesn't want a deadline, I apologize. To my mother and daughter, who wonder where their mom and daughter has disappeared, I may emerge. To my elder son, who knows exactly where I am four nights a week for four years, I will see you in class. And to my husband, who is doing without home cooked meals, doing his own laundry, and cleaning house for four years while I indulge my fascination for copyright, I love you.

For David: 1979-2003.

Introduction to the 4th Edition

Why did you pick up this volume? This isn't light reading, though it may be an excellent soporific if you need to get some sleep. Copyright, to many, is deadly dull and grossly frightening at the same time. Many are convinced that a copyright violation cannot ever happen in their schools, and they will loudly proclaim the fact as they photocopy sheets from a workbook or pop the Disney tape into the VCR during rainy day recess.

The fact is that copyright is an everyday dilemma, and one that can only be solved by significant education. I enjoy doing copyright workshops; I feel they are some of my best teaching. This book is an attempt to share what I do in a workshop, but without the funny faces, silly voices, and other human-interest types of stories that I toss in. I even omitted the jokes. Sorry, but they just come across as odd when reduced to print.

This edition of *Copyright for Schools* updates aspects of the law that affect schools. In addition, I have continued "Copyright catechism." The dictionary defines the term "catechism" as learning through questions and answers. I've included representative questions about facets of copyright that I have answered in my *Copyright Question of the Month* columns from the journal *Library Media Connection*, and others that I am asked during presentations to educators and librarians. These aren't answers to specific, real-life quandaries and certainly don't substitute for competent legal advice, but these hypotheticals can guide you as you wrestle with your own copyright conundrums.

As I've stated in previous editions of this book, I am not an attorney. I've been researching and writing about copyright laws and schools for about 18 years now. I started researching my obligations under the law in response to a technological installation. I was astounded at the requirements that I had never learned but which put me and my faculty and administrators at risk. Fortunately, I had a supportive principal and an ethical faculty. All this isn't to say we were always "copyright clean" but we had a building expectation of compliance, we regularly trained our staff, and we monitored our materials and uses with an intent to comply with the various laws. Since that time I have continued to read, question, and try to understand. My quest led me to the only place possible to get all the information in the right way—law school. Attending law school gives you a new perspective and appreciation for the law, and its interpretation, and how different courts will view similar sets of facts in totally opposite ways.

This monograph presents the safest position—that level of practice considered to be within legal limits by the most conservative application of the law. Certainly you might choose to stretch the recommendations, and you might never be challenged. In some instances, the recommended practices might even be considered ultraconservative. The National Commission on New Technological Uses of Copyrighted Works (a.k.a. CONTU) Guidelines, for instance, if followed to the letter, might deny some user an arguably legitimate interlibrary loan. Some interpretations must necessarily be a judgment call, and they will be so noted.

Don't feel so frightened of copyright that you fail to employ every available opportunity to provide resources to your students, teachers, and colleagues. But the further afield you go from conservative interpretation, the stronger your rationale and your documentation should be. You will need both, if challenged. Don't confuse rationale with rationalization (in the Webster's New Collegiate Dictionary sense of "to attribute one's actions to rational and creditable motives, without adequate analysis of true motives"). Infringers frequently rationalize their acts in regard to copyright. Such explanations will not stand up to legal scrutiny.

Above all, stand fast. The easiest road is not always the right and proper way. For many reasons, our government and the governments of dozens of countries around the world have protected authors and enabled educators to utilize intellectual property for research and teaching. The interests of one group influence and restrict the rights of the other. The balance is fragile. As educators and librarians, we want to provide whatever our patrons desire. As teachers and citizens, we have an obligation to model ethical and lawful behavior for our students. Make no excuses.

The information presented in this volume is not intended to substitute for qualified legal advice, but rather as a way to help you determine if you need to consult an attorney for detailed guidance on a given situation. If you have any doubt that your activities are within the law, first read the law itself. It is available online from many sites. The suggestions and guidelines contained within this book can help you decide if you are erring on the side of conservatism, or if you might be straying to the hazardous side of the street. If in doubt, consult an attorney—preferably one who specializes in intellectual property (commonly listed as copyrights, trademarks, and patents or some combination of those terms). Because copyright and intellectual property are not required courses in law school, often specialists in educational law are unaware of the multitude of layers of copyright protection. I know of several instances in which school district attorneys gave advice that was inaccurate based on even the most liberal interpretation of copyright law. Many copyright attorneys will consult with you for an hour, providing authoritative legal advice, for the sum of a couple of hundred dollars. When dealing with your professional livelihood, two or three hundred dollars is a small sum to pay for a good night's sleep and it can provide enough dependable backup for a firm stand against those who would have you participate in questionable activities. All these rules and regulations may seem to be too complicated to be worth the trouble. After all, you haven't been caught so far, right? Cease and desist letters are on the rise, and reported cases of schools violating copyright from computer software piracy (Los Angeles Unified School District) to photocopying workbooks (Beaumont, TX, Independent School District) are only the beginning of the story.

Perhaps a parable will put the whole copyright problem into perspective.

Two second graders are fighting over a ruler. One child is on each end of the ruler, pulling alternately.

"It's mine!" one yells, pulling the ruler.

"No, it's mine!" yells the other, pulling harder in the opposite direction.

The teacher steps in, claiming the disputed ruler. She determines to whom the ruler belongs, turns over the item, and sends him on his way. Taking the other child in tow, she scolds him sternly.

"You don't take what isn't yours without asking first!"

You don't take what isn't yours without asking first.

That's all copyright is about.

— *Carol Simpson*
January, 2005

Chapter 1

The Law

It has a name: Title 17, United States Code, Public Law 94-553, 90 Stat. 2541, as amended. Kind of dry sounding, isn't it? Who would guess that this could be one of the most obtuse, complex and arguably the most hated law affecting schools today? But that is it: US copyright law.

If you are reading this book, you have somehow been affected by the law. Either you want to use someone else's material, and you were stopped/cautioned by a colleague or superior, or you are reading about it for a class you are taking, or perhaps you have been assigned duties dealing with copyright protected materials and you want to protect yourself and your institution. Regardless of the reason, you need to know something about copyright law and you need to know it quickly. Quickly may be more than you can expect, but getting to know the law is a matter of a few key concepts. Once you have those in mind, they apply fairly regularly to just about any situation you might encounter.

History

Copyright dates back several centuries, to English common law. Tradition holds that the Statute of Anne is the first true copyright "law," though there had been attempts prior to that date to control copying of materials. Even chaining books to shelves and restricting the copying to trained monks in monasteries was a form of copyright enforcement.

Origin in the U.S.

As early as the beginning of the 18th century, publishers and authors in England had a legal right to control reproduction of their works. The United States based its original copyright law on the English version as well as providing protection through wording in the U.S. Constitution: " . . . securing for limited times to authors . . . the exclusive right to their . . . writings . . ." (Article I, Section 8). While many school people may be surprised, Washington actually signed the first U.S. copyright law in 1789. Most people believe that copyright is a much more recent invention. The U.S. law has been rewritten several times over the ensuing years. The last major revision occurred in 1976, with minor modifications in the years since.

What it is now

Copyright has changed over the years. From the first U.S. copyright law signed by George Washington in 1789, to the current iteration passed in 1976 and tweaked almost annually since, copyright has had a significant impact on the U.S. But knowing what happened before is only useful in obtuse cases dealing with old material. For most school employees, 99.999% of their copyright questions can be addressed by the current law. So what you need to know is: What does a copyright owner own, and what must I exercise caution in using?

Rights of a copyright holder

The six rights that a copyright owner owns are the rights of: reproduction, adaptation, distribution, public performance, public display, and digital transmission of sound recordings. Knowing what a copyright owner owns is key to understanding how to interpret most copyright situations. Starting initially as simply a right to copy (hence the term "copyright") or print, the rights of the copyright holder in the United States have gradually expanded to be six rights accorded to the original creator. Should someone infringe, or violate, a copyright, a single infringement may violate all six rights at the same time, but copyright is violated if even one of the six exclusive rights is abridged.

What the creator does with the rights given in a copyright is his own business. Rights are similar to property rights in that the owner may rent, lease, lend or sell outright any or all of the rights in the work. The rights may be sold as a bundle, or can be meted out, either as an exclusive or non-exclusive basis. For example, if you purchase a video program with public performance rights, it is unlikely that you would be the only person who has purchased those performance rights. It would be likely that the copyright owner has offered a public performance license to many people, besides you.

It is also possible that the right(s) sold/licensed are not for an infinite period of time. It is not unusual for an author to sell the rights to a book to a publishing company. However, in the contract of sale there may be a clause that states the rights to the work revert to the author if the book does not remain in print for a specified number of years. Why is that significant to schools? It's not uncommon for a teacher to have a favorite book of short stories or a spelling workbook, or other teaching tool, which is many years old. The work will likely be out of print. Nevertheless, the teacher would like to use several sections of the work in class. Because the use will be repeated from term to term, the teacher would need to get permission to use the materials or pay a royalty since the plans she has for the material exceed the permitted educational limits. The choice of permission or royalty belongs to the copyright owner. However, the publishing company may be out of business, and there appears to be no one from whom to get permission or to whom to pay a royalty. In such a case, it would be worth investigating the author(s) of the work as the copyright may have reverted to the author when the work went out of print.

In discussing the various rights, starting on page 17, consider that this is a baseline discussion of what the copyright owner owns, and does not take into consideration any possible exemptions found in the law or in associated guidelines. In addition, rights may be modified with permission or license. With a license granted to do any of the actions prohibited in the discussions of the rights, the end user can do whatever they have gotten permission, or paid a license, to do.

Reproduction

The right of reproduction is the fundamental right of copyright, and was the initial impetus for the law. Reproduction in all formats is controlled by the copyright owner or his assigns/agents. The law specifically mentions various formats when identifying this right by indicating that non-print reproduction ("phonorecords") is also a right reserved to the copyright holder.

An important fact to remember is that copies need not be exact to be considered reproductions. If you were to make a drawing of Mickey Mouse on a piece of paper, and if such drawing were recognizable as Mickey Mouse, for the purposes of this portion of the law, the drawing would be of Mickey Mouse. Just because a few details (colors, words, notes) have been changed doesn't mean that the use is beyond the restrictions of this right. Making a change in format such as recording a book or digitizing a photo could also be considered to be making a copy or an adaptation or derivative work. Don't assume that the word "copy" only means photocopy. The law was written in this form long before photocopiers were in common use. In the case *Hearn v. Meyer* (664 F. Supp. 832) the court ruled that manual copying was as much an infringement as photocopying. More details on this aspect will be seen in the chapter on Fair Use.

Adaptation

Adaptation is changing a work in some way, or creating a derivative work based on the original. Derivative works are new works created from older, possibly protected works. JK Rowling gets paid a lot of money to write books, but she gets paid a lot more when those books are adapted into screenplays and produced as movies or plays. Some authors are very protective of this right, while others take the phrase "imitation is the most sincere form of flattery" to heart. Taking a popular song and writing new words is adaptation. Turning a picture book into a play for the second grade to perform for the PTA is adaptation. Taking the characters of a book and extending the story is adaptation. Scanning a print work into a digital copy is both reproduction (making a copy) and adaptation (changing the format). The same thing happens when a student modifies the work of an artist to create a new piece of art, or a teacher converts a cartoon into digital format for a PowerPoint™ presentation. All of these instances create derivative works. Not all of these uses may be illegal, depending on the surrounding circumstances, but on the surface all these activities potentially infringe on the author's right of adaptation and should be examined by the user.

Other common derivatives are indexes, translations, concordances, abridgements, and recordings of musical works. Some derivative works, however, are entitled to copyright protection themselves (at least on the added value portions of the work and especially when the original work has fallen into the public domain) so one must not assume that all derivatives are under the control of the original copyright owner.

Distribution

When a teacher creates copies of a graphic in a book, the right of reproduction comes into play. When the teacher passes out those copies to her class, the action is affected by the right of distribution. Distribution can occur in many ways. Mailing home newsletters is distribution. Loaning books from the library is distribution. Sending video around the building using the video distribution system is distribution. Putting computer software on the campus network is distribution. Forwarding an e-mail is distribution. Putting student work on the Web is distribution to the world.

Limitation on right of distribution: first sale doctrine

If the right of distribution were absolute, you couldn't give a book to your niece for Christmas, nor could you have a yard sale. Cutting up a calendar with lovely photos would not be possible, nor would weeding a library of obsolete materials. In fact, loaning books from the library would be a violation of the author's right of distribution as well. So how can we do all of those things and still stay within the law? We rely on a nifty piece of legal doctrine known colloquially as the "right of first sale."

Before we can understand the first sale doctrine, however, we must understand what one owns when one owns a book, for example. When you purchase a book at the local bookstore, you have purchased paper, ink, binding, and a license to read the words until it wears out. You have not purchased the words themselves, nor the expression of the ideas discussed within. First sale doctrine explains that the right of distribution ceases with an item's first sale, meaning that you can do whatever you wish, physically, with the book. You can wrap it up and give it to your niece; you can rip out the pages and wallpaper your study; you can try to get a decent price for the book at a yard sale; you can donate it to the Friends of the Library book sale; you can even toss that book into the dumpster if you are so inclined. You own that one physical (as opposed to intellectual) copy of that book, and the copyright owner can do nothing at all to stop whatever private use you make of that physical copy. The copyright owner can attempt to stop you from using that work to make commercial advantage if, for example, you were to carefully remove the plates in a book of photography and frame them to sell in an art gallery. Such use is not private, and could potentially interfere with the copyright owner's own commercial use of his work.

A group of recording artists challenged the first sale doctrine several years ago when they tried to boycott used CD stores. They claimed that the stores were making money on their previously sold works, without paying royalties. The protest died, however, when it was pointed out that they had received their sales royalties the first time the CD was sold, and they no longer held any control over those copies. A case that was controversial and troubling for librarians was decided in 1997. The court held that a library could be found guilty of infringement via distribution. The LDS Church had purchased a single set of research materials, and made copies which it distributed to its branch libraries. The branch libraries allowed researchers to use those materials only within the confines of the branch library.

The distributed materials were later found to be illegal copies, and the library was held to be liable for distribution of the illegal materials even though the copies were never removed from the library (*Hotaling v. Church of Jesus Christ of Latter-Day Saints*, 118 F.3d 199 (4th Cir. 1997)). The ruling stated: "When a public library adds a work to its collection, lists the work in its index or catalog system, and makes the work available to the borrowing or browsing public, it has completed all the steps necessary for distribution to the public. At that point, members of the public can visit the library and use the work." (*Hotaling*, 1997, p. 203) Such a ruling makes libraries, in particular, concerned that the materials they hold are legal and legitimate.

Public performance

The right to perform a work publicly is reserved to a copyright owner. "Performance" indicates a work of film, video, dance, theatre, music, etc. A work need not be performed in its entirety to be considered "performed." In fact, a recent posting on the CNI-Copyright e-mail list discussed the amount of a work that must be used to be considered significant. One lawyer replied that if the work is recognizable, enough has been performed to be considered "significant." Naturally, disagreements over that amount would abound, which is why such definitions are hoped for in court rulings.

What is "public"?

Key to understanding both public performance and public display is comprehension of the legal definition of the term "public." The law defines a public performance as: to perform or display it at a place open to the public or at any place where a substantial number of persons outside of a normal circle of a family and its social acquaintances is gathered; or to transmit or otherwise communicate a performance or display of the work to a place specified by [the previous] clause or to the public, by means of any device or process, whether the members of the public capable of receiving the performance or display receive it in the same place or in separate places and at the same time or at different times.

What you do in the privacy of your own home, in the company of your family and your intimate friends, is not considered "public" for the purposes of our discussions of copyright. So, when discussing a performance of a film, for example, if you were to have the showing in your home, with your spouse and your children present, such a showing would not be considered a public performance and the showing would not be controlled by the copyright owner. Inviting the next-door neighbor, his wife, and their two children over to your home to see the same film would also likely not be considered "public." However, the farther you reach beyond an intimate group such as this, the more "public" you become. If you invite your entire church

---

Q: A magazine article encouraged students to use discarded books by using them to create covers and new artwork. Some of the books almost didn't even look like books when the students were finished! However, what about the copyright issue of changing the format of an existing work?

A: Actually, the students in this project weren't changing the format of the work. They were using the book itself as a building block of a work of art. Because of the first sale doctrine, the physical copy of the book belongs to the first person who buys it. Without the first sale doctrine, libraries wouldn't be able to loan books to patrons! The copyright owner has no further control over the physical property of that book. The book owner can give the book away, loan it, sell it, destroy it, or rip it apart. The copyright owner still owns the intellectual content of the work, but the paper, ink and binding belong to another. In this case, the students were using the physical book to create new artwork, not using the intellectual content of the book (the part that is protected by copyright).

school class and their spouses over for a party, and you show *The Passion of the Christ*, you may be skating on very thin ice regarding the public performance right. Certainly a public school classroom is considered "public." No matter that we may want our students to view the school as "home" and "family-like," the fact remains that the school is a public place. Gatherings such as a Boy Scout or PTA meeting would be considered public. In fact, an important federal court ruling known as Redd Horne set the standard for private and public when the court ruled that a performance of a video in a private, closed viewing room in a commercial video store was, in fact, a public performance. Performances in public places are controlled by the copyright owner under the right of public performance.

Public display

Like the right of public performance, the right of public display controls works displayed in public places. Displays outside the home are controlled by the copyright owner. A display is of something static, such as a painting, photograph, or sculpture. It could also apply to literature if the work were exposed to public viewing, such as on the Internet. Section 109 (c) of the law allows legally acquired copies of artwork to be displayed where that work is located; so you can hang a poster you have purchased, or you can display the books that the library owns, but you can't scan those into a Web page and display them around the world. This limited exception to public display does not carry over into public performances of things like movies, videos, sound recordings, or music, etc.

Digital transmission of sound recordings

The newest of the copyright owner's rights, the right of digital transmission of sound recording, came into being with the enactment of the Digital Millennium Copyright Act. The right is a reaction to the loss of control over sound recordings when they are in digital formats. Users would listen to Internet radio stations that streamed pristine digital recordings, and while listening they would capture the audio files. As you know, each digital copy is just as perfect as the original. Users could burn their own CDs of their favorite songs rather than going to the music store to purchase copies. As a result, earnings in the music industry began to decline. Users were getting the music without paying any fees whatsoever.

As a result, based on the number of listeners, Internet radio stations are required to pay hefty royalties to record companies (the copyright owners) through rights brokering organizations. Such fees are not new. Analog (AM and FM) radio stations have paid licensing fees for many years. However, the mandatory fees imposed on digital transmission were many times higher than those paid by analog stations, primarily because of the ability to copy perfect quality transmissions. Record companies felt that they should get their share of the profits one way or another. This new right allows them to do just that.

Moral rights

A new group of rights was granted by Congress in 1990 called "moral rights." These rights apply to certain types of visual artwork (painting, sculpture, etc.) that are produced in limited quantities (fewer than 200). In such cases the author can require that his/her name remain with the object. In addition, the artists have some power to prevent their artworks from being defaced or destroyed. In one case a sculptor successfully sued a municipality when a large sculpture, installed on city property, was destroyed without his permission. Moral rights would be significant for a school if the school had students paint a mural, or other artwork. The students would own the copyright in the work, and could demand that their names be displayed with the work. In addition, if the work was damaged or destroyed, intentionally or unintentionally, the students would have grounds to sue the school for a violation of moral rights. Painting over the work, remodeling the building, or even allowing other students to deface the work with graffiti could be taken as potential causes for action. Censoring copies of a work, such as putting pants on the naked boy in Maurice Sendak's *In the Night Kitchen* would not fall under this aspect of copyright since that copy is not the original artwork. It would, however, be an act of censorship, but that is a topic for another discussion.

How does one get a copyright?

In the years up to 1976, authors had to proactively register their works in order to achieve copyright protection. There were certain requirements for a copyright notice, paperwork to be filed with the copyright office, a limited amount of time in which one had to file for the copyright, a determination if the work had been published prior to registration, and appropriate fees to be paid. If any of the points were not accomplished in exactly the prescribed manner, the copyright registration was null and void, and the work then fell into the public domain.

With the enactment of the 1976 copyright law, a work became protected as soon as it was "fixed in tangible form." The term "tangible form" means that the work is retrievable—that it isn't ephemeral. A work may be fixed by being:

- *written on paper*
- *painted on canvas*
- *saved to disk*
- *recorded on tape*
- *exposed on film*
- *or any other method that creates a permanent record of the creation*

Any creative work that is recorded in such a manner is automatically granted the protection of copyright for the author/creator. Other types of creation, such as skywriting, or extemporaneous performances that are not recorded, cannot be protected by copyright. In order to get the protection of copyright, no notice is required, nor is registration essential.

These changes came about as a result of the United States signing the Berne Convention in 1988, a worldwide treaty that provided agreement among nations for each to protect the copyrights of the others under a country's own laws. This agreement made copyright enforcement easier because one only needed to know the copyright laws of one's own country rather than those of hundreds of nations. For example, if you were to write a book and publish it in the United States, you would only have to make appropriate registration here in the U.S. France, Germany, and Egypt (among many others) would protect your work under their laws as if the work had been registered in all of those countries. This agreement also makes copyright compliance easier from a user's point of view in that we only have to know the copyright laws of one country—our own. The U.S. protects the

Q: Why would I want to go to the trouble to register my creation?

A: While registration is not required to achieve a copyright, it is needed before a suit is filed.

Q: Do students own the copyright on the works they create?

A: Yes. Original student works are protected by copyright just as any other creative work. Because most public school students are minors, however, parents or legal guardians must grant permission in writing for schools to use student work in publications, exhibits, and other public uses. Displays inside the classroom don't require the extensive permission.

copyrights of all the Berne signatories under the laws of the U.S. In most instances, we needn't learn the copyright rules of France, Germany, and Egypt or any of the other countries signing the treaty.

HOWEVER, if one wishes to be able to sue for damages should the copyright be infringed, "timely" registration of the copyright is required. The necessary information on registration of a copyright is available from the Copyright Office in Washington, DC (**www.copyright.gov**).

Registration requires submission of a number of copies of the work to the Copyright Office, along with a completed form and the necessary fee. The fee varies from time to time and from type of work registered, but typically it is about $30 per work. Works can be registered as a "collection," so someone who writes short stories or haiku can rest assured that they won't go broke registering each small item.

What can't be protected by copyright?

An important concept in copyright law is that facts are not protectable. Facts are owned by all mankind, and no one person owns, for example, the multiplication tables, or the list of the 10 longest rivers in the world. However, if someone were to write a narrative about either of those two factual representations, as long as there was a modicum of creativity involved, the expression of those facts would be protected by copyright to the extent that the expression was creative.

Works that have not been fixed in a tangible medium of expression, such as dance that has not been codified or recorded, or an improvisational speech that has not been transcribed or recorded, cannot be protected by copyright. Recent upheaval about university note-taking services such as **cramster.com** have emphasized that course lecture notes are protected by copyright because they are fixed, but the actual delivery of the lecture (unless the notes are read verbatim) is not protected. Professors who tape-record their lectures or who have them stenographically recorded may own the copyright on those lectures.

Q: We'd like to print and sell a recipe book for a fundraiser. What copyright implications are there?

A: Recipes consisting of lists of ingredients and simple assembly instructions may be freely reproduced as they are not protectable by copyright. In fact, similar recipes in published cookbooks may be used. The copyright on most cookbooks is primarily a "compilation copyright"— a copyright on the selection and arrangement of the items, not on the items themselves.

Titles, short phrases, names, common symbols or designs (like a stop sign), slight variations on type styles, lettering or coloring, or lists of ingredients cannot be protected by copyright. Ideas, procedures, methods, and discoveries are not protectable, but descriptions or illustrations of these items may be protected by copyright. Works containing only non-protected material with no original authorship, such as plain calendars, lists of common facts, charts of measures, etc. are not protected.

Works created by the U.S. Government may not be protected by copyright. This prohibition involves works created by members of Congress within their congressional duties, or employees of federal agencies as part of their job responsibilities. Some federally funded projects written by non-federal employees may have copyright protection, so it is always wise to investigate the copyright status of any work before making free use of it. The works of state and local governmental agencies may or may not be protected by copyright.

Check thoroughly

Works that are not creative cannot be protected by copyright. In 1991, the Supreme Court held that a traditional alphabetical telephone directory did not contain enough original, non-factual materials to be considered eligible for copyright protection (*Feist Publications, Inc. v. Rural Telephone Service Co., Inc.*, 499 U.S. 340 (1991)).

Work for hire

Now, I will tell you that I have lied to you. While it is true that a copyright vests at the moment of creation, it doesn't always go to the creator. Take, for example, a classroom teacher who teaches fourth grade science. For her class, she creates a series of science worksheets. The worksheets are particularly effective, so the teacher would like to compile the worksheets into a book that she will offer to a publisher. The only catch to this plan is that the teacher's district owns the copyright in the worksheets, barring any contract or agreement that would restrict that arrangement. The reason this is true is that the worksheets were created as part of the teacher's job. This concept is known as "work for hire." Just about anything that a teacher does within the context of his or her job could be claimed as the intellectual property of the school. A common question is to inquire if doing the work at home or on weekends or vacation makes any difference in the work for hire rules. Actually, no, it makes no difference. If the work was done "within the scope of employment" it matters little where or when the work was done. If the work was for fourth grade science, in this example, the school could make a very good case that the work belonged to them. However, if you are teaching fourth grade science, but write a college physics textbook in your spare time at home, the school would be hard pressed to convince a court that this work was part of your work as a fourth grade science teacher.

Since a teacher doesn't own the copyright in the work made for hire, he has the same limitations on materials he created as the average teacher-on-the-street. If the teacher changes districts, he should ask the district he is leaving if he may have permission to continue to use and/or adapt those materials. Get that permission in writing.

An idea to create something isn't sufficient to achieve a copyright since ideas themselves are not protectable, but the actual creation of the work is. So if you came up with an idea for some exam review materials or flash cards, but other district employees actually write the items themselves, you would likely not have a claim on the copyright in those items. If there are other contributors to the work, such that no one person is responsible, you would have difficulty claiming ownership of the copyright even if the initial idea were yours. If this work were mounted within an online site, for example, Web designers, instructional designers, etc. can all be considered partial "authors," and if they are district employees, there would be a strong case that the district is the owner of the work.

A clause in teacher contracts regarding copyright ownership can forestall later disagreements. On the other hand, contract work may or may not be work for hire, depending on the contract written. Specific types of work such as parts of a collective work (e.g. book chapters), part of a film or other audiovisual work, a test, an instructional text, a translation, etc. (though not a sound recording) can be considered works for hire but only if there is a written contract so stating. So, a teacher who works over the summer under a supplemental, piece work contract to produce a curriculum guide might, in fact, own the copyright to the guide produced. The school would want to have a written agreement, signed by all parties, to assure that the copyright of the resulting product belongs, in fact, to the school. Some schools have encountered problems with this facet of copyright law when dealing with volunteers (adult or student) who work on school Web pages. Forewarned is forearmed.

Duration of copyright

Copyright, as of the publication date of this book, lasts for the life of the author, plus 70 years. If there are two or more authors, the work is protected for the life of the longest lived author, plus 70 years. For works of corporate authorship (such as a film where there are dozens of contributors, or a committee report or other internal document of an organization), works for hire and pseudonymous works, copyright protection extends for 95 years from the date a work is published or 120 years from the date it was created, whichever is shorter. For works published by a group (the National Education Association or the Association for Supervision and Curriculum Development, for example) or works of diffuse authorship such as a film (there is a producer, director, actors, editors, musicians, set designers, wardrobe, make up, etc. who all contribute to the final product) the duration of copyright is 95 years from the date of creation of the work. Works published before 1923 are currently in the public domain in the United States. Those created prior to 1923 but never published may still be protected. Those created between 1923 and 1978 have varying periods of copyright protection. The time of creation (or registration) determines if, and how long, a work is protected. Laura Gasaway, librarian and law professor, has a Web page that explains when works pass out of the protection of copyright at: **http://www.unc.edu/~unclng/public-d.htm**.

The durations identified above pertain to works created after October 27, 1998 when the Sonny Bono Copyright Term Extension Act went into effect. A work created today will not be in the public domain within our lifetimes if the effective term of protection is not shortened. In fact, under this law the work will not be out of copyright protection before almost every human currently alive on the planet has died. Considering the Constitutional wording of "to preserve for a limited time…," life plus seventy years certainly seems like forever.

A Supreme Court ruling on the constitutionality of the law was prompted by a lawsuit filed by publisher Eric Eldred. Publisher Eldred contended that the term of copyright no longer met the "limited time" requirement now that the term had been extended for 20 years. The Supreme Court ruled that as long as there is a finite time imposed by the law, the law meets the constitutional requirement (*Eldred v. Ashcroft*). Other cases are being prepared to fine tune the challenge, so more deliberation on this topic is possible in the future.

How do you know if a work is protected? If a work was created in the United States after January 1, 1978 you know that the work was automatically protected by copyright at the moment it was "fixed" or written down, saved to disk, painted on canvas, etc. After 1989, there need be no "C-in-a-circle" mark (©) or other notification of copyright, and the author need not have registered his work with the Copyright Office in order to own a life-plus-70 years copyright on the work. For works created prior to January 1, 1978, a notice of copyright and registration with the Copyright Office were required to obtain valid copyright protection. Those works published without such notice were considered to be in the public domain—without formal copyright protection. For various other periods of time back to 1923, different rules and durations of copyright protection were in effect. See Laura Gasaway's chart for more detailed information. For unpublished works (such as private letters and diaries, manuscripts, family

Q: I wrote a detailed instructional unit for teaching a novel. This unit was used in my ninth grade English class, but I wrote it entirely on my own time and at home. Do I own the copyright in this unit?

A: The answer is "maybe." If this unit was created independently of your teaching duties, and you just happened to use it at a later date, you could make a good case that the copyright is yours. However, if the unit was created expressly for your ninth grade class, the district would have a good case for ownership of the unit. Since "within the scope of employment": doesn't specify hours and days, and since most teachers do grading, etc. at home, the school could assert this was within the scope of your employment. Agree in advance who owns these types of projects.

photos, etc.), however, notice and registration are not required, and the works retain their copyright protection for many years.

The process for registering a copyright is set out by type of material. All require a $30 registration fee, plus some copy of the material being registered. The requirements for the various types of registrable materials can be found online at **http://www.loc.gov/copyright/circs/**.

Since notice of copyright can be an important factor in determining responsibility for willful infringement, the Digital Millennium Copyright Act included strict new regulations regarding removal of what the Act calls "copyright management information." Such information can include the actual copyright notice affixed, but also might include the names of the author and copyright holder, performers, writers, title, etc. Removal of copyright information will be especially important in cases of school and library photocopying. Under previous iterations of the law, a simple notice of possible copyright was sufficient to protect from complicity in copy infringements. Most libraries used a basic ALA-approved stamp stating "NOTICE: This material may be protected by Copyright Law (Title 17 U.S. Code)." Under DMCA this warning would no longer be sufficient. If a work's copyright notice can be found, the entire notice must be included (either photocopied or hand written) with the copies. If no copyright notice can be found on the work, the former stamp would be sufficient.

Recent laws

Copyright hasn't stayed static since the passage of the 1976 revision. In virtually every session of Congress, someone introduces (and often passes) a bill that tweaks copyright law in some fashion. Recent changes have brought significant changes to how copyright is administered and interpreted. Supreme Court and other federal court rulings have created de facto law under which some or all of the country have to live. (United States District and Circuit Court rulings are only binding for the area of the country the court covers. Only U.S. Supreme Court rulings are binding for the entire United States.)

The United States also signs treaties that impact copyright practice. Most require matching legislation to make U.S. law dovetail with the requirements of the treaty. One of the most important recent copyright treaties is the Berne Convention,. Under Berne, the countries agreed to protect the works of other signatory countries under the laws of the other countries who signed the agreement. For example, a French work being used in the United States would be protected under the laws of the United States. This practice simplifies matters in that we in the U.S. only need to know U.S. law to know how we can use materials from other countries. Some of the more important copyright-related laws passed since 1976 include:

Q: I want to use a book but it is out of print and the publisher is out of business. Is the book now free to reproduce?

A: Out of print is not the same as out of copyright (or public domain). If the work is (or might be) still protected by copyright based on its original date of publication (after 1922), someone may own the copyright. Use the Copyright Office files to locate the current owner for permission. Some publishing contracts allow out of print books to revert to the author. Try contacting the author(s) as well.

Q: Could you give me a simplified version of just what the international copyright law says? I'm in an international school in the UAE and the amount of copying from texts here has really surprised me.

A: There is no such thing as "international" copyright law. Each country has its own laws. If the country signed the Berne Convention, they protect the intellectual property of other countries under their own laws. You need to find out what UAE copyright law is, and if they signed Berne. Then you will know where you stand.

Net Theft

The "No Electronic Theft" Act, signed into law on December 16, 1997, closed a loophole in earlier criminal law that allowed those who intentionally shared copyrighted computer software via the Internet to be exempt from criminal prosecution if the suspect made no profit on the exchange. Reproduction of copies worth, in total, over $1000 brings the act into play. Trading software with a total value of more than $1000 also is covered under this law. NET Theft first declared that reproduction and distribution may be by electronic as well as physical means (UCLA, 1998; United States Department of Justice, 1998). "Computer software" in this law includes MP3 files, so those who trade illegal digital audio files over the Internet could fall into the criminal category established in this Act.

Visual Artists Rights Act

Passed in 1990, the Visual Artists Rights Act puts artists in control of their works in more ways than standard copyright allows. It is significant for those who create derivative works, because the artist has complete control over attribution of his work, even when the physical work has been sold. It is also significant if you have art, even student produced art, in your school.

The artist has the right to both claim authorship in his work when such attribution has been denied, as well as deny authorship when work has been misattributed or the artist's own work has been changed to the point that the artist feels attribution would be harmful to his reputation. In addition, the artist has the right to prevent the intentional modification of a work, or the destruction of a work of "recognized stature."

Rights granted by VARA exist until the close of the calendar year in which the artist dies, and are not transferable to anyone. Even if the artist sells the physical art and/or the copyright in the art, the artist retains the rights granted by VARA. The rights apply to paintings, drawings, prints, photographs, or sculpture, created as unique items or in limited editions of 200 or fewer copies. Certain types of art are specifically excluded from the grant of rights under this act (Hoffman, 2002).

DMCA

Signed into law in October, 1998, the Digital Millennium Copyright Act (DMCA) was opposed from its inception. Library, scientific, and academic groups have long found the provisions of the act to be overbroad and far-reaching.

Basically, the DMCA updated copyright law to account for the Internet and digital technologies. Key provisions included:

- *you may not "break" copy protection on software (computer or DVD) (known as the "anti-circumvention" section).*

- *libraries and schools may crack software or to access purchased/licensed software that is not working properly, or to view the list of blocked Web sites in an Internet filter ONLY.*

- *schools that provide Internet access can be protected from copyright infringement claims if they register an employee as the district's agent with the copyright office and follow a set of procedures in the event of a claim.*

- *you must pay a statutory fee to "webcast" sound recordings.*

- *the Register of Copyrights was ordered to undertake an overview of digital distance learning provisions and prepare a report of recommendations to Congress (UCLA, 2001). Note: this was accomplished and the resulting report developed into the TEACH Act.*

- *include the complete copyright notice of the original on copies of protected materials (Lutzker, 1999).*

- *a computer technician may make a RAM or backup copy of computer software while doing computer hardware repair.*

- *libraries and archives can make up to three digital copies of works for preservation purposes (this assumes the works are out of print and in danger of destruction from age or condition), but the works may not be used or distributed outside the premises of the library or archives.*

- *establishes statutory fees for digital transmission of sound recordings and making the ephemeral copies that are necessary for such transmission (Band, 2001).*

- *libraries may migrate works held on obsolete media to current technologies, but the transfers may be made only if you can't buy the same work in a non-obsolete format (Harper, 2001). "Obsolete" means that the hardware to perform or display the work must no longer be available for purchase in the marketplace. Eight track tapes and Beta format videotapes are obsolete. VHS videotapes and phonograph records are not. (Note that this permission is given to libraries but not to schools or other organizations. A school library can claim both the library and educational exemptions of the law, but only for those items held in the library.)*

As you can see, the DMCA created extensive changes in copyright practice as far as digital materials are concerned. Libraries and other groups were not pleased about many of the provisions reported here, and still seek modification of the law.

Sonny Bono Copyright Term Extension Act

The Sonny Bono Copyright Term Extension Act (CTEA) went into effect after it was signed by President Clinton in October, 1998. The Act extended the copyright of all items under copyright as of the date of the implementation of the Act. Because of the impact of this Act, no published works will enter the public domain until January 1, 2019, at which time all works published in 1923 will enter the public domain. Before the implementation of this Act, the term of copyright was life of the author plus 50 years. The Act extended the term of copyright to life of the author plus 70 years, or 95 years of date of creation for corporate works, films, etc. The bill was heavily promoted by the Disney companies because Mickey Mouse would have entered the public domain (through the expiration of the copyright in Steamboat Willie) on January 1, 2003.

The Act was heavily opposed by librarians and publishers of public domain works, and publisher Eric Eldred chose to challenge the Act by requesting an injunction. In January 2003, the U.S. Supreme Court ruled that the Act was constitutional, paving the way for its implementation. (Eldred v. Ashcroft, 537 U.S. 186, 2003).

Digital Performance Right in Sound Recordings Act

This Act, passed in 1995, granted the sixth right to copyright holders. The right limits the digital transmission performance of a sound recording. Digital transmission would include Internet transmissions and certain digital satellite transmissions.

TEACH

The Technology, Education And Copyright Harmonization Act (TEACH Act) established the rules under which copyright protected materials could be used in online education. The Act is the result of a requirement of the DMCA under which the Register of Copyright conducted hearings around the country to determine what legislative action was needed to facilitate the use of copyright protected materials in distance learning. Under the 1976 iteration of copyright law, "transmission" of a copyright protected work was prohibited, therefore rendering online transmission of copyrighted works illegal without explicit permission even when a face to face showing of the same work for educational use would meet the fair use exemptions. The TEACH Act established a set of criteria that, if followed by schools, would allow the use of limited amounts of copyright protected materials when used in qualifying educational situations.

Penalties for infringement

Should a person choose to ignore the law, the penalty for copyright infringement is not a minor inconvenience. Damages can be actual (true financial damages suffered) or statutory (set by law), depending on how the suit is filed and whether the copyright to the infringed work was registered before the infringement commenced. Statutory fines range from $750 to $30,000 per infringement, with each individual work or event constituting a separate act of work infringed. A limited exception permits truly unwary infringers (also called innocent infringers) to have their fines reduced to as little as $200 per work infringed, but such reduction in penalty is at the discretion of the court. To qualify for such an exception, an infringer would have to present a strong case that they truly believed (with reasonable justification) that their use of the work was not infringing. The presence of a copyright notice would, for example, be an excellent reason to believe that an infringement was intentional. If the court decides the infringement was knowledgeable and intentional, statutory damages can run as high as $150,000 per instance. Legal fees and court costs can escalate the true cost of losing a copyright infringement case, since an infringer may be required to pay the copyright holder's attorney fees and court costs as well as the statutory penalties. Of course, there is no cost that can be put on lost sleep and worry. Most copyright suits are civil matters, but in 1992 the penalty for criminal infringement of computer software copyright (commonly called "piracy") was raised to felony status, with fines up to $250,000! To become a criminal offense, 10 illegal copies with a total value of $2,500+ worth of software are all that is required. For complete information about potential penalties and liabilities, see Chapter 5 of U.S. Copyright law at: **http://www.loc.gov/copyright/title17/ chapter05.pdf**. As of April, 2005, taping a film in a theatre and distributing all types of non-print works being prepared for commercial distribution were also criminalized via the Artists' Rights and Theft Prevention Act. See Brad Templeton's "Ten Big Myths about Copyright Explained" for more surprising information about copyright at: **http://www.templetons.com/brad/copymyths.html**.

Some examples of different types of infringement would be:

Innocent infringement — A teacher reads in a journal that an item has fallen into public domain and makes copies. In truth, the journal confused two items of similar title.

Standard infringement — A librarian makes copies of an article for a class many months in advance without making any attempt to contact the copyright holder and obtain permission.

Willful infringement — A principal asks permission to reproduce copies of a journal article for the faculty and is denied. He makes the copies anyway without a reasonable basis to believe he didn't need permission.

When a court finds that a copyright has been infringed, it may take one of several courses of action. An injunction prohibits the infringer from making any further use or copies of the work infringed. This penalty is used primarily in cases of large-scale use or copying for profit. The court might also impound or destroy infringing copies. Of course monetary damages are generally sought, and those damages may be actual or statutory. Actual damages are usually requested only in large-scale piracy cases, since the copyright holder must prove lost profits. However, if a school were to do something egregious such as making mass copies of workbooks, lost profits might be more appropriate than the legally established fines. Statutory damages are the type most often requested in suits against schools and school personnel, and since the costs are applied per item copied they can mount up quickly. Court costs may be assessed to the loser of a copyright action. Attorneys' fees of the prevailing party may also be charged to the loser of an infringement suit, but a prevailing plaintiff will only get the fees if the copyrighted work in dispute has been registered with the Copyright Office within the time frame prescribed by law. A prevailing defendant can get fees and costs whether or not the copyright was filed in a timely manner. The court must make the determination of fees.

Is there an easily accessible record of suits against schools that one may consult? No. While it is true that court decisions are generally public records, the vast majority (maybe 99.9%) of copyright infringement actions are settled out of court. Out of court settlements are between the parties involved, especially when there are no criminal actions involved. The parties may choose to keep the negotiations private, in which case neither party will talk about the events. For that reason, it is difficult to determine how much a school is typically fined for copyright violations. One hears of schools who have been required to purchase legal copies of all software found to be installed illegally, or to purchase a license to show entertainment videos when those had been shown without public performance rights. Other situations may involve punitive fines for illegal reproduction of workbooks or other print materials.

If someone in the district or building violates copyright, that person pays the fine, right? Well, not exactly. Copyright watchdog groups report the results of infringement actions, both as spoils of victory and warnings to potential infringers. Most of the reported cases indicate that the classroom teacher or librarian is only the beginning in naming liable parties. Many suits go right up the chain of command, from librarian, to principal, to curriculum director, to superintendent, to the board of education under the assumption that these parties are aware of and responsible for the actions of their employees. The copyright owner looks for the "deep pockets" in most instances, but when suing schools the copyright owner is more likely to be making a statement or setting a precedent. They want to make an impact on all educators who will hear of the suit.

Two supplemental forms of liability enter the picture at this point. School employees can be considered contributory infringers if they assisted or helped the infringer to do the infringing act or if they were in a position to control the use of the copyrighted work. An example of such a situation would be a librarian who loaned two videocassette recorders and a set of patch cords with knowledge that they would be used to copy a copyrighted video. The librarian helped the infringer to perform the act by providing equipment to aid the infringement. Why would someone want two VCRs and patch cords except to copy a video? The new dual deck VCRs or DVD-R machines present a problem. While a VCR DVD player is convenient to check out because it can handle every technology, if the machine can copy media from one format to the other, you are presenting an infringement technology when you check it out. In addition, the librarian may have provided the program that will be copied with knowledge that the tape will be infringed. If the librarian is in a position to refuse the loan, but makes the loan anyway while knowing that an infringement will occur, she can be considered a contributory infringer.

Employers would be vicarious infringers if they had reason to know an employee was violating copyright and had the power to stop the infringement but took no action. An example of vicarious infringement would be a principal who had been notified that an infringement was taking place but who took no action to stop the theft. Both vicarious and contributory infringers are just as liable as the person who actually made the copies or used the material.

Liability

The teacher's liability— Teachers control many copyrighted works: books, workbooks, video, computer software. Misusing the copyright protected materials puts the teacher at the center of a copyright controversy. The teacher may or may not need assistance to violate copyright, but for the most part the teacher will be the beginning of a chain of copyright liability.

The technician's liability— Technicians exert control of many aspects of technology. During the course of their jobs, they are aware of certain file transactions, programs installed, and other activities of the network environment. If a technician knows that students (or teachers) are trafficking in illegal materials of any kind, but take no action to stop the activity, they may be found to be complicit.

The librarian's liability— We've all heard of "chain of command." Liability works in much the same way. If infringing copies are made on library-owned equipment, it's a good bet that the librarian who loaned the equipment could be involved in the infringement action. A case could be made that the librarian knew (or should have known) that the event would be an infringing action. Only with the support of a strong copyright policy, good record keeping, and thorough staff training would the librarian (and administrators) be able to prove that the infringer was acting as an individual.

The principal's liability— The principal is the instructional and administrative leader in the school. As such, the principal must be aware of curriculum, student issues, staffing and personnel responsibilities, extra curricular activities, equipment and resources, and dozens of other issues affecting the building. With such a vast array of knowledge it's understandable that when a copyright infringement occurs in a school, the copyright owner will assume that the principal had at least passing knowledge of the event or control over those persons committing the infringement. In either case, the principal could be at minimum a vicarious or contributory infringer. Such a possibility raises the likelihood that the principal will be named in any potential infringement action against the school.

As you can see, the technician, librarian, and administrator are at some risk from the illegal activities of others. To that end, it is worthwhile to establish and maintain clear and thorough copyright records, and to inform school personnel and patrons of their obligations under the copyright law.

Administrators, once schooled on copyright, would probably appreciate notification when violations are observed. This isn't to say that the librarian, teacher, or computer technician becomes the "copyright police." On the contrary, these staff members aren't charged with enforcing the copyright law. That falls to the FBI and the Justice Department. But the librarian and the technician are doing the students and staff of the school and the district a disservice to ignore a potentially damaging and embarrassing legal situation. Apprising a principal of a legal violation is akin to notifying her of a fire code violation so it may be corrected before the fire inspector arrives for inspection. Forewarned is forearmed.

State copyright laws

Until 1978, both the state and the federal governments could prosecute most copyright infringement cases. When the 17 U.S.C. § 301 came into effect, anything within the scope of copyright became part of the federal jurisdiction. The legislative history of this section states: "(a)s long as a work fits within one of the general subject matter categories (of federal statutory copyrights), the bill prevents the states from protecting it even if it fails to achieve federal statutory copyright because it is too minimal or lacking in originality to qualify, or because it has fallen into the public domain." States do retain some laws to protect sales of sound recordings (most of which are not covered in federal copyright protection, although the underlying printed music is) and videos under piracy statutes (USDOJ, 1997).

Related laws

Copyright law doesn't exist in a vacuum. Other types of laws may be factored into any analysis of a situation involving copyright. Those other aspects of the law may include state contract laws, state and federal privacy laws, and federal trademark law, among others.

Contract law

Contract law is the big gun when it comes to trumping an issue of copyright. U.S. copyright law provides certain rights and obligations on the part of copyright owners and those who would use copyrighted materials, but any of those may be swept away by a valid contract. Contract law is, of itself, quite complex; however, it is important to understand that one may sign away virtually all fair use rights given under copyright law just by signing a license (a form of contract) that abrogates those rights.

Privacy statutes

There are a few federal privacy statutes; most deal with how the government can use and control information that it keeps on citizens. There are dozens of state laws that protect privacy. Laws in states such as California and New York, where many celebrities live, tend to be more restrictive of personal information than in states with fewer notable persons. Whereas copyright may protect a photograph, privacy laws protect a person's likeness and image. So while a photo of Marilyn Monroe, for example, may be in the public domain, the privacy statutes of California might prevent anyone from using that photograph (and hence her likeness) for commercial advantage without the permission of Monroe's estate (EPIC, 2004).

Trademark law

Akin to copyright, but dealing with identifiable items related to business, short phrases, symbols, logos, etc., trademarks are their own universe of intellectual property. Administered by the United States Patent and Trademark Office, these marks may be maintained perpetually. As long as the trademark owner uses the mark actively and defends it from falling into common use as a generic term (such as what happened to the trade name of "Aspirin") the mark may be reserved for the trademark owner. Trademarks, just like copyrights, may be sold, traded, etc. Service marks, identifying services rather than products, are also part of the body of trademarks (Legal Information Institute, 2004).

Why is any of this significant for schools?

A school may find itself in copyright hot water in any of several ways. Most common is to receive a cease and desist letter. Such a letter may be sent from a company or its attorneys, and generally states that the company is aware that you have violated copyright in some manner. The letter usually goes on to state what you are alleged to have done, and what demands the company is making for reparation.

It is not a good idea to ignore such a letter. In most cases the letter will demand some response from you by a given date. If the company does not receive a response to their allegations by that date, further legal action may be taken. If you feel that the allegations are unfounded, you should take this opportunity to present your side of the case to the company or other representative of the copyright holder. But don't take such a step without advising your administrators so they can be prepared for possible legal action. They may also prefer to involve the school's legal counsel in any discussions with a potential litigant. One word of caution: copyright courses are not required in most law schools. Your school's counsel may have taken many courses in education law, but none at all in copyright. Urge a consultation with a copyright specialist if you are uncomfortable with the advice your counsel is giving.

Another way schools may find themselves in trouble might be when a representative of a copyright holder directly contacts someone in the school who is believed to be a wrongdoer. This author was paid a visit by a software company representative who alleged that the library in which the author was working used illegal copies of a popular computer program. When appropriately licensed copies were produced, the company representative politely left. If one can easily resolve the potential conflict with a little cooperation and open discourse, that should be the appropriate tack.

The last way a school might find itself in trouble is to have an attorney or process server appear at the school. They may be accompanied by or be represented by the FBI and/or federal marshals. Situations such as this require immediate attention of your administration and legal counsel. As a rule, such incidents do not occur without cause, and there is generally sufficient evidence that the plaintiff has convinced a federal judge that there is likelihood of wrongdoing on the part of your building or district and that evidence will likely be concealed or destroyed if not seized. This is the most serious of cases.

How is a school prosecuted?

Schools may be sued for real or actual damages, or they may be sued for the fines set forth within the law. For a school to be sued for real or actual damages, the amount of material used and the possible loss in value (tangible or intangible) to the copyright holder would likely exceed the damages set forth in the law (statutory damages). Attorney's fees and court costs get added to the fine amount. Because most cases of use in schools don't involve amounts over $30,000, few cases demand actual damages. Cases where schools systematically duplicate workbooks without paying royalties, or have vast amounts of illegal computer software are two types of copyright actions in which actual damages would be more beneficial to the copyright holder.

What if there is no trial?

The vast majority of copyright cases (both involving schools and others) are settled out of court. While such a settlement is always a relief to the school, the rest of us are disappointed because a definitive court ruling helps to define the boundaries of copyright. Copyright is an ever-changing landscape, with shifting borders. A court ruling helps attorneys and consumers to understand what can be considered appropriate behavior regarding copyright protected materials.

Out of court settlements aren't necessarily inexpensive, however. A recent case against Los Angeles USD was settled out of court for $300,000 in fines plus attorney's fees (Business, 1999; Blair, 1998). In addition, the school was required to purchase at retail value all the computer software that had been installed illegally. The total cost for the incident amounted to about $5 million! So while an out of court settlement may reduce stress simply to have it behind, the option may not be a good one in terms of finances. A good attorney who specializes in intellectual property is the best person to consult in such a situation. He or she can analyze the situation and determine if the likelihood of winning a court case might make out of court settlement a poor idea.

Why worry, why bother?

So your school doesn't comply with copyright. What difference does it make? Do you feel that no one will ever know in most cases, and no one will even care? Perhaps you have heard that schools are such "small potatoes" that big producers and publishers don't really care because a school doesn't have deep enough pockets for anyone to get a big settlement. You may have even heard that schools are exempt from copyright suits.

Don't believe it! Schools encounter copyright actions on a daily basis. Most are quickly resolved in a professional manner, and no public record exists. These types of actions are the type for which one can do no research. The author maintains a database of copyright infringement actions against schools at: **http://www.school-library.org**. There you can see a sampling of a variety of copyright actions told in the voices of those close to the situations. If you know of a copyright action, from a cease and desist letter to a full-blown lawsuit, please add it to the database of cases so we can all share in the information of what is actionable, and how other school districts dealt with the situation.

Copyright compliance is as much an ethical issue as a legal one. Does one take something that belongs to another and appropriate it? Of course not! One also would not walk into the crowded lunch line in the cafeteria and take a dessert without paying for it. "Taking something that doesn't belong to me?" the teacher declares indignantly. "I would never do such a thing, especially with students watching!" But the same person might stand in front of a class and instruct, "See how we can right click on this graphic and save it to our disk to use however we desire?" Under these facts, taking the work of others appears to be only inappropriate in certain circumstances.

Copyright law is federal law. Perhaps you live a long way from the District of Columbia, and you don't think anyone there will know what is going on in your small district. The law is a pain to keep up with, and there are few clear cut rules, so you might just as well pretend it doesn't exist. However, your district probably has a policy regarding copyright compliance. If you feel that Washington it too far away to be a threat, what about your local school board? The penalty for violating a school board policy can be loss of a job. If Washington doesn't frighten you, perhaps the fear of being caught violating board policy would. The fact remains; the law is still the law, even if we don't like it. Those who don't like the law should work to change it, not just ignore it.

Works cited

Band, Jonathan. (2001). *The Digital Millennium Copyright Act.* Washington, DC: Association of Research Libraries. Retrieved June 19, 2004 from http://www.arl.org/info/frn/copy/band.html.

Blair, Julie. (1998). *Pirated software could prove costly to L.A. District.* Education Week. Retrieved June 14, 2004 from http://www.edweek.org/ew/vol-17/43soft.h17.

Business Software Alliance. (24 February 1999). *Five Southern California Organizations Settle Software Copyright Claims.* Retrieved January 5, 2004 from http://www.bsa.org/usa/press/newsreleases/Five-Southern-California-Organizations-Settle-Software-Copyright-Claims.cfm.

Eldred v. Ashcroft, 537 U.S. 186, (2003).

Electronic Privacy Information Center. (2004). *EPIC Archive – Privacy.* Retrieved August 3, 2004 from http://www.epic.org/privacy/.

Feist Publications, Inc. v. Rural Telephone Service Co., Inc., 499 U.S. 340 (1991).

Harper, Georgia (2001)

Hearn v. Meyer, 664 F. Supp. 832

Hoffman, I. (2002). The visual artists rights act. Retrieved June 18, 2004 from http://www.ivanhoffman.com/vara.html.

Hotaling v. Church of Jesus of Latter-Day Saints, 118 F. 3d 199 (4th Cir. 1997).

Legal Information Institute. (2004). LII: *Law About ... Trademark.* Retrieved August 3, 2004 from http://www.law.cornell.edu/topics/trademark.html.

Lutzker, Arnold. (1999). *Memorandum.* Retrieved June 18, 2004 from http://www.arl.org/info/frn/copy/notice.html.

UCLA Online Institute for Cyberspace Law and Policy. (1998). *The 'No Electronic Theft' Act.* Retrieved June 18, 2004 from http://www.gseis.ucla.edu/iclp/hr2265.html.

UCLA Online Institute for Cyberspace Law and Policy. (2001). *The Digital Millennium Copyright Act.* Retrieved June 18, 2004 from http://www.gseis.ucla.edu/iclp/dmca1.htm.

United States Department of Justice. (1997). *Criminal Resource Manual 1844 Copyright Law—Preemption of State Law.* Retrieved August 3, 2004 from http://www.usdoj.gov/usao/eousa/foia_reading_room/usam/title9/crm01844.htm.

United States Department of Justice. (1998). *The 'No Electronic Theft' Act.* Retrieved June 18, 2004 from http://www.cybercrime.gov/netsum.htm.

Chapter 2

Public Domain

What is it?

A work not protected by copyright is considered to be in the public domain. A work can be missing copyright protection in any of several ways.

How does something get into the public domain?

A work can become part of the public domain (PD) through different means. The work may not be eligible for copyright protection at all. It might not be "creative," or it might not be created by a person. Other factors come into play when considering copyrightability as well.

A work must be considered "creative" in order to qualify for copyright protection. For that reason, facts are not eligible for the protection of copyright. For example, a simple list of the 10 longest rivers in the world is factual, and not eligible for the protection of copyright. However, if you were to write an essay about the 10 longest rivers, and describe their surroundings, and their ecology, and talk about the important economic benefits each provides for its watershed, the expression of the facts regarding the rivers is creative and protectable. However, anyone is free to make use of the factual material included within the essay. The most important court case to discuss this concept is know as the *Feist* decision, decided by the U.S. Supreme Court (see section on Related cases at the end of this chapter.)

A work created by a gorilla or an elephant, for example, can be highly creative, but because it was not created by a human the work does not qualify for copyright protection. To be protected, the work must be created by a human being. In this day of computer-generated text, questions may arise about works created by computers.

Works created by U.S. Federal government employees during the course of their duties are not eligible for copyright protection. Speeches of the U.S. President, acts of Congress, booklets prepared for various federal agencies, U.S. Government Web pages, all would be free from copyright protection. Use caution in gathering material from government sites, however, as they may have used licensed art (such as from Microsoft Office) or other materials in their works. Also, it is a common misconception to think that because federal government documents are in the public domain, that all governmental entities also place their materials in the public domain. This is not the case, and should be investigated on a case by case, agency by agency basis. Some school districts and state agencies claim no copyright in their curriculum guides, policies, etc. Others protect and defend their documents strongly. When in doubt, ask.

Works, created during the period when a specific type of copyright notice was required, fell into the public domain if the notice was defective. For example, a copyright notice had to have the c-in-a-circle mark, or the word "copyright" to be considered valid. If your typewriter didn't have a copyright symbol and you typed a letter c between parentheses instead, your notice was considered to be defective and your copyright invalid. In such cases, the work immediately fell into the public domain if the work was published with the defective notice.

Works whose term of copyright has run the full course are no longer eligible for copyright protection. This class of works would include all those published before January 1, 1923. Shakespeare' plays, for example, aren't protected by copyright in their original form as they were published before 1923. If notes, commentary, or background information have been added to the play, however, those portions of the works may be covered by copyright (provided they were written after 1923), as would be contemporary illustrations. Reprints of old novels or classic fiction may have new copyrights based on new illustration, or new introductory matter. Some unpublished works—previously protected under common law copyright but now released under new legislation—started entering the public domain in 2003 if their 70 years-after-death period had lapsed. Watch for diaries, photographs, manuscripts, etc. to appear in the future as the life + 70 terms run their course.

Works whose copyrights were not renewed, if they were covered during a period when copyright renewal was required, lost their copyright protection when the copyright was not renewed. Many silent films were not renewed after talking pictures became popular, so they are now in the public domain. Some other materials post-1923 are also now in the public domain as a result of non-renewal. The non-renewal may have been a slip-up on the part of the copyright owner or his agent, but the results are the same. One must research to find which ones are not protected.

Some materials are dedicated to the public domain by their authors. The Creative Commons (**www.creativecommons.org**) is a good example of such works. Scholars contribute their works to this archive of public domain materials, in the hope that they will benefit scholarship and society as a whole.

Caveat: Just because a work has no notice of copyright does not mean that the work is in the public domain. Since 1989, the fact that a work has no copyright notice should not be taken to mean that the work is not protected by copyright. In fact, because the World Wide Web was created after 1978, most things you see on the WWW are protected by copyright unless they were created by some entity forbidden to hold copyrights (such as U.S. government agencies) or are a verbatim reprint of some public domain work such as old (pre-1923) literature. Some scholars also state on their Web pages that works published there are in the public domain.

How long does public domain last?

Since "public domain" means that a work is not covered by copyright, the rules regarding the length of copyright coverage do not apply. Currently, once a work has lost its copyright protection and has passed into the public domain, copyright protection cannot be regained on that work. Therefore, the public domain lasts, in effect, forever. There is an exception in Section 104 (a) that covers a particular class of unpublished works by foreign authors, but that exception will seldom apply in a K-12 school situation.

What can you do with public domain materials?

Public domain materials have no copyright restrictions. If a work is in the public domain, it may be reproduced, adapted, distributed, performed, displayed, and transmitted. However, it is essential to understand that only the ORIGINAL public domain work has these options. Subsequent modifications and adaptations may gain for their adaptors or creators a copyright on the additions or changes. For example, the original works of Beethoven are long in the public domain. However, no high school orchestras perform the ORIGINAL works of Beethoven. In the first place, Beethoven wrote for instruments that are no longer used. In the second place (and even more relevant) the original scores are far too difficult for most high school orchestras. To play these works, someone has adapted the works into versions that are less complex and less difficult without losing the original melody and tone of the piece. While the original parts of the piece are still in the public domain, anything new that is added or modified in the derivative work may be protected.

How do you find public domain materials?

Public domain materials are everywhere! There are even publishers who specialize in public domain materials. Educational publishers use many public domain materials because there are no costs to use them, and the publishers can edit the materials as they choose. English textbooks, for example, use materials by Shakespeare, Keats, etc. because they are free, as well as notable.

There are several sources to locate public domain materials. Not all the sources are free to use, though the public domain materials they help you locate are free to use, once you locate them in the original versions. Some of the best, such as Public Domain Report (**www.pubdomain.com/index2.htm**), are subscription Web sites. But they do offer samples of music, art, children's literature, drama, film, and literature. All have been scrupulously researched as to PD status. The company has a public domain sheet music service, as well. Remember, you can arrange, translate, modify, publish, etc. any of the public domain materials they provide, so the cost is negligible if you use the service to any degree.

It is possible to do your own searches for public domain status, but that really means not finding anything in the copyright office database, plus having definitive information about actual publication date so you are certain that the version you are working with is the original. Be cautious, especially if you plan to sell or adapt material for public performance, that you are certain the version you are using is in the public domain.

What is the difference between "copyright free" and "royalty free"?

A work that is "copyright free" is in the public domain. There are no restrictions on its use. It may be copied, adapted, distributed, publicly performed or displayed, and transmitted digitally if it is a sound recording. A work that is "royalty free" may still be protected by copyright (and usually is), but the copyright owner has elected to forgo collection of royalties for certain uses of the material.

Q: Is the Bible considered public domain? If it is copyright protected, who would own the copyright?

A: The answer depends on the version. The King James version is in the public domain—at least in the original translation. New translations may still be protected. Check the copyright date of the version you are using. Anything copyrighted before 1923 is public domain. (Watch out for "enhanced" versions, though. The Bible text itself may be public domain, but the notes, etc. may still be protected.)

How can I use royalty free materials?

Royalty free materials are usually governed by license. The license will explain in detail how the collection of materials can be used in your case. Typically, you can use the royalty free art, or music, in standard broadcast situations or productions/publications without additional payment. The most usual prohibition on use of royalty free material is to employ the items in another collection of similar items. For example, many collections of clip art are royalty free, but they are not copyright free. The artist or copyright owner does claim a copyright on the works, but the owner does not elect to charge a per use fee on the art as long as the person using the art abides by license restrictions. Upon reading the software license for the clip art, one discovers that use of the art in publication, Web pages, derivative works, etc. may be permitted, but it is expressly prohibited to use the work in another collection of clip art. Such a common prohibition might cause problems for teachers or librarians who are in the habit of collecting art from various free Web sites or clip art collections, and gathering them together by theme for their students to have a one-stop-shopping location for project art. The teacher might put up a page of elephant clip art, for example, if her third graders were doing multimedia projects on elephants. By putting the royalty free art into a clip art collection for her class, she has violated the license and the copyright of the art.

Related cases

Feist Publications, Inc. v. Rural Telephone Service Co., 499 U.S. 340 (1991)

In this case, a publishing company was collecting listings of names, addresses, and telephone numbers to publish in a private telephone directory. The telephone company objected, contending that the work was their creative property. The Court held that collections of facts, by themselves, are not copyrightable, and that some modicum of creativity is required. A simple alphabetical arrangement of names and telephone numbers was insufficient to qualify as "original."

Chapter 3

Fair Use

T he law—Title 17, United States Code, Public Law 94-553, 90 Stat. 2541, as amended—
gives citizens special exceptions to the strict legal copyright requirements. The
purpose of these limited exceptions to the exclusive rights of copyright holders is so that
knowledge and scholarship might advance. These special exceptions are called "fair use."
Fair use, as defined in the law, has certain aspects that apply to everyone, and others that
apply only to certain classes of use, such as use in nonprofit schools.

Copyright law provides several instances in which reproduction of copyrighted items is
permissible. These exceptions to Section 106 (the section where the rights are defined) are
considered the "fair use exemptions" and are found in Section 107 of the law. This section is brief
enough to be reprinted here:

Notwithstanding the provisions of sections 106 and 106A, the fair use of a copyrighted
work, including such use by reproduction in copies or phonorecords or by any other means
specified by that section, for purposes such as criticism, comment, news reporting, teaching
(including multiple copies for classroom use), scholarship, or research, is not an infringement of
copyright. In determining whether the use made of a work in any particular case is a fair use the
factors to be considered shall include:

1. *The purpose and character of the use, including whether such use is of a commercial
   nature, or is for nonprofit educational purposes;*

2. *The nature of the copyrighted work;*

3. *The amount and substantiality of the portion used in relation to the copyrighted
   work as a whole; and*

4. *The effect of the use upon the potential market for or value of the copyrighted work
   (17 USC , §107).*

These four factors are also known as the four tests of fair use. Basically what the law is
saying is that Congress intends to protect the rights of the author while still allowing legitimate
educational and research uses of copyrighted materials.
Fair use is the most misunderstood aspect of copyright law, at least as far as schools are concerned.

Common misconceptions about fair use include:

Misconception #1 — *Schools can use any copyright protected materials they wish, because they are schools.*

Misconception #2 — *Using materials is OK if you don't make a profit.*

Misconception #3 — *Promoting someone's work by distributing copies is justification for free use.*

Misconception #4 — *Materials used "for the good of kids" absolves one of copyright liability.*

Fair use is a balancing act. The idea is to balance carefully the need for an author to protect his right to exploit his work commercially (or privately), and the need for the public to have access to the fruits of knowledge so we (the public) can advance scientific and creative endeavors. If authors weren't able to profit from their creations and discoveries, few would create or research. However, in exchange for a limited time exclusive right, the author or discoverer must allow limited use of the work so that others may build on the creation or discovery in an effort to increase human knowledge. It is a noble effort, and one with which the courts struggle. To preserve as many of the rights of each side of the equation as possible is a Herculean task.

What is it?

Fair use provisions of the copyright law grant users conditional rights to use or reproduce certain copyrighted materials as long as the reproduction or use of those materials meets defined guidelines. Fair use goes hand in glove with the intent of copyright "to promote the progress of Science and Useful Arts." As defined in the law, fair use balances the First Amendment free speech right with the rights of the author to control the use of his copyrighted work.

Fair use is not a right given to educators or any other person. Fair use is a defense applied in court to a charge of infringement. When a court considers a claim of fair use, it considers both the rights of the user and the rights of the author. The burden of proving fair use falls to the educator using the material, so thorough knowledge of copyright law and associated guidelines is essential for librarians and educators using copyrighted works. As there is seldom a clear-cut fair use situation it is incumbent upon the educator to know the conditions under which one may claim fair use.

Difference between fair use and guidelines

Essentially there are two kinds of fair use:

1. *Fair use as defined in the Copyright Act (statutory fair use). Every person in the United States can avail themselves of this concept of fair use. The law defines the factors that you must consider when making a claim of fair use. Four factors are defined in the law, and the rights of both the creator and the person wishing to use the material are considered. While the law does not indicate that any of the factors is to be considered with any more weight than any of the others, in practice courts have used some of the factors as more significant than others.*

2. Fair use as defined by several sets of guidelines designed for educators and librarians. These guidelines apply only to educational and library use of materials. Some guidelines are codified within the law itself (AV guidelines, TEACH Act) while others are agreed upon by outside organizations (multimedia guidelines).

For purposes of simplicity, guidelines are easier to learn and administer than going through the fair use tests, but if the guidelines don't permit a projected use, one can always fall back on the "four tests" fair use assessment to determine if a particular use might be fair, regardless of the limits suggested by the guidelines. For example, the multimedia guidelines permit teachers and students to use video clips of 3 minutes or 10% of the whole if used in a multimedia presentation (additional requirements figure in this analysis). If the teacher or student wants to use a clip that lasts 3 minutes and 15 seconds, is that use possible? Since this use exceeds the multimedia guidelines, the educator or student can then apply the four tests of fair use to determine if the use might be fair under that assessment.

Since educators have two forms of fair use available (statutory fair use and guidelines), assess a proposed use from both aspects to see if one will allow the use before abandoning the idea or attempting to license the use. Keeping the maximum fair uses available to educators is essential if they don't wish to enter into a period when fair use is abandoned in favor of licensing.

> **Q:** *I'd like to copy an outline map of my state. What copyright implications do I face?*
>
> **A:** Simple outline diagrams and maps are not eligible for copyright protection. You may copy these types of materials at will. More complex diagrams and maps require the same evaluation process as graphics.

Examples of fair use analysis

Making a fair use assessment based on the factors outlined in the law (statutory fair use) is not a simple prospect. The law identifies four factors that must be considered in any fair use assessment. Some of the factors have sub-factors that must also be considered. While the law doesn't specify that any one of the factors has a greater weight than any of the others, in actual practice courts have given more consideration to at least one of the four. We will discuss the four factors, then go through a sample analysis.

It may be easier to visualize this as a process of weighing. Imagine a scale, with a plate on each side. One plate is "us" (the educators) and the other is "them" (the copyright owner). Between the two plates are four weights that freely slide from side to side, similar to the scales you remember from the doctor's office. The first weights are not much different in size but the last weight is bigger than the others. You don't want to move that one: just as at the doctor's office you get very apprehensive when the nurse moves that large weight at the back!

The weights are the four factors that affect a decision on fair use. Following

Fair Use Factors Pro and Con
(many variations of weight are possible)

Disfavoring Fair Use — Favoring Fair Use

Published — Unpublished

Creative — Factual

Whole work — Part of work

Affects profits — Non-profit educational

FAIR USE BALANCE

are commonsense definitions to help you understand how to adjust those weights. Remember, one must evaluate ALL four factors before deciding which way the scales will tip. And a weight needn't be pushed all the way to one end of the scale or the other. Precious little in copyright is black or white, pro or con, and fair use is no exception. It isn't necessary to "win" on all four factors to get a favorable fair use conclusion. In coming to a reasonable conclusion, it is essential to apply the tests in the way a court would apply them, not as we might wish they would be applied. Gratuitous justification is the surest way to get oneself and one's organization in hot water.

Factor 1: Purpose and character of use

This first factor of fair use is probably the easiest one to assess. It is a two-part test, and either half could result in a determination of a favorable outcome on this test. As with all the tests, apply this one objectively.

The first test of fair use encourages educational use of materials, but it has been interpreted to favor "transformative" uses, such as putting a quotation in a term paper.

A recent court case stated that making low-resolution thumbnail-sized copies of images available elsewhere on the Internet was a "transformative" use. *Kelly v. Arriba Soft Corp.*, 280 F.3d 937 (9th Cir. 2002). Even multiple copies of non-transformative uses can be acceptable in limited numbers. See the chapter on print materials for more details on multiple print copies. Keep in mind that, in the absence of specific guidelines, all four tests of fair use will be considered in determining an appropriate application of the fair use doctrine. Factor 1 is actually fairly insignificant when all four factors are applied to a given situation.

Part 1: nonprofit educational use

Are you in a nonprofit public or private school, and is the use you are proposing for this entity? Such a use would get a favorable assessment on this portion of this factor, but even with a positive result here, one must continue to the other half of this factor plus the other three. For-profit schools, such as Edison Schools, some charter schools, and some private schools would not receive a favorable assessment on this portion of factor one. Even if you don't qualify on this portion of the test, continue to the rest of the assessments.

Part 2: criticism, commentary, news reporting

Any of these choices can qualify a use on this half of the first factor. For example, if a for-profit newspaper uses an excerpt from a novel when publishing a book review, this portion of the first factor can be met. Criticism involves making critical judgments about a work, and usually will have portions of the work included to make the critic's points. Commentary involves writing explanations about a work, and may or may not be critical. News reporting is exactly what it states. While intended to apply to the news industry, this selection could apply to the school newspaper, school television reports, etc.

Note that both halves of this factor do NOT need to be satisfied in order for this factor to move to your side of our metaphorical scale. For example, the local television station can still use a portion of a movie in a review under this factor (taking into account the rest of the factors, of course) even though it does not satisfy the first half of this factor regarding nonprofit educational setting.

Factor 2: Nature of copyrighted work

Factor two of the four is a two-pronged question. Neither half eliminates consideration as fair use, but having both on your side greatly enhances your fair use defense.

Part 1: Factual or creative?

This question wants to know the content of the material being infringed. As we discussed before, facts cannot receive copyright protection. Therefore, appropriating facts from a copyright protected work would be less hazardous than taking portions from something creative. Materials that would lose on this factor would be literature (novels, poems, drama), art, music, etc. Materials that would tend to draw this factor on your side of an evaluation would be newspaper accounts, almanacs, maps, and other factual representations of information. An important point to note is that while the facts themselves are free to use, the expression of those facts is not. For example, an encyclopedia article is written from and about factual material. The facts contained in the article are free to use, but the way the author of the encyclopedia article has expressed those facts is not. Also, a work such as an almanac is composed primarily of facts. The facts themselves are free to use, but the selection and arrangement of those facts, plus the expression of the facts if presented in narrative or graphic form, is the basis for the copyright in the almanac.

Part 2: Published or not published?

The second half of this factor asks if the work is published. One might assume that since an author/creator who has published a work expects it to be seen and used by the public, there would be slightly more protection given to published works than to unpublished ones. In reality, unpublished works are more closely protected because the author/creator obviously did not wish the material to be made public. Unpublished materials would be such things as letters, diaries, family photographs, e-mails, unpublished manuscripts, etc.

"Published" in copyright parlance may not have the meaning generally attributed to the word. The 1976 law defines "publication" as: *the distribution of copies or phonorecords of a work to the public by sale or other transfer of ownership, or by rental, lease, or lending. The offering to distribute copies or phonorecords to a group of persons for purposes of further distribution, public performance, or public display constitutes publication.* A public performance or display of a work does not of itself constitute publication. Something offered for sale in the marketplace is obviously "published," even if no one buys it. However, there is no clear legal assessment if a Web page is published when it is mounted on the web, or if something distributed to family, friends, or even within an organization such as your school is officially "published." (Note that out of print isn't the same as unpublished.)

Factor 3: Amount of work used?

This factor is a little clearer to understand. The question is basically, how much of the work will you use? As a matter of practicality, the less you use, the better. If you want to use a short paragraph from a large Tom Clancy novel as an example of a metaphor, you are probably OK here. However, if you want to use a haiku, you are going to be using ALL of it. Any time you use *all* of something, there are going to be questions about this factor. Any time you use *most* of something, you will also get an unfavorable evaluation here as well.

When there are analyses of this factor, the phrase "significant amount" appear frequently. For example, when asking how much of a musical recording would be considered "significant," a copyright attorney explained that if one can tell what song is being used, the amount is "significant." That amount could be even a few bars. How much of a work is "significant" is a judgment call, and one that a court would adjudicate. Common sense would tell you that copying 10 pages from a picture book is a far more significant extract than 10 pages from a novel.

Essence of work

The term "essence of the work" is often tossed about when discussing how much one may use under the fair use defense. This term is used to explain a short segment of a work that embodies the spirit of an entire work. A scene of a movie, or a phrase of a song, or a section of a book might all be considered to represent the "message" or "spirit" of that work. If one uses something that embodies the entire piece within a small segment, one has—in essence—used the entire work.

This concept may be explained with some examples. If you are aware of the book, *Rosie's Walk* (Aladdin, 1971), you will recall that the entire text of the book is spread across two pages at the beginning. The rest of the book consists of pictures of Rosie the hen being pursued across the barnyard by a fox, blithely ignorant that she is on his dinner agenda. The mishaps that befall the fox in his pursuit of Rosie are featured in the pictures, but there is no text to describe what happens. So if one were to copy the two textual pages from this 32-page book, you would have copied a small portion of the book, yet you would have copied the text in its entirety! These two pages would easily be considered the "essence" of the work.

An important Supreme Court case on this issue involved former U.S. President Gerald R. Ford. President Ford, after he left office, wrote his autobiography entitled, *A Time to Heal* (*Harper, 1979*). His publisher, Harper & Row, negotiated an agreement with *Time Magazine* to publish an excerpt from the book at or near the time of publication of the book. The excerpt was to cover the section of the book in which former President Ford explained why he pardoned former President Richard Nixon. This was a hot issue of the day, and much sought after information. Somehow, *The Nation* magazine managed to get a copy of the unpublished manuscript, from which they published a 300-word excerpt before the *Time* article could appear. This excerpt scooped *Time's* article.

Harper & Row sued *The Nation* claiming they had violated the fair use provisions in copyright law. The U.S. Supreme Court held that *The Nation* had, indeed, violated the copyright of the work. They ruled that the 300 words chosen were sufficient to be considered "the essence of the work" and that the use of unpublished material was significant in the assessment (*Harper & Row, Publishers, Inc. v. Nation Enterprises 471 U.S. 539 (1985)*).

On the other hand, the Supreme Court held that the band 2 Live Crew could use a substantial part of the song "Pretty Woman" in a parody of the song, so how much is "too much" varies from case to case (*Campbell v. Acuff-Rose Music, 510 U.S. 569 (1994)*). Excessive copying can only be determined after taking into account the other three factors and the circumstances as a whole. Just remember that this is only one of four factors, so the use of a large portion of a work is not always a completely disqualifying point. This case also cited the "transformative" nature of the resulting work as significant in the analysis. A transformative work is one that puts the borrowed material to a new or novel use.

In still another case, a schoolteacher copied 11 pages of a 24-page handout from another teacher's copyrighted work on cake decorating. The courts held that the 11 pages was too much of the copied work to be classified as fair use, as well as the fact that the 11 pages comprised the most important sections of the work copied. The new work also competed directly with the original since both were educational for a similar audience (*Marcus v. Rowley, 695 F.2d 1171 (9th Cir. 1983)*).

Schools will want to note that common problems under this factor include using identifiable portions of songs, using graphics (because generally the entire graphic is used), and using poetry. Of course, any time one uses *all* of anything, you should seriously consider this factor. Just because you may have an unfavorable outcome on this single factor doesn't mean you won't prevail on the other three, but it is worth significant deliberation.

Factor 4: Effect of use on market for or value of work

This factor is the "eggplant that ate Chicago" of the four factors. Courts, of late, have given this sole factor more importance than the other three even though the law does not indicate that one of the four factors is more significant in a fair use assessment. In essence, if your use would deprive someone of sales, this factor would come into play. Courts actually consider potential damage, rather than actual damages, when weighing this factor.

One must also consider that the "value of" fits in here. If your use would somehow disparage the original author, or his work, even in ways you might not imagine or agree with, this factor can become significant. Some people like to rationalize by saying that their use of a work actually *promotes* the original work. However, it is not up to you, the person borrowing the original work, to make that decision. The copyright owner alone has the right to decide where and when his work will be publicized. A wise person once advised, "If the copyright owner wants you to help promote his work, I promise you he will contact you!"

Q: I'd like to copy something from the Web to put on a local server. Since the Web author doesn't charge any money for the site, I'm not affecting the market for the work, right?

A: Perhaps you are affecting the value of the work. If, for example, the author receives funding based on "hits" to the Web site, by copying the information and distributing it, you may impact the funding by draining hits away. You, as the person borrowing material, don't get to decide whether your use affects the market for the work.

Commercial use

Any commercial use of a work or portion of a work will yield a poor result on this factor (Crews, Message 23, Oct. 26, 1998). For schools, that would mean any use that transfers money, even if there is no net profit. For example, if you sell yearbooks, and you have used unlicensed/unpermissioned copyrighted graphics in the yearbook, this use would be considered "commercial." The same would hold true if you are selling CDs of the band concert, or t-shirts with a cartoon on them, or any other transaction involving copyright protected materials used without license or permission.

Misrepresentation

An important case to understand regarding "loss of value" is the *Ticketmaster v. Microsoft* case (Ticketmaster v. Microsoft, United States District Court for the Central District of California, Civil Action Number 97-3055DPP). In this case, Microsoft had created a link to the Ticketmaster ticket-ordering page, a page deep within the Ticketmaster Web site. Ticketmaster sold advertising on its home page, but not on the pages deep within its site. Ticketmaster and Microsoft had negotiated to have a relationship between the two companies that would be represented by Ticketmaster links within a new Microsoft Web site, but negotiations had broken down. Microsoft went ahead and made the link to the Ticketmaster ordering page, anyway. Ticketmaster claimed that Microsoft was using the Ticketmaster trademark and logos without permission, and implied a relationship that did not exist. Microsoft contended that the use of the link was fair use.

Because Microsoft used frames on the Web site, Web pages belonging to Ticketmaster appeared to be part of the Microsoft Web site. The correct URLs do not appear in the Location window when using frames, only the URL of the master site, in this case Microsoft's Seattle Sidewalk. Ticketmaster contended that such obscuring of the origin of the Web pages, and the use of the Ticketmaster trademark and logo were misrepresentations, and not subject to a claim of fair use (Netlitigation, 1998). This case was eventually settled out of court. The settlement had Microsoft agreeing to only link to the top page of Ticketmaster's site, where there was advertising and other indications of the ownership of the content (Smith, 2000).

The significance of this case for schools lies in the fact that there are often Web pages deep within online sites that may be useful for schools. However, creating links to such pages may result in implied relationships and/or misrepresentation of relationships that are offensive to the owners of the sites to which pages are linked, especially if using framing technology that hides the URL of the original site. To be sure, it is always safe to ask permission to deep link, but relying on fair use in this situation can be problematic.

What would happen if everyone were to…

In analyzing a complex copyright situation, a copyright attorney once advised that the court, in assessing the final factor of fair use, must assess what would happen to the "market for or value of" the work as if *everyone* was to do what you are proposing to do. In other words, the idea that you are just a small classroom in a rural school in middle America isn't the issue. The issue is that if everybody were to repeat this same behavior with the same fair use defense, what effect would *that* use have on the market for or value of the work.

Looking at a case from this standpoint makes sense. For example, if an English teacher duplicated an editorial in today's newspaper for her class, the use is minimal for that class. But if every English teacher across the country were to do the same thing, would that affect the market for the newspaper? Likely not. People would still want to read the comics, check out the want ads, and get the scores from the ball game last night. The use of making copies of that editorial would not likely affect the market for the paper.

However, if a second grade teacher made copies of an entire picture book for her class, and the court extends that view to be what would happen if every teacher were to distribute copies of the entire picture book to his or her class, you can easily see how the broad reproduction might affect the market for the book. Why purchase a book when your teacher is going to give you a copy for free? In addition, there is the issue of the value of the work. The copyright owner may only want that book printed in hardback because the cost cutting that must occur to get an affordable paperback copy reduces the quality of the outstanding illustrations—a significant part of the book. The copyright owner does not want the reputation (or value) of the book to be abridged by substandard reproduction.

Various types of guidelines

In addition to the statutory fair use tests, various sets of guidelines have developed over the years. Since the text of the law was too vague to be of much help in deciding if a particular use were permitted, the U.S. House of Representatives and the Senate held hearings in an effort to determine an equitable balance between the rights of copyright owners (who may or may not be the actual creators of the copyrighted works) and those of the general public.

The hearings resulted in a set of guidelines (often referred to as the "Congressional Guidelines" or the "fair use guidelines" **http://www.musiclibraryassoc.org/Copyright/guidebks.htm**) that, while they are not law, are interpreted to be the Congress intent in enacting the law. The courts have taken this statement of intent into account when deciding cases of copyright infringement. The House report on Congressional intent was quite explicit on the amount and types of copying that could be considered fair use. These specific limits will be discussed in the section on print.

In addition to the Congressional guidelines that dealt with primarily print, there are also guidelines that have emerged from the wording in the law describing fair use of audiovisual materials. Following those guidelines came regulations on interlibrary loans and resource sharing, components of an active library program. As technology advanced, presentation packages such as PowerPoint and Hypercard stretched the limits of fair use. Pressure from educators on producers finally yielded a set of guidelines to govern the use of copyright protected materials in these types of presentations. (See Chapter 7 for details).

The Digital Millennium Copyright Act established some guidelines for schools that put materials on the Web, through the creation of a copyright agent program. Each "online service provider" (most schools qualify as an OSP) can protect themselves against copyright actions by establishing a position called the agent. The agent follows certain procedures to monitor copyright claims for the site, and the sponsoring organization is rewarded with limited immunity from prosecution.

Guidelines took a giant leap forward with the passage of the TEACH Act, codifying guidelines for using copyrighted materials in distance learning situations. The new advance in course distribution required a parallel reorganization of fair use permissions to enable online classes to have similar fair use of materials that face-to-face classes had enjoyed for many years.

Each time technology took a leap forward, fair use guidelines followed behind, trying to keep up. Unfortunately, when guidelines were created to handle the newer technologies, older guidelines were not updated to match. Hence, you will find that what is OK in one medium is not OK in another. This disconnect is a major reason why so many people find understanding and administering copyright to be so confusing!

To whom does it apply?

As you go through the various guidelines, there are several things to keep in mind. The first will be: to whom does this apply? As we discussed before, the statutory "four tests" of fair use may be applied to any citizen at any time. Some of the guidelines that we will discuss in upcoming chapters may apply only to teachers, or only to librarians, or only to students. When making assessments, it is very important to remain clear about whom you are talking.

Situation will also be an important consideration. Where, when, and how are these materials going to be used? What may be fair use in one instance may not be fair use in another. Pay particular attention to situation when you are looking at the guidelines that will follow.

Remember, it is permissible to "shop" for the fair use evaluation that is most favorable to your use. If guidelines don't permit the needed use, you can always fall back to the standard fair use assessment to see if your additional use can be justified. It is important to always press for the maximum permitted use, since those rights not used will eventually erode away.

General public vs. schools

Sometimes the restrictions of guidelines will not allow enough of some medium to meet the teaching need of a student or teacher. For example, the multimedia guidelines allow using up to 30 seconds or 10% of a song in a multimedia presentation, whichever is less. For a typical rock song, 10% is 18 seconds, so the limit is the lower of 18 and 30. However, suppose that a musical phrase that the teacher wants to use is 20 seconds in length. Does that mean the segment is out because it exceeds the 18 second limitation? Or does it mean that the teacher must truncate the phrase to be able to use it? Not necessarily. The teacher can go through the four-test analysis that is available to all citizens. If the use can pass the four tests, she can use the 20 seconds with confidence.

Schools vs. libraries

As pointed out earlier, everyone has certain fair use rights. Schools get a special set of fair use rights to help them educate students. Libraries get another set of special guidelines to help them achieve their civic mission. School libraries get the best of all possible worlds, since they can claim the school exemptions, the library exemptions, and the fair use exemptions afforded all citizens. The school library exemptions don't extend to the parent school, however. Only activities within the library are acceptable candidates for the library exemptions.

The best part of having the library exemptions may be that if you have a library you probably have a librarian. School librarians are the only educators who routinely receive an education on copyright law during their training. Even school administrators seldom get more than a cursory copyright education. Of course, having an education doesn't make the librarian the copyright policeman. The librarian is a resource person who is able to help students, faculty, and administrators to puzzle out the conundrum that is copyright. Look upon your librarian as the copyright consultant, not the copyright cop.

Works cited

Campbell v. Acuff-Rose Music (92-1292), 510 U.S. 569 (1994).

Crews, Kenneth. 1998. Bloomington, IN: *Indiana University Online Copyright Tutorial.*

Harper & Row, Publishers, Inc. v. Nation Enterprises, 471 U.S. 539 (1985).

Kelly v. Arriba Soft Corp., 280 F.3d 937 (9th Cir. 2002).

Marcus v. Rowley, 695 F.2d 1171 (9th Cir. 1983).

Netlitigation | Cases | Ticketmaster v. Microsoft. 1998. [Retrieved August 9, 2004 from] http://www.netlitigation.com/netlitigation/cases/ticketmaster.htm

Smith, Margaret Kubiszyn. 2000. [Retrieved August 9, 2004 from] *Gigalaw: Emerging Legal Guidance on "Deep Linking."* http://www.gigalaw.com/articles/2000-all/ kubiszyn-2000-05b-all.html.

Ticketmaster v. Microsoft, United States District Court for the Central District of California, Civil Action Number 97-3055DPP.

Chapter 4

Print Materials in Schools

Because the four factors cited in Section 107 were less than clear, representatives of affected education and publishing groups met to work out much more specific explanations of the law. The result was endorsed by Congress when it was read into the Congressional Record. These Congressional Guidelines (1976) <**http://www.musiclibraryassoc.org/Copyright/guidebks.htm**>, as they are called, are not law, per se, but they were written to indicate legislative intent and are used as benchmarks against which copyright infringement is gauged. The guidelines state minimum standards of fair use; certain other types of copying may be permitted. Exactly what those other types of copying are and how much is tolerated would vary depending on the judge and jury hearing the case. Yes, the final arbiter of what is permitted is a court of law. While you might be convinced that the pages you plan to copy fall under the fair use exemption, the copyright owner may have entirely different views. The most conservative line is generally safe, whereas straying very far afield of these guidelines is an open invitation to litigation. One might make an analogy to driving. Going 31 miles per hour in a 30-mile-per-hour zone probably wouldn't merit a ticket, but going 50 miles per hour in the same zone would likely alert even the most laid-back patrolman. In a school situation, sometimes one is more comfortable giving teachers and students clear directions and numbers on which to judge appropriate behavior. These Congressional guidelines do just that—provide specific limits to acceptable behavior.

These guidelines were developed primarily for print materials, because print material was predominant in 1976 when the guidelines were written. While there are specific limits and restrictions based on the format of material, there are also some general tests imposed on all educational uses of copyrighted works. These tests are more concrete and easier to apply to educational and library copying than are the fair use factors. The additional tests are those of brevity (defined by specific lengths and numbers of items), spontaneity (see following questions), and cumulative effect.

There should be an affirmative answer to both of the following questions before a claim of fair use may be made under these guidelines:

1. *(or display) is at the instance and inspiration of the individual teacher,* and

2. *The inspiration and decision to use the work and the moment of its use for maximum teaching effectiveness are so close in time that it would be unreasonable to expect a timely reply to a request for permission.*

Essentially these spontaneity questions restrict educators from having materials (or television programs) copied in anticipation of demand. All requests for duplication, whether photocopies or off-air taping, must come directly from the teacher involved. In other words, an administrator, department head, librarian, or other person in a position of authority may not direct teachers or librarians to copy materials under the fair use exemption. In addition, a teacher's superior may not dictate to the teacher that copyright protected materials must be copied. A supervisor may suggest specific materials, but it is the responsibility of the individual teacher to decide to make the copies. This requirement is often called a "bottom up" copying scheme as opposed to a "top down" order.

What typical activities are covered?

The photocopy machine is probably the biggest danger spot in the school from the standpoint of print copying. Teachers photocopy materials at an astounding rate, and they do not always have the authority to make multiple copies of the items they are copying. While the print guidelines are very specific about how much and how many times something may be copied, and also specify items which may never be copied, few teachers or administrators have ever seen the guidelines. If someone were to do an audit of the copies made at the copy machine in a given week of the second semester of school (or possibly even the second marking period), one would find that the vast majority of the copies being made were infringing.

Typical school activities (permitted and not permitted) that will be addressed by the rules in this chapter include:

- *copying teacher-made tests/worksheets/letters*
- *copying commercial workbook pages/worksheets*
- *copying coloring book pages/sheets*
- *copying sheet music*
- *copying graphics onto bulletin boards freehand or via a projection device*
- *copying articles from professional magazines to distribute at faculty meetings*
- *copying graphics/maps/charts onto transparency film*
- *copying test booklets for assessment*
- *copying textbooks when there are not enough for every student*
- *copying magazine articles/newsletters for students (Weekly Reader, etc.)*
- *copying activity cards, instructional materials when there are not enough for every student*
- *copying test sheets (SRA kit sheets, etc.) when the original supply runs out*
- *copying flyers with graphics for PTA, etc.*
- *scanning book covers for library Web pages*

This is not a complete list of the types of print copying activities that are possible or even common in schools. But knowing the rules for these activities will provide guidance to other types of activities.

Q: As English coordinator, I would like to require all the high school English teachers to copy and distribute an editorial from the local newspaper to use as a standardized test writing prompt. Since this is a small portion of the newspaper, would this be permissible?

A: This small copying would be acceptable if the classroom teacher was making the copying decision, (see question 1), but because this copying is being directed by a higher authority, such copying is not permitted under the fair use guidelines. As an alternative, you could suggest the use of the editorial, and allow the individual teacher to make the decision to use that particular resource with her class.

Photocopying—issues

Typical photocopying issues to which schools will want to pay particular attention include:

- *photocopying consumable materials such as workbooks (whether or not the book is still in print or in adoption)*
- *photocopying more materials per term or year (depending on the length of the course) than allowed in the guidelines*
- *using photocopies to substitute for purchase of materials (as in making copies of textbook chapters rather than buying a copy of the text when you are a few short)*
- *administrators or curriculum coordinators directing teachers or entire grade levels or courses to photocopy protected materials. Such decisions may only be made by the teachers themselves, individually.*
- *not getting permission to repeatedly copy materials after the first fair use.*
- *copying student work to retain as exemplars*

Phonorecords—issues

No, we aren't talking about 12-inch black vinyl discs. Not all copying involves the photocopier. An audio-recording of a print work is called a "phonorecord." It is important to note that reading a book onto a cassette tape is exactly the same thing, according to the law, as putting that book on the photocopier and copying every page. Most educators recognize that photocopying a book is not a fair use, yet they feel entitled to make an audio recording of a book for a student who is a struggling reader.

The types of phonorecord issues that will interest schools include:

- *reading library books onto cassette tapes to assist struggling readers*
- *reading books onto cassette tapes to assist visually impaired students*
- *reading the newspaper onto tapes to take to senior citizens, as a service project*

Graphics—issues

Nothing perks up a tired worksheet like clip art or other graphics. However, using graphics can be problematic in certain situations. While the guidelines do address graphics for instruction, many of the graphics used in schools are used for decoration, not for instruction. The guidelines and the fair use tests are designed to support use of copyright protected materials for direct instruction, but making your school or classroom look "cute" or "welcoming" is not a stated purpose of fair use.

The types of graphics issues that schools will need to pay particular attention to include:

- *copying/enlarging cartoon characters, greeting card graphics, images from books/coloring books for the purpose of decoration of bulletin boards, classroom walls, etc.*

Q: As principal, I want to have teachers read the latest professional materials. I propose having my faculty maintain a notebook of articles that I select, but they photocopy. Is this permitted since I will not be doing the copies?

A: Probably not. As the teacher's supervisor, you may suggest they read the articles, but the decision to copy the materials must be left up to the teachers themselves. For you to order them to make the copies, you would be instituting a "top down" copying scheme which is prohibited under the copy guidelines. However, a teacher is permitted to make a copy of an article from a magazine if making that copy is the teacher's choice.

Q: *A teacher has plastered his walls with newspaper cartoons. Is it a copyright violation for teachers to cut out cartoons and display them?*

A: Presuming that the teacher bought the book or newspaper, she may cut it up and post the cartoons on her wall. The teacher may also make a single copy of a cartoon for her personal use or for teaching. That single copy can be on transparency film. The cartoon may also be scanned into a multimedia authoring program (see the chapter on multimedia for details).

- *using graphic characters on school t-shirts, book bags, signs, etc.*
- *using characters from library books to create murals, or other decorative elements.*

Murals—issues

Murals are lovely ways to decorate school walls. They warm up walls that otherwise would have a definite "institutional" feel. As long as students, teachers, or outside artists are creating or copying their own work, murals are not a problem. When you need to be concerned is when the mural artist uses the work of others in the mural. The work of others can be famous paintings (painted after 1923 and not in the public domain) or uses—more commonly—famous book characters such as the *Cat in the Hat*, or Disney characters. These instantly recognizable characters are not only protected by copyright but they are also protected by trademark in most cases. The artists/copyright owners may aggressively protect these characters. In fact, a librarian in Florida reported that representatives from Disney actually arrived with paint and painted out a mural that contained Disney characters.

Scanning—issues

Changing format on the scan is the biggest problem you will encounter with this method of reproduction. When one creates a scan, not only do you create a copy but you create a digital copy of an analog work. Digital copies may be copied infinitely without any of the degradation that is common to analog copies such as photocopies. Producers are exceptionally nervous about allowing their material to be digitized, fearing that it will "escape" and be lost forever.

Common activities involving scanning that you will want to watch:
- *scanning photos for yearbooks, Web pages, newspapers*
- *scanning book covers for library catalogs and Web pages*
- *scanning maps for Web pages*

What rights are affected?

Of the reserved rights of the copyright holder, several are of particular import in issues of print reproduction. Those rights include:

Reproduction

- Making copies is how a print copyright owner makes money. If you make the copies locally, the copyright owner gets no money from your copies.

Distribution

- Where do the copies you make go? Copyright owners get to decide where (or if) their works will be distributed. Especially in matters of out-of-print works, copyright owners may not wish these materials to be available because they are out of date, or not fashionable, or the publisher has other materials with which this work may compete. All would be valid reasons not to wish the work to be available in the marketplace. Perhaps the publisher feels the work is inappropriate for the venue in which you propose to distribute the works. Such decisions are reserved for the copyright owner, alone, to make.

Adaptation

- When you make changes in print materials, you are adapting them. Perhaps you want to take a book and turn it into a play to present to parents for a PTA meeting. Or you wish to translate a work into Spanish for your Hispanic students. Or you wish to take a cartoon and turn it into a large paper "run through" for the football or basketball team. Naturally, you will want to adjust the picture to put the characters in the team uniform. You might write new words to go with a piece of sheet music. All these typical activities are considered adaptation and are within the rights of the copyright owner.

Display

- Print materials are displayed when they are put in a public place. Display could include book covers on bulletin boards; posting student work in the halls, or on a Web page; newsletters and yearbooks.

What guidelines affect print materials?

When considering what fair uses one may make of print materials, there are several things to keep in mind. First, is the material protected at all? Remember, that anything published before 1923 is in the public domain in the United States. Materials published after 1923 but before 1976 that were not registered appropriately, or not renewed are also in the public domain. You may use public domain materials for any purpose whatsoever.

If you find that the material is, indeed, protected, you may decide to seek a fair use defense to your use of the materials. You have two choices: find a set of guidelines that apply to the materials you wish to use, or apply the statutory four tests of fair use. Finding that the materials are print, you may elect to use the print guidelines to see if your proposed use is within the limits of the guidelines. If your use exceeds the guidelines, you may go through a fair use analysis to determine if your use may be considered fair via that route.

When the 1976 law was passed, there were no guidelines. There was only the fair use section of the law (section 107). The law is cryptic and difficult for laypeople to understand. Representative Kastenmeier of the House Judiciary Subcommittee headed a House committee that worked with publishers and education representatives to clarify the fair use definitions codified in the law, and to give educators understandable, workable limits for fair use. These limits are known collectively as the Kastenmeier report, the classroom photocopying guidelines, or sometimes the print guidelines.

Kastenmeier report

The first half of the report covers print works (specifically books and periodicals) and the second half includes guidelines on the use of printed music. Also appended are short guidelines on replacement copying and repair of damaged materials (Special Interest Video Sales Group, 1995).

Details of report

Single copies for teachers

A teacher may copy (or ask to have copied) for the purposes of research, teaching, or preparation for teaching any of the following:

- *A single copy of a chapter from a book;*
- *A single copy of an article from a periodical or newspaper;*
- *A single copy of a short story, short essay, or short poem, even if it is contained in a collection;*
- *A single copy of a chart, graph, diagram, drawing, cartoon, or picture from a book, periodical, or newspaper.*

The teacher may retain the single copies of these materials in files for personal or research use or for use in teaching. This interpretation would permit reading the material to a class. A liberal, but not unjustifiable, interpretation of the guidelines would allow the teacher to write the material on the blackboard or overhead projector for use in teaching, as well.

The preceding permissions seem quite generous. The Congressional guidelines, however, provide some limitations on these options. There are four significant prohibitions to the print permission, three of which have application to single copies for teachers:

- *Copying shall not be used to create or to replace or substitute for anthologies, compilations, or collective works. Such replacement or substitution may occur whether copies of various works or excerpts therefrom are accumulated or reproduced and used separately.* (Note: In other words, you can't create your own books by gathering bits and pieces from other sources. This would include notebooks of editorial cartoons, comic strips, series of essays, and the like.)

- *There shall be no copying from works intended to be "consumable" in the course of study or of teaching. These include workbooks, exercises, standardized tests and test booklets and answer sheets, and like consumable material.*

- *Copying shall not: substitute for the purchase of books, publishers' reprints, or periodicals; be directed by higher authority; or be repeated with respect to the same item by the same teacher from term to term.*

The prohibitions are significant because they deal with guidelines often breached in daily school and library practice. A teacher may find some particular item that seems relevant to a course. While copying some portion of the text is acceptable, copying more than the limited chapter, article, essay, or chart described in the law above would be considered to be substituting for the personal purchase of the work and would therefore be in violation of the Congressional guidelines and of the copyright law itself. Financial loss to the copyright holder is the overriding consideration when a court is asked to consider a ruling of fair use, so anything beyond minimal copying would tend to tip the scales away from a justifiable claim of fair use. Though the law doesn't specify that any of the four factors of fair use is "more equal" than others, in reality courts hold the "value" test to be more significant in application. Sometimes a work may be out of print, and a teacher will attempt to justify copying the entire work because it is not available in the marketplace. However, out of print is not the same as out of copyright. There may be many reasons a work goes out of print: perhaps demand for the work has dwindled, and it isn't economically reasonable for the publisher to keep the work in print. Or the publisher may have a similar work by a different author that they would prefer to promote, and they let the earlier one lapse out of print. The book you have may be inaccurate. Whatever the reason, it is the prerogative of the publisher to print or not print a work the publisher owns. By making unauthorized copies beyond the chapter/essay/article limit, the teacher bypasses the permissions and royalty to which the copyright owner would be entitled.

Similarly, since copying may not be "directed by higher authority," an administrator, curriculum director, supervisor, or department head cannot direct a teacher or other staff member to copy copyrighted materials under fair use for whatever purpose. An individual teacher must initiate the copying for that teacher's use. An example of violation of this aspect of the guidelines would be a principal telling a teacher to copy a specific article on an aspect of classroom management. The principal may ask the teacher to read the article but cannot order the teacher to copy the article. The teacher may, however, decide to copy the article for files or for reading at a more convenient time. This decision originated with the teacher; hence, there is no violation.

Another example of violation would be a department head directing teachers to copy the instructions from a set of standardized tests so that only one set of instructions will need to be purchased. Not only is this a violation of the prohibition on copy orders coming from a higher authority, it also is a direct attempt to deprive the copyright holder of sales, violating the fourth fair use factor: "the effect of the use upon the potential market for . . . the copyrighted work."

Q: The speech and debate team would like to make several copies of numerous pages from books that state "no portion of this book may be reproduced or copied without written permission of .....". Is this "fair use"?

A: A notice in a book cannot override federal law regarding fair use. However, a signed contract or license can. It is impossible to answer the question without knowing the book, where it came from, how it was acquired, etc. etc. Here are some things to consider.

Copying for classroom use, in limited amounts as suggested in the print guidelines, is permissible. Going far beyond that limit is probably NOT fair use. This appears to be, from the description in your question, an extracurricular use. In that case, all the classroom guidelines go out the window and you fall back on standard fair use—the four tests. You have to consider if this work is creative, if it is published, if the use is nonprofit, how much you are using of the work, and what effect the use will have on the market for or value of the work. HOWEVER, if you have licensed these materials, and the license says they can't be copied, all bets are off. The license controls.

Multiple copies for classroom use

Copying in multiple units for student use in a classroom setting is completely permissible if certain tests are met. An instructor may not make more than one copy of the item for each student in the course, and each item copied must be used for classroom use or for discussion. Additionally, each copy must include a notice of copyright. To clarify this point, if a teacher has 30 students, she may not make 45 copies assuming that some of the students will lose or mutilate their copies before the assignment is finished. The teacher must actually use the copies for a specific activity or discussion. She may not make the copies just to include them for their literary or cultural value, or as a non-required (enrichment) supplement.

The requirement of notice of copyright is the most often neglected aspect of this section of the guidelines. Each copy must have a notice of the copyright holder. Ordinarily this can be as simple as a notation on the margin of the page such as "Copyright 2001, Big Publishing Co." Failure to include this notice is a violation of the Digital Millennium Copyright Act because it removes what is known as copyright management information.

The three tests that each instance of copying must meet are brevity, spontaneity, and cumulative effect. These tests are very specific in nature, and each copy must meet all the criteria for each test. This wording is specified in the guidelines and indicates legislative intent, so fudging significantly on the limits is probably not a good idea.

Brevity

Poetry: If a poem is less than 250 words and is printed on not more than two pages, it may be copied in its entirety. If the poem is longer than 250 words, only 250 words may be copied. The law does allow an unfinished line to be included if the 250-word limit should happen to fall in the middle of a line.

Prose: If a complete article, story, or essay is less than 2,500 words, it may be copied in its entirety. For other types of prose, such as a play, a novel, or a letter, a copy must not be more than 1,000 words or 10 percent of the whole, whichever is less. No matter how short the work, one may legitimately copy an excerpt of 500 words. In other words, if a work is only 1,000 words in total, a teacher may copy 500 words even though that amount exceeds the 10 percent guideline.

Exception: The type of literature, composed of text and significant illustrations, commonly called "picture books," is generally much shorter than the 2,500-word limit for complete copying. The law provides a specific prohibition against copying works of this type in their entirety (and it specifically includes similar works intended for adults). Only two pages of a picture book may be copied as long as those two pages do not comprise more than 10 percent of the text of the book. Graphic novels were not invented when these guidelines were written, but one could make a good case that they would fall into a similar exception.

Illustration: One chart, graph, drawing, cartoon, diagram, or picture may be copied per book or periodical issue. These copies must be photocopies or other exact copies. Modifying the illustration in any way violates the author's right of adaptation. Note that teachers may make a single copy of an illustration or chart for use in teaching under the Single Copies for Teachers rules. That single copy can be on a transparency or scanned into PowerPoint and used in that format.

Q: Is it OK for a teacher to record a picture book and let kindergarten students listen to the story on the tape while looking at the book?

A: There is a special exception to copyright law for handicapped users that allows this practice, but the person for whom you are recording the book must be blind or otherwise physically unable to use a book. The copy must also be made on a special recorder designed for handicapped users. (See 17 USC § 121) Making a copy of a book by recording it is the same (according to the law) as making a copy by photocopying it. Remember that for picture books there is a copy limitation (under the classroom guidelines) of two pages or 10% of the text, whichever is less.

Spontaneity

The idea to make multiple copies must be initiated by the individual teacher. In other words, the department head cannot make copies to give to each teacher to use in class, nor can the principal copy copyright protected materials to hand out in certain classes. The guidelines even go so far as to state that the making of multiple copies must be at the inspiration of the individual teacher, implying that the department head or supervisor cannot even give the classroom teacher a list of appropriate items to be copied without violating the letter of the law. This doctrine is consistent with the prohibition of copying directed by a higher authority, as discussed earlier.

The rationale for the spontaneity rule is that the idea and decision to use the work and the moment it will be used for maximum teaching effectiveness are so close in time that it would be unreasonable to expect a timely reply to a request for permission. "Unreasonable" and "timely" are subject to some degree of latitude. How long should one expect to wait for permission to reproduce? Are two weeks enough? A month? A semester? As a rule of thumb, allow about two weeks for a reply. If teachers know at least two weeks ahead of time that they will need to copy something for use in class, they should write for permission. If they do not receive a reply in time, they could then proceed with the copying since there is not sufficient time to send a second query. Obviously, if an article, illustration, poem, or other printed matter comes to the attention of the teacher a matter of days before the time of optimum use, the teacher could make multiple copies for the class without writing for permission. The teacher may not, however, use that same article, illustration, or poem in subsequent semesters or years without permission.

Cumulative Effect

The last test that an instance of multiple copying must pass is that of cumulative effect. The guidelines want to assure that copying is not substituting for purchase of books and periodicals. Again, the law wants to protect authors and publishers to assure there is a market for materials. To comply with this test, the copying must be done for only one course. For example, a teacher may make copies of a poem for all freshman English classes (one copy per student), but may not copy the same poem for her sophomore English classes.

The guidelines limit the number of copies that may be made from a single source or author during a school year (or a semester or quarter if this isn't a full-year class). A teacher may make class copies of one short poem, article, story, or essay or two excerpts from the same author during one term (year or semester or quarter). If the copies are taken from a collective work (a book of poetry or essays by multiple authors, for example), the teacher is limited to three or fewer items during a class term. Periodical articles are also limited to three or fewer items copied from one periodical volume (not issue) during one term. Current news articles from newspapers and magazines are exempt from this requirement. When an item ceases to become "current news" is not defined, but a two-month window would be generous. While the above rules are very specific, you must also consider the four prohibitions to the print permission when determining fair use. (Three of them were quoted on p. 54).

Q: Our tenth grade English teachers require their students to create an anthology of poetry, essays, short stories, and articles on one thematic aspect of the Holocaust. Since the law states that copying should not be used to create or be a substitute for anthologies, compilations or collective works, is this a violation of copyright law?

A: The print anthologies restriction is addressed more to teachers who simply photocopy the world rather than purchase textbooks. If the students make only a single copy of the materials for their own projects, the students make the choice of what to copy, and the projects revert to the students at the end of the assignment, there should be no problem.

1. Copying shall not be used to create or to replace or substitute for anthologies, compilations, or collective works. Such replacement or substitution may occur whether copies of various works or excerpts therefrom are accumulated or reproduced and used separately.

2. There shall be no copying from works intended to be 'consumable' in the course of study or of teaching. These include workbooks, exercises, standardized tests, test booklets, and answer sheets, and like consumable material.

3. Copying shall not
   — substitute for the purchase of books, publishers' reprints, or periodicals;
   — be directed by higher authority; or
   — be repeated with respect to the same item by the same teacher from term to term.

4. No charge shall be made to the student beyond the actual cost of the photocopying.

In addition, no more than nine instances of such multiple copying can occur for one course during one class term.

The intent of these prohibitions is to protect authors and publishers from teachers who would substitute copies for purchased books or workbooks.

Examples of acceptable multiple copying

As a result of confusing reports about a nominee to the Supreme Court, a teacher requests the librarian to make 32 copies (one per student enrolled in the course) of a one-page excerpt (approximately 475 words) from a book to give to each student. The students will use the excerpt as a basis for a written exercise in editorial writing. Each student's copy is free, and each copy includes a notice of copyright.

An elementary teacher asks the clerical aide to make 19 copies (one per student) of a timeline of the American Revolution. The students will include the diagram in a notebook they are creating to follow the events of the Revolution from beginning to end. Each copy includes notice of copyright.

An English coordinator suggests that a particular poem might be good to teach the skill of identification of meter. The decision to use the poem is left up to the individual teacher.

Last year, a first grade teacher copied a word game out of a children's magazine for her students to use as they studied a specific letter sequence. This year she wants to use the same game. She plans in advance and writes for, and receives, permission.

Examples of unacceptable multiple copying

A teacher copies a column from five consecutive issues of a magazine, making a booklet of articles for each student in a class. This practice violates the prohibition against creating anthologies as well as the cumulative effect test against copying more than three articles from a periodical volume.

Every year an elementary teacher makes copies of the poem "There's a new kid on the block" to give to students on the day that a new student arrives in class. Using this poem every year violates the prohibition against copying the same item from term to term.

A teacher wishes to teach the concept of sequencing. To help students visualize the process, the teacher copies a short picture book for each student and then mixes up the pages. The students must put the book back into the correct sequence. This practice violates the limit on brevity in that only two pages or 10 percent may be copied from a picture book.

 A debate teacher requests copies of several selected articles for students to use in preparing a defense. The copies cost $4.57 at a local copy shop. To make matters simpler, the teacher charges the students $5. The extra money goes into the fund used to buy ribbons for the debate tournament. This practice violates the fourth prohibition to multiple copies. The student may not be charged beyond the actual cost of the copies.

 A month before the school year started, the school decided to teach a new class. There wasn't time to order textbooks. The teacher had to come up with all the teaching materials herself. She copied chapters from different books plus articles from magazines in order to give students learning materials. This example violates the admonition against more than 9 instances of multiple copying per year or term (depending on the length of the class).

 A principal reads an article appropriate to a staff development concept. She asks the secretary to make copies for all the teachers and place them in their mailboxes. This instance violates several regulations including "top down" prohibitions. Also, the teachers aren't students enrolled in a class—they are employees. Copying for the purpose of staff development seldom merits a fair use exemption. It could be a fair use, however, if the four factors test of section 107 are met.

Copies for handicapped students

A modification to the rule against copying and adaptation permits institutions serving the blind and physically handicapped to acquire or make adaptive copies in Braille or other formats (17 USC § 121). There are specific regulations about the format of the copies and who may use them. These rules cover students who are unable to use standard print works because of visual deficiencies, or because they are physically handicapped and cannot hold a book or turn its pages. It does *not* address the needs of the dyslexic or slow learner. Those students who qualify under this law must be identified through the Library of Congress Division of Blind and Physically Handicapped, or through one of the state library branches. Application requires certification of the disability by medical personnel. The "other formats" includes reading books onto cassette tapes, but one must pay particular attention to the format of tape specified in the law. While consumer grade cassette tape plays at $1^3/4$ inches per second (i.p.s.) using 2 track tapes, the format specified in the regulation is $^{15}/16$ i.p.s, using 4 track tapes. The $^{15}/16$ i.p.s. 4 track standard is used in the Recording for the Blind program that is established through the Library of Congress and the various state libraries. Special players are required to play these slow, multi-track tapes. The players are available for free when the application is approved. Digital copies are also permitted under this section of the law, such as those made for

Q: If it is a violation of multiple copying if you copy the same poem for your class year after year, is it a violation of copyright law to show the same video to your class year after year? I've heard that it is OK to show the same video every year as long as the school has purchased a legal copy of it. But, I've heard that practice is not acceptable without a performance license.

A: No, it isn't. Print copying is covered under the Kastenmeier report, while AV use is covered under section 106 of the law. The print guidelines (the Kastenmeier report) specifically state that copying may not be repeated from term to term. But the AV use guidelines do not address re-use. Perhaps the act of copying is what they feel makes the two uses different, but they are treated differently for school use purposes.

Kurzweil machines. The law cautions that copies in whatever format made under this exception may only be used with students certified as eligible.

As of December 3, 2004, a new amendment to copyright law came via the Individuals with Disabilities Education Improvement Act of 2004. The new requirements allow certain technologies to be employed to assist "print disabled" (which would include diagnosed dyslexic) students. These materials will be able to be produced locally only if such materials are not available for purchase. The law also provided for the establishment of the National Instructional Materials Access Center under the auspices of the American Printing House for the Blind. The law directs a new standard, the National Instructional Materials Accessibility Standard, that will be available solely for the conversion of print materials into accessible formats for print disabled students. However, the new standard and exemptions only apply to required textbooks. Library materials and supplementary materials are not addressed in the new law. Authorization for services under this law will remain certification through the State Library or the Library of Congress Division of Blind and Physically Handicapped. Both require certification by a medical professional that the individual is unable to use standard print materials. (Individuals, 2005).

Print permission issues

If a teacher knows that a particular item will be used year to year or term to term, the safest course is to write for permission. The same holds true if the teacher plans in September, for example, to use a particular poem at Thanksgiving. This knowledge gives the teacher ample time to request permission from the copyright holder, likely the publisher. In such an instance, requesting and receiving permission is mandatory prior to copying, not optional. However, if the teacher requests permission but gets no response by the time the material is needed, the teacher may make the needed copies—once. If the teacher hasn't gotten permission to make copies by the second time the materials are needed, she needs to locate something else to use.

Always remember: a copyright owner is not required to respond to your request for permission. If you don't get an affirmative response, the safest course is to assume the answer is "no." The landmark Kinko's case (see section on Related Cases in this chapter) supports that statement where the court explains that Basic Book's failure to respond to requests for permission was not to be interpreted as a license to copy. *Basic Books, Inc. v. Kinko's Graphics Corp.* 758 F.Supp. 1522, 1540 (S.D.N.Y.,1991).

Consumable materials

Consumable materials comprise much more than workbooks. The category includes workbooks, tests, standardized tests, answer sheets, and worksheets among other forms of consumables such as cut-outs, templates, and patterns intended to be destroyed in making the item. The prohibitions on multiple copying state that "there shall be no copying of or from materials intended to be consumable." Pattern books, such as knitting books or woodworking plans, probably don't qualify as consumable and would likely be afforded the protection of other printed works, but dress patterns printed on tissue are likely intended to be destroyed to an extent in making the item.

The problem is that there are multiple items in the school teacher's bag of tricks that can be considered consumable yet are still copied, albeit illegally. Schools often draw on the "no-profit" defense when copying consumables, but such a defense doesn't take into consideration the other tests of fair use. All aspects of the fair use exemption must be considered when making copies under fair use. Here are some common examples of improper use of consumables:

 A teacher buys a single copy of a book of worksheets and copies one of the worksheets for students to use when they have a substitute teacher.

A teacher buys a book of worksheets, then cuts the worksheets apart to create a new sheet, duplicating that new worksheet for the class.

 A computer program provides a package of questionnaires on which to record responses to questions. These sheets may or may not be suitable for insertion into an automatic scoring machine. The publishing company sells replacement packages of the required questionnaires. When the supply of questionnaires runs low, the librarian photocopies a new supply from one of the originals, keeping an original on file to make future copies.

 A new math series comes with a package of standardized tests. In order to stretch a limited budget to buy a set of manipulatives, the school buys one package of the tests (enough for one classroom) and duplicates enough additional copies so all students in the grade level can take the test on the same day.

These uses (and infinite variations) are all out of compliance. Each of these violations could come into compliance simply by receiving permission from the publisher of the material. Since the publishers are in the business of selling consumable materials, it is unlikely they would grant blanket permission to reproduce their consumables. However, since printing their products involves materials and labor costs to them, they might be willing to work out a discount arrangement for a school to undertake the actual duplication of the material under a license agreement. It can't hurt to ask. The worst they can do is say "no."

Periodicals

Copying periodical articles (including newspaper articles) falls into the same basket as copying most print materials. Periodical articles are mentioned specifically in the guidelines concerning making single copies for teachers. An article from a periodical or newspaper is considered to be within limits of acceptable copying. In addition, copying a chart, graph, diagram, drawing, cartoon, or picture from a periodical or newspaper is also legal. Under the Guidelines, current news articles are exempt from permissions requirements; however, an item is only "current" for a short time. The two month suggested lead time for permission requests is probably sufficient for this use, as well. It's important to acknowledge that news doesn't stay "current news" forever.

The guidelines on multiple copies for classroom use are much more specific with regard to types of acceptable copies, whether from books or periodicals. The guidelines for brevity apply equally to items copied from periodicals and newspapers.

Poetry taken from periodicals must meet the guidelines for poetry: if a poem is less than 250 words and is printed on not more than two pages, it may be copied in its entirety. If the poem is longer than 250 words, only 250 words may be copied. The law does allow an unfinished line to be included if the 250-word limit should happen to fall in the middle of a line.

Q: A Special Ed teacher has a textbook that he uses with his class of 5 or 6 inclusion students. From the book publisher he requested a CD that reads the book to the student so they can follow along in the book. The publisher sent one CD free-of-charge. He wants to burn more copies of the one CD so more than 1 student can use it at a time. Can he legally burn copies of the CD?

A: He can't make that copy under fair use (it copies the entire work, the work is creative, and the copy is to avoid purchasing a legitimate copy). The copy doesn't follow the classroom exemption, either, because the CD is of the entire work, not just a chapter. He can contact the publisher for permission to make the copies, or to order more copies directly from them.

"The distinction between "fair use" and infringement may be unclear and not easily defined. There is no specific number of words, lines, or notes that may safely be taken without permission. Acknowledging the source of the copyrighted material does not substitute for obtaining permission."
–U.S. Copyright Office. 1999.

Prose taken from periodicals must meet the test for prose: if a complete article, story, or essay is less than 2,500 words, it may be copied in its entirety. For other types of prose, a copy must not be more than 1,000 words or 10 percent of the whole, whichever is less, with a minimum acceptable copy limit of 500 words. In other words, if a work is only 1,000 words long, a teacher may copy 500 words even though that amount exceeds the 10 percent guideline.

Graphic material in periodicals may also be copied provided the copying meets the test for illustrations: One chart, graph, drawing, cartoon, diagram, or picture may be copied per periodical issue. Beware of copying an item, a cartoon for example, from several issues of a periodical. The allowed limit is three per periodical volume. The number of issues comprising a volume varies from periodical to periodical, but it generally encompasses one 12-month period defined by the publisher.

The test of spontaneity is also applicable to copies from periodicals. The making of multiple copies must be at the "instance and inspiration" of the individual teacher. A supervisor may not direct a teacher to make multiple copies of material from any periodical. In addition, the decision to use the work and the time of its use in class must be so close that it would be unreasonable to expect a reply of permission from a copyright holder. Again, the three-week window for permission would appear to be adequate.

The guidelines also specify a test of "cumulative effect" to limit the number of instances of copying allowed.

Those guidelines affecting the copying of periodical materials are:

- *The copying must be done for only one course;*

- *Only one entire article or two excerpts may be copied from the same author;*

- *No more than three items from the same periodical volume may be copied during one class term (year or semester, depending on the course); and*

- *No more than nine items may be copied in multiples per course during one class term.*

Some examples of these rules applied to typical classroom uses of periodical copies would be:

- *The American history and American government teacher finds an article that would be applicable to both courses. She may not reproduce the article for both classes. She may post the original article on the class bulletin board, however, and ask students to read it there.*

- *A biology teacher has already handed out two excerpts of works from Stephen Jay Gould for her class's study of evolution when she finds a new article in the journal Science that is even more enlightening. She may not make multiple copies of the work without permission. She may, however, place her copy of the magazine on reserve in the library and require students to read it.*

- *A third grade teacher has copied two different articles from this year's Zoo Books for her science class. In preparing a unit on poetry, she finds a poem in one of this year's issues. She may copy the poem, but no more items from that volume of the periodical for this term.*

- *A sociology teacher uses magazines as a primary resource, copying articles to use as discussion starters and essay support. So far this term he has copied eight articles to hand out to his classes. In a new issue of National Geographic there are two articles about primitive societies that he would like his students to compare and contrast. He may not copy both these articles since that would exceed the nine-items-per-term limitation.*

Documents in the public domain, such as periodicals or monographs from the Dept. of Education or ERIC, do not count in the total copies per year as there is no restriction on duplication of public domain materials.

The general prohibitions on multiple copying apply to periodicals, also. Those prohibitions specify that copies may not be used to create or substitute for anthologies or compilations. The prohibitions state that the copies do not have to be "accumulated" to fall under this rule. "Accumulated" in this case means collecting the copies and distributing them all at the same time, as if they were together in a booklet. The articles may be copied and used separately and still violate this prohibition.

Additionally, copying must not substitute for the purchase of a subscription to the periodical or publisher's reprints; it must not be ordered by a higher authority; and the same items may not be copied in succeeding class terms. Of course, the student may not be charged for the copies beyond the actual cost of the copies. The most significant consideration in this list is that of financial impact on the copyright owner. If the proposed fair use copying were to be repeated widely by many others, would such copying have an adverse effect on the copyright holder's revenues? If so, the use is undoubtedly not fair.

The lone exception to the rules on copying from periodicals is that of articles from current news periodicals (e.g. Time, Newsweek) and newspapers and the current news sections of other periodicals. Using the Guidelines for guidance, copying such articles is in compliance. The only question would be how "current" the article is. While no guidelines exist to specify the amount of time allotted to "currency," a window of two weeks would not be inappropriate and would certainly be justifiable, especially around vacation periods where an article might be published but the class does not meet for a two-week span of time.

Graphics

The term "graphics" can cover a lot of territory: paintings, photographs, lithographs, serigraphs, etchings, maps, diagrams, charts. Posters and illustrations can all be considered graphics. Graphics pose a major source of potential copyright problems for schools. Section 106 of the copyright law reserves six rights to the copyright owner: reproduction, adaptation, distribution, performance, display, and digital transmission of sound recordings. The rights of reproduction, adaptation, and display are the most problematic for schools as far as graphics are concerned. In certain instances reproduction of graphic material may fall under the "fair use" provisions. Making a single copy of a graph or illustration from a book is acceptable if the copy is for personal research or study, and multiple copies of a single graphic are authorized for a class under the standard print fair use guidelines:

- *Copying must be at the instance and inspiration of the teacher and so close in time to the required use that receipt of permission would be impossible;*
- *The copy is for only one course in the school;*
- *There are not more than nine occurrences of multiple copying for that course; and*
- *Not more than one graphic is copied per book or periodical.*

Adaptation is a bigger dilemma. Graphics producers make much money from adapting their works for other media. Disney characters adorn everything from drinking cups to nightshirts to posters. Cartoon and advertising graphics decorate paper goods, greeting cards, and billboards. All of these appealing images are attractive to children, and teachers wish to capitalize on their students' recognition of the popular characters and themes. This desire is made all the more realizable because virtually every teacher has available the means to incorporate these designs in bulletin boards, handouts, notes to parents, and other decorative uses in the classroom or library.

Q: *The art teacher at our school would like to put samples of famous artworks on her Web page. If the artist is long dead (i.e. VanGogh, Renoir, etc.) can she copy the work from another Web page and put it on her own in order to provide samples for her students to view?*

A: *She can copy the artwork itself (as that is in the public domain if the work was published before 1923), but the image from someone's Web page MAY be protected by copyright. And if it is protected by copyright and the owner has watermarked the image, your art teacher friend could get into a lot of hot water for taking and redistributing an image.*

A photo of a public domain work that employs no creativity in angle, lighting, etc. cannot be protected by copyright because the photograph doesn't meet the requirement for minimal creativity. Some photographers and museums, however, don't believe that and insist their works are protected. They can be very litigious if they find you are using their digital images. That would mean a lot of expense and stress to fight the suit. Depending on your aversion to risk, you might want to scan your own images from photographs as long as they meet the requirements stated above.

Copyright law doesn't look kindly on such unauthorized uses. By taking an artist's work and enlarging, modifying, or converting it to another medium, a teacher usurps the creator's (or more accurately, the copyright holder's) right to determine how the image will be used.

The library may be a contributory infringer in most school-based instances of copyright violation in this area. The primary tool in this misdeed is either the opaque projector, the overhead projector, or the document camera. If the librarian lends that equipment with the knowledge that it will be used to infringe copyright, the librarian is considered a contributory infringer because he or she has knowledge that copyright is being or will be infringed, and even contributes to the infringement. As a contributory infringer, the librarian or anyone else with knowledge that the infringement is taking place could be liable for damages. A good plan would be to post the standard copyright warning notice usually affixed to photocopiers on all equipment that could potentially be used to make contraband copies, adaptations, or derivations. The wording of these notices is specified by law, and is reprinted in Appendix E. Preprinted adhesive labels and stand-up signs are sold by the major library supply houses. In this instance, one could make a case that the opaque projector and the overhead projector could be considered "unsupervised reproduction equipment." Libraries (as opposed to schools) aren't held liable for unsupervised reproduction equipment, so the librarian might have a viable defense from contributory liability if the standard disclaimer is attached to any library-owned equipment capable of making reproductions.

Graphic infringements occur when:

- *A teacher uses the opaque projector to enlarge a greeting card illustration for a bulletin board decoration.*

- *A librarian photocopies an image from a coloring book as part of a worksheet she is creating.*

- *The PTA uses a pantograph or overhead projector to enlarge a poster to wall size as a hall decoration.*

- *The art teacher creates stuffed animals of popular picture book characters.*

- *The principal scans a cartoon from a magazine into the PTA newsletter.*

- *The cheerleading squad creates a paper "run-through" for the basketball team. The "run-through" features a popular cartoon character dressed in the team uniform.*

- *The librarian scans images from books to put on the library Web site (a single copy from a book for use in the library is fine, but distributing copies to the world is likely beyond the scope of fair use).*

As you can see, potential for copyright infringement of graphics is quite broad. The best prevention is to insist on original or public domain graphics.

The Internet discussion group for school librarians, LM_NET, carried the following message from Corinne Smith, director of audiovisual services at Penn State University. Dealing with copyright of visual material on a daily basis, she has a unique perspective on this issue:

> "So far, there have been no comprehensive guidelines issued regarding the scanning or importing of copyrighted materials into your own work—except for the obvious 'derivative work' that you are making, presumably illegally.
>
> "Most of us live by the rule of asking permission for everything we copy into computer or interactive video programs, even if we're just going to use it in a classroom situation. Some folks have charged us for classroom use, others are just happy we asked for permission."

> "As for copying fictional character images, you're playing with fire there! Both Disney and Warner Brothers have lawyers combing the country just looking for violations. Their cartoons are both copyrighted and trademarked, so they can get you any way they want to. Look at Garfield or Snoopy cake pans, even, and you'll see some sort of copyright notice on the box it came in. Look at those nifty Bugs Bunny and Tasmanian Devil cartoon shirts, and you'll see a copyright and trademark notice at the bottom of the shirt. The latest story I heard about fictional characters involved an "illegitimate" Barney imitator who appeared at a local restaurant. The restaurant was issued a cease-and-desist order because that was not a legal Barney running around to greet the kids."

Scanners

The scanner is a new computer-based technology that has jolted the world of print copyright. Virtually any image can now be transformed into bits and bytes for incorporation into graphics packages, desktop publishing documents, and multimedia presentations. As stated previously, the original copyright holder retains the rights of reproduction, adaptation, and display, among others. Scanning a copyrighted illustration may be a copyright violation of any of those three rights. A student may use a scanned copyrighted image in a report, but the student must retain ownership of the report once it is graded. The teacher may not retain that report (or a copy

Q: Our art teacher would like to have her elementary students paint a mural in the library combining characters from children's literature. These would not be a direct copy from a book, but rather a combination of characters within an orginal setting. None of the characters would be Disney, but rather from artists such as Tomie dePaola, etc. This would be an educational effort, to teach art skills. There would be no financial gain to this. Is it OK?

A: No financial gain isn't the big consideration here. Note that many artists are just as aggressive about protecting characters as Disney, Shel Silverstein, etc. What you are doing is creating a derivative work. Students have the right to do this for their own education (art skills), but the copies must vest with the student. You are planning to do a daily public display of these characters, and the daily display has nothing to do with coursework. The copies will not be with the students, rather they will stay at the school, and the purpose is to avoid paying for licensed copies of artwork. None of these is a reason in your favor.

I wouldn't recommend this project to you. As an alternative idea, the students can read several versions of a tale (*Cinderella*, for example) and then draw THEIR OWN versions of the characters. However, remember that the students own the copyrights to their own work, and you will want signed releases from the students' parents (because the students are minors) to retain and display the work. I would probably add that you have all rights to the work so that at some point in the future you can decide to paint over the mural, thereby destroying it.

of it), nor may he or she reproduce it for a workshop. If the work is a multimedia presentation, it may only be displayed for the students and teachers in the class for which it was prepared. Presentation before what would amount to an open audience is considered a public performance. The student may not grant permission for such a performance because, while he owns the copyright to his own portion of the work, he may not give permission for that which he does not own—the copyrighted material he has "borrowed" to enhance his own work.

A staff member cannot scan a cartoon or article into a newsletter for distribution to the faculty or parents. A scanned copy of a famous photograph cannot legally be modified by computer graphics into a similar, or even quite different, image. There is no amount of modification that can be made to an original image to make the format conversion "OK." In short, just because the technology exists to reproduce an item electronically, the user of the technology does not have the right to do so.

Resources for understanding

Fair Use of Print Materials Glossary

Accumulation: Gathering together reproductions to be distributed at one time. Accumulated copies do not count as one; they count as the total of the parts. Also, copies do not have to be distributed at once to be considered an anthology.

Collective work: A work written by two or more authors, each of whom contribute separate, identified portions of the work.

Current news: Descriptions of events that have happened in the recent past. Some magazines and newspapers contain nothing but current news, while others mix current news with commentary, essays, and personality pieces. Only current news is offered a special exemption from copy limits.

Notice of copyright: Required notice on fair use reproductions of copyrighted material. The notice must include the name of the copyright holder and the date of copyright, such as "Copyright 1997, Linworth Publishing." The notice must appear on each copy.

Periodical volume: The binding increment of a periodical. Most periodicals assemble volumes based on a 12-month period (though the volume may start in January, July, or any other month), but others use a two-volume-per-calendar-year arrangement or other increment.

Term: The length of time to complete a course. An English class might span an entire school year, while an elective class such as psychology might meet only for a semester or quarter. The term of the English class is a year, while the term for the elective is either a semester or quarter. One must consider the term of the course when evaluating the ability to reproduce materials for that course.

Related cases

Some landmark cases have been ruled upon in the last few years. Understanding these cases will help develop a mental framework to understand the scope of fair use.

***American Geophysical Union v. Texaco Inc.*, 37 F.3d 881, 900 et seq. (2d Cir.) *(Jacobs, J., dissenting)*, amended & superseded, 60 F.3d 913 (1994), cert. dismissed, 116 S.Ct. 592 (1995).**

One of the most important cases regarding photocopying, the case involved a corporate library (Texaco) that made photocopies of magazine articles on the request of scientists who worked for the company. American Geophysical Union and 82 other publishers of scientific and technical journals sued, claiming that photocopying was not within the bounds of fair use. The courts agreed, citing that this was "institutional, systemic" copying, with the intent to avoid paying for additional copies of the magazines.

***Princeton University Press v. Michigan Document Services, Inc.*, 99 F.3d 1381 (6th Cir. 1996).**

The ruling in this case found that using photocopies of copyright protected excerpts of works to assemble "coursepacks" for college courses is a copyright infringement and does not meet the tests of fair use. The coursepacks were assembled by a for-profit copy shop near the university campus, and no permissions were sought and no permission fees were paid through third party clearinghouses.

***Basic Books, Inc. v. Kinko's Graphics Corp.*, 758 F. Supp. 1522 (S.D.N.Y. 1991).**

The court held that Kinko's violated the copyright of several works by making copies for coursepacks without requesting permission or paying appropriate fees. The decision lists the actual works copied, and the pages copied. Most of the works were out of print and out of stock, but copying a single chapter from a book was found to be excessive. Note that Kinko's is a for-profit enterprise, even though the use was nonprofit. This case has significant implications for school and library copying. The court stated: "Plaintiffs in copyright infringement action had burden of showing defendant's "willfulness" in order to receive statutory damages, and could sustain that burden by showing that defendant recklessly disregarded plaintiffs' rights or that defendant knew or should have known it infringed their copyrights." Pay particular attention to the "should have known." In this context, the court defines "willful" as "with knowledge," not necessarily meaning malicious. If a reasonable person might figure out that an action was infringing, everyone will be held to that standard. This case is also a good example of the courts upholding use of the Classroom Guidelines when considering an infringement case.

***Hotaling v. Church of Jesus Christ of Latter-Day Saints*, 118 F.3d 199 (4th Cir. 1997).**

This court held that a library could be found guilty of infringement if it allowed researchers to use materials only on the premises. The materials were later found to be illegal copies, and the library was held to be responsible for distribution even though the copies were never removed from the library.

Works cited

American Geophysical Union v. Texaco Inc., 60 F.3d 913 (2nd Cir. 1994) (LOISLAW) 1994. [online] http://www.law.cornell.edu/copyright/cases/60_F3d_913.htm [accessed 8-15-04].

Basic Books, Inc. v. Kinko's Graphics Corp., 758 F. Supp. 1522 (S.D.N.Y. 1991). 1991. [online] http://fairuse.stanford.edu/primary/cases/ c758FSupp1522.html [accessed 4-15-05].

Hotaling v. Church of Jesus Christ of Latter-Day Saints, 118 F.3d 199 (4th Cir. 1997). 1997. [online] http://caselaw.lp.findlaw.com/scripts/getcase.pl?navby=search&case=/ data2/circs/4th/961399p.html [accessed 8-15-04].

Individuals with Disabilities Education Improvement Act of 2004, PL 108-446, December 3, 2004, 118 Stat 2647 (2005).

Princeton Univ. Press v. Michigan Doc. Servs. 99 F.3d 1381 (6th Cir. 1996). [online] http://fairuse.stanford.edu/primary_materials/cases/michigan_document_services/ [accessed 8-15-04].

Special Interest Video Sales Group. 1995. *Fair use doctrine.* [online] http://www.sivideo.com/9fstsleb.htm [accessed 8-15-04].

Chapter *5*

Audiovisual Materials in Schools

T he law defines audiovisual as follows:

"Audiovisual works" are works that consist of a series of related images which are intrinsically intended to be shown by the use of machines, or devices such as projectors, viewers, or electronic equipment, together with accompanying sounds, if any, regardless of the nature of the material objects, such as films or tapes, in which the works are embodied. 17 USC § 101

Section 110 of the Copyright Act of 1976 was written, in part, to address the needs of producers of audiovisual materials who were concerned that their property was not being adequately protected under the old law. The new law clarified many ambiguities, though often not in favor of educators.

The same fair use guidelines that apply to print materials do not apply to audiovisuals. There are differing guidelines for print, audiovisuals, multimedia and distance learning, and the guidelines are not at all consistent. Because of the nature of the audiovisual medium, producers worry not only about unauthorized copies but also about losing profits from unauthorized performances of the protected works. Unauthorized performances aren't generally a concern of print publishers, with the exception of those who publish plays and music. Producers of music recordings, movies, and television programs make their money from licensing those works for public exhibition and broadcast as well as from direct sales, so they are especially wary about what end users will do with the copy they have purchased. Had Congress allowed as free rein for copying audiovisuals as they permitted for print materials, these media producers feared they would be cheated of profits that were rightfully theirs.

Aside from playwrights and composers, copyright owners of print materials needn't worry much about their performance rights because performance of print materials is not much of a problem. The right of adaptation is reserved for the copyright holder in all circumstances, and mounting a performance of a print work is no simple feat. In order for a print work to be "performed," it must be adapted for a play or painting or sound recording—a straightforward violation of copyright. But if graphic or illustrative materials are involved, a "performance" is as simple as a display. Simply tacking up a copyrighted work, when not associated with an educational fair use exemption, would be a technical violation of copyright if the display was intended for others to view.

Q: *A very long term teacher constantly shows videos in class. They are not coming from the library, they are not being shown on library equipment, etc. I have talked to her hundreds of times, approached 5 different principals about the problem in the last 17 years, but it never ceases. She told me, "They will have to catch me!" The class is watching* The Client *right now. This is a child development class, so I'm sure it doesn't apply to the curriculum. How much harm could she do to me and my district?*

A: As long as you have documented the warnings to the teacher and to the principal, the danger to you is minimal. The danger to the DISTRICT, however, could be serious. Students talk outside of class. Anyone could report this to Movie Licensing USA, the enforcement and licensing arm for entertainment producers. The only link I can see here might be child-rearing (the child is the client) but that would be pretty thin. Even if the district could mount a fair use defense, there would be legal expenses and public embarrassment. If settled out of court, it would likely cost in the 5 figures in fines (based on other cases I have heard) plus attorney's fees. In addition, your principal could be charged personally with vicarious infringement since s/he was notified of the infringement, had the power to stop it, but did nothing. I'm not saying it would happen, but it could. On top of that, if the district has a copyright policy that is being violated both the teacher and the principal could face dismissal for violation of district policy. Doesn't sound very pretty, does it?

The key to understanding the audiovisual guidelines is recognizing that Congress, when writing the law, wished to provide support to teachers in a classroom while presenting content to students. Beyond that, they had little sympathy for a school's request to be exempt from the requirements of copyright. As long as the direct teach piece is included, teachers are fairly free to use video and its cousins within the classroom. The primary problems teachers have with the guidelines are that teachers know there is more to school than just class, and there is more to learning than the set curriculum. Enrichment, reward, and relaxation are all valid parts of the educational experience, but they are not ones that Congress elected to support through exemption from the requirements of copyright law. Once that basic concept is internalized, the audiovisual exemptions fall into place.

What typical activities are covered?

It is very important to remember that this section of the law covers video, filmstrips, sound recordings, graphics and all other nonprint formats that are not multimedia or distance learning.

Because school is a public place (in other words, it is not a private home), any performance of a copyrighted work in a school is considered a public performance. Public performance is a right reserved to the copyright holder. Certain types of public performances, however, are permitted under the exemptions for audiovisual performances included in section 110(1). If a particular showing should happen not to meet the requirements for exemption, does that mean the audiovisual work cannot be shown? Not at all. It just means that the showing isn't exempt from the requirements of public performance. Public performance of audiovisual media requires one of three things:

> *1. permission from the copyright owner to hold a public performance*
> *2. a license from a rights broker that covers the work to be shown*
> *3. payment of royalties to the copyright owner or his agent*

The kinds of school activities that will be covered by the guidelines in this chapter include:

- *showing films/video/television to present or summarize content*
- *showing films/video/television to reward students*
- *showing films/video/television to entertain/babysit students*
- *showing films/video/television in connection with extracurricular events*

Movies—issues

The primary issue involved with showing films is non-instructional showings or peri-instructional showings. A secondary issue involves archival copies. For example:

- **rainy day recess**—*what do you do with a group of squirmy 3rd graders who can't go outside? Show them a movie! It will keep them quiet and still.*

- **general cultural value showings**—*after lunch each day, some students are finished first and get restless. So to keep everyone in one location, you show a film on some educational topic, even though it may have no relation to their classwork.*

- **entertainment showings**—*The PTA offers a babysitting service during the PTA meetings. They show cartoon films to keep the little children occupied and quiet in another room.*

- **peri-instructional showings**—*the band must take a commercial bus to the state band competition. The bus is equipped with a video player and monitors, so the band director plans to show the movie,* Mr. Holland's Opus, *on the long drive.*

- **extracurricular activities**—*the middle school cheerleaders are having a lock-in in the gym, and the sponsor plans to show the film,* Cheer.

- **copies of video**—*video is perceived as being fragile and expensive, and owners want to protect their investments. Some teachers and librarians want to make backup copies of videos they own so they will have a replacement copy if something should happen to the original.*

The issues above are all common, typical school uses of audiovisuals (mostly video) and they all make management and economic sense. Unfortunately, they are all copyright violations! The key thing to keep in mind as you go through the explanations and rationale for the audiovisual rules is that the members of Congress who passed these rules must report to both educators and publishers/producers. Alas, because educators consume resources and publishers/producers create them and pay taxes on the income derived from them, Congress leaned toward the side of producers in this aspect of fair use.

TV/cable/satellite—issues

The issues surrounding television and cable programming are similar to those involving film and video. Non-curricular and peri-curricular showings are common, though non-permitted. Because many of the useful curricular-related programs show at night and on weekends, teachers would like to tape programs for showing at a better time of day, or a better time of the school year (when they are studying the topic of the program). Recording

Q: Our school will charter large, commercial busses for an extended field trip. The busses have VCRs and TVs. We would like to show a tape of a movie owned by one of the teachers to keep the children occupied while we make this lengthy trip. Is this legal?

A: Probably not unless performance rights were acquired with the tape. This use of video is not face-to-face instruction. It probably involves some people who are not students and teachers in the class, such as a bus driver or chaperones, and the bus might be considered a bit strange for an instructional locale. The copyright holder, however, could grant (or sell) you one-time public performance rights. Additionally, the bus company may have a public performance license that will cover your use. Investigate your options.

programs and retaining them is a different issue than just showing the program, as in the case of video and film. With off-air recording, you are actually making a copy of the program as well as performing it.

Typical uses include:
- **recording news programs**—*a 20-20 program on gang warfare is appropriate for a Home and Family Living class.*

- **recording movies**—*the English teacher wants to tape this weekend's NBC playing of Mel Gibson's* Hamlet *to show to her class at the conclusion of their current unit on the play.*

- **recording sports programs**—*the gymnastics coach wants to tape all the Olympics gymnastics events to show students proper form. She will retain the tape and use it every year.*

- **recording cable broadcasts**—*the drama teacher wishes to record an Arts & Entertainment broadcast of* Rent *to show her advanced technical theatre class.*

Recording is the major issue here, since most schools don't subscribe to premium satellite and cable channels. Occasionally the local cable company will provide a feed of the basic cable lineup, and showing those programs live is perfectly OK since you are a subscriber. However, subscribing at home allows you to tape and retain programs for use at your convenience, but use at school (of programs taped at home or at school) is for public performance and therefore does not enjoy the same permissions as recording for private use at home. See more about taping from cable/satellite in the section on off-air taping.

Web—issues

Until the TEACH Act was enacted, "transmissions" of audiovisual works were prohibited. Now, under the requirements of TEACH, some transmissions of audiovisual materials are allowed. See the chapters on the Internet and distance learning for complete details.

Sound recordings—issues

Sound recordings include both music and spoken word recordings. The recordings may be on any type of medium, from wire recordings to vinyl to digital recordings. While digital recordings have amazing clarity and depth of sound, a person can copy a digital sound recording with perfect reproduction an infinite number of times. The recording industry felt the effects of this simple technique as far back as 2002, citing significant drops in sales and profits (RIAA, 2002).

Typical activities involving sound recordings include:
- *Choir director purchases one copy of a CD of a musical that the school will perform, and makes a copy for each cast member so they can review the songs before rehearsals start.*

- *School webmaster streams a copy of the song the Senior class has chosen as Senior Song.*

- *Reading resource teacher makes a backup copy of the tapes in all the book/tape sets in the reading resource room.*

What rights are affected?

Producers of audiovisual materials are anxious about their materials. They apply various technical protection measures to prevent copying or illegal performance of their works. Their reasons include potential violation of the following rights:

Reproduction

Copies, especially digital copies, mean unlimited reproduction at perfect quality. With the history of the decline of the recording industry after MP3 filesharing, producers are understandably nervous about allowing copies for any reason.

Distribution

Going hand in hand with reproduction, distribution of copies is the copyright owner's biggest worry. The copies made could be distributed via networks like MP3 files are, or on tape/CD/DVD. Distribution of television programs and video can occur when using a video distribution system, or through cable networks or microwave transmission.

Adaptation

Any time you change the format of a work, you have created an adaptation. Changing a work from VHS to DVD or streaming video is an adaptation. So is taking clips and making a separate tape of excerpts (equivalent to an anthology of print works). If you expurgate a work (remove offensive words or scenes) you have also created an adaptation. Creative people, including directors, are highly offended when someone dares to change their work. Moral rights, while not terribly strong in the U.S., may come into play in such a situation.

Public performance

Any performance that happens in a school is a public performance. The key to understanding what is public and what is not is who attends and where it occurs. A performance that occurs in the home may be private. A showing that occurs where the public may go cannot be private. Courts have ruled that a private viewing booth at a video store is a public place (*Columbia Pictures Industries v. Redd Horne*, 749 F.2d 154 (3rd Cir. 1984)), so a room in a public school is certainly public.

Virtually any copyrighted work may be performed publicly, be it music, drama, dance, motion picture, literary work, or other audiovisual expression. A public performance need not be a gala event in an auditorium. Something as seemingly trivial as popping a cassette into a boom box can be classed as a public performance, given the proper circumstances. Those circumstances are clearly defined in the law:

> *… a place open to the public or at any place where a substantial number of persons outside of a normal circle of a family and its social acquaintances is gathered. . .*

Any display or performance of a copyrighted work under these circumstances would require a license. The gray area of this definition is the "substantial number." How many people outside the normal circle of a family does it take to cross the line into public performance? Unfortunately, the law and the fair use guidelines don't quantify this number. Court precedent doesn't give much guidance, either. However, a major movie studio did attempt to sue a woman who showed one of the studio's movies to the guests at her child's birthday party saying that this event exceeded the exemption afforded a family and its social acquaintances. Alas, the movie studio dropped the suit because of extensive unfavorable publicity before a court could make a determination of the number of "friends" it takes to cross the line into public performance. The *Redd Horne* case indicates that no one in addition to the viewer need be present to create a public performance. Only one person viewing a video in the private viewing room of a public video store created a "public performance" according to the ruling in that case, so a classroom of unrelated students viewing a film in a public school would certainly be a public performance as well. Putting motion media onto the open Web can certainly be considered a public performance since you have made it accessible to the world via the Web.

Public display

Section 101 of 17 USC defines a display:

> To "display" a work means to show a copy of it, either directly or by means of a
> film, slide, television image, or any other device or process or, in the case of a motion picture
> or other audiovisual work, to show individual images nonsequentially. (17 USC § 101)

Where a display becomes "public" has always been an issue of concern. Obviously, the same definition of public applies here as it does for public performance. Anything beyond a family and its circle of social acquaintances is public, therefore any display at a public school would also be public. So would any display on the Internet. Remember, however, that there will be some fair use and guideline exemptions that will come into play.

Digital transmission

Digital transmission was added to the rights of the copyright holder with the passage of the Digital Millennium Copyright Act. Digital transmission had been a concern of music producers once they realized that Internet radio was streaming perfect digital copies of their songs to anyone who cared to save the files on their local computer systems. Since (with tongue firmly in cheek) a CD only has perhaps one good cut, why pay for an entire CD when you can grab the "good one" for no cost via Internet radio.

As a result of this concern, significant royalties must be collected for each listener of a recording digitally transmitted. The DMCA did not provide for any specific educational exemptions for digital transmission, but the various media would still fall under the existing TEACH Act if they met the requirements thereof.

What guidelines affect AV materials?

Rules for using audiovisual materials are included in section 110(1) of 17 USC, the current copyright law, so this will be a question of law, not one of externally developed guidelines. The actual wording says:

> Notwithstanding the provisions of section 106, the following are not infringements of
> copyright:
>
> (1) performance or display of a work by instructors or pupils in the course of face-to-face
> teaching activities of a nonprofit educational institution, in a classroom or similar
> place devoted to instruction, unless, in the case of a motion picture or other
> audiovisual work, the performance, or the display of individual images, is given by
> means of a copy that was not lawfully made under this title, and that the person
> responsible for the performance knew or had reason to believe was not lawfully made;

The rules are written in legalese, not in eduspeak, so it may take a bit of translation to explain the significance of the five factors included.

5 yes/no questions

Explaining how to base an audiovisual fair use assessment on the paragraph excerpted on page 74 is really fairly simple. The result can be condensed into five yes/no questions, based on the factors set forth in the law. The form in this section (See Figure 5.2) gives you a shorthand way for a teacher to go through the fair use analysis, but since rationalization often justifies a recreational showing, an instructional leader is always a good check to verify appropriate use. See the definitions below for details on how to answer the questions on the form. ANY answer of no on the form means that public **performance rights** are required to show the film in that circumstance.

1. nonprofit educational

The use here must truly be nonprofit. Interestingly, you don't have to make a profit to be "for profit." You only have to TRY to make a profit. So if your band is collecting admission for a music video party, or the film club is taking donations to watch the Oscar™ nominees from 10 years ago, they are "for profit" even if they don't break even. This also means that for profit daycare centers and schools don't qualify for this factor.

2. classroom or similar place

A "similar place" could be the auditorium, gymnasium, cafeteria, multipurpose room, library, theatre, band hall, natatorium, field house, etc. A "similar place" probably would not be the local pizza parlor (unless this were a business class and they were watching a film on restaurant management) or on a bus on the way to a band competition.

3. instructors and pupils

This factor means that only members of the class are involved; no quest, visitor, or other students not in the class are permitted under a fair use showing.

4. legally acquired copy

There are many ways to legally acquire a copy of an audiovisual work. Basically this factor only wants to assure that the copy isn't pirated. As long as someone has legitimately paid for the copy, you are probably clear on this factor. Ways you can get a "legally acquired" copy include:

a. Library
You may use a copy of an audiovisual work owned by your school library.

b. student or teacher
You may legally use a copy of a work owned by a teacher, a student or a student's parents, as long as the work isn't taped from cable or off-air beyond the taping guidelines (see off-air taping section).

c. borrowed from library
You may use a copy borrowed from the public library, a university or community college library, or from a regional media library.

d. rented from video store

A copy rented from your local video store may be used as long as the teacher can answer YES to all 5 of the AV exemption questions. Long ago, video stores required you to sign a contract before you could check out videos. That contract sometimes restricted what you could do with the video you rented. If your video store still requires such a contract, check it to see if you might be in violation of the contract if you show the video to students at a public school. If your store doesn't require a contract at all, the videos are legally acquired, so they would be OK to use.

e. taped off air

A video taped off an over air channel or from a cable/satellite channel with permission of the copyright holder is an acceptable source to answer YES to this question. (see off-air taping guidelines section).

While the librarian needn't demand receipts from students and teachers, a cautious approach would dictate that outside videos be accompanied by a statement from the owner verifying ownership (Figure 5.1).

Should the copy later be determined to be fraudulent, the school and library then have a solid case that they had no knowledge that the tape was in violation.

Of course, common sense would tell you that if the tape is not in a standard commercial case or is obviously re-taped, the program is probably not legally acquired. In such a case the librarian would be wise to refuse to show such a program, or to provide equipment to do so. A school or district policy addressing videos not owned by the school is an essential part of effective copyright compliance. The policy should be approved by the board, supported by the principal, and annually called to the attention of the faculty.

Such a policy would give the librarian a firm foundation to deny a faculty member's request to use questionable material.

5. face-to-face teaching activities

This factor of AV fair use is generally the most difficult to meet because this is where Congress states that they expect to see the direct teach piece in the analysis. In other words, the display of the work must be related to the lesson at hand, not simply related to some type of lesson past or a lesson to come. For example, the freshman English curriculum might require the students to read Shakespeare's *Romeo and Juliet* in September each year. However, the English teacher needs some time to prepare final exams later in the semester, so she decides to show the Franco Zefferelli film of the play to occupy her students while she works on the exam months after the class has studied the play. Such use of the video would probably not be within the fair use exemption since the class is no longer studying the play. A good rule of thumb to determine if use of a video is acceptable is to ask, "Is this an integral part of the unit I am teaching right now?" If the answer is "no," then the showing is probably a public performance. Beware of loose or questionable links from audiovisual material to lessons. Showing *Babe* because the class has been studying the farm is not a reasonable tie-in unless your local farms have talking animals. The same rationale would apply to showing *The Lion King* during a study of Africa or the great cats. There are many more curriculum-appropriate materials you could select.

Figure 5.1 — Copyright verification form

I, _____ , certify that the videotape/film,

_____

belongs to me/my household. This tape was purchased by/for me, and is a legally acquired copy of this program.

I am lending this program to _____

as part of the educational program with the understanding that the program will be used for instructional purposes only. I release the staff and students of _____

liability for damages that may occur to my tape.

Signed _____

Date _____

Applying this factor kicks out the most common uses of media in schools: reward ("If you work hard on this project all week, we will have a movie on Friday afternoon), recreation ("It is too cold/hot/rainy to go out for recess today, so we will watch an educational movie instead), and babysitting ("We need to talk to the parents tonight at the PTA meeting, so let's send the little kids to the gym and let them watch a movie while we discuss the bond issue.") Extracurricular activities are also suspect under this factor because they are not direct teaching. Extracurricular activities such as film clubs are valuable recreations, but they are just that: recreations. Some universities have been cited for similar activities, so it is possible that public schools could also be targeted. You might just want to mark this factor as "unknown," but that doesn't yield the five YES answers required for an affirmative decision. At that point, you want to assess your aversion to risk. Do you want to take a chance that no one associated with the film producers will ever find out?

Umbrella licenses

Unless there is a specific teaching goal documented in a district curriculum guide or state standard, one may reliably count on the need for a performance license. Several vendors sell so-called "umbrella licenses" which permit the school or library to show non-curricular films and videos from limited lists of producers. There are pros and cons to these licenses. A library-only license makes the librarian (and the library) the local "babysitter." Whenever the PE teacher is out, the kids are sent to the library to see movies to keep them entertained. If you have a building-wide license, teachers become lax in their use of video. The primary vendor of these licenses is Movie Licensing USA. See the Appendix for contact information.

Additionally, beware of what might be called "general cultural value." Certainly there are many wonderfully educational videos on the market and perhaps in your library or personal video collection. However, showing these types of videos to a class without a specific curricular objective is not permitted under the "face-to-face" rule. If the objective isn't specified in the curriculum guide for this particular class, showing a video on that topic is a public performance and license or permission is required. Keep in mind that what is "curricular" for one class might not be part of the curriculum for another, no matter how "educational" the topic might be. For example, a French class might be able to show the movie *The Red Balloon* as an example of French culture (part of the curriculum for that class), while an English class would have difficulty tying in this wordless film to its literature objectives.

Home use only

Many videos have a "home use only" notice. Some libraries and schools are fearful that using tapes so labeled will place them in jeopardy. The truth is that simply placing a "home use only" notice on a video does not restrict a school from lending a copy owned by the library or using the program if the use otherwise meets all of the fair use criteria set forth previously.

Once a tape has been sold, the "right of first sale" states that copyright owner's exclusive distribution right to that copy has ceased (Reed, 1989, p. 2). The transfer of the right of distribution is the essential transaction that allows libraries to lend books and other materials. Note that only the right of distribution has ceased. The right of performance and display still resides with the copyright owner. In other words, the purchaser of a film or video may lend, sell, or give the copy to whomever she wishes without worry. Performances of the film or tape, however, must still comply with the law regarding performances or displays.

Caution: Watch carefully for producers or suppliers who sell you a license to a program rather than the program itself. Licensing a program is a way for a copyright owner to retain the distribution right since there is no actual sale. If you purchase a license to a program, you will be subject to any restrictions the copyright owner may choose to impose, including restricting your right to lend the program.

Mary Hutchings Reed, consultant to the American Library Association, recommends that "home use only" labels be allowed to remain on videos owned by a library (Reed, 1989, p. 2). A library would not want to appear to encourage copyright infringement, lest it be considered a contributory or vicarious infringer. The "home use only" label will remind patrons that the video is not licensed for public performance, and while any lawfully acquired film or video may be used in a qualifying educational setting, these videos are still subject to copyright restrictions in the matter of public performance. Some practices that are never acceptable with film or video include:

- *Making an anthology or collection from clips or excerpts;*
- *Transferring the work to another medium, e.g., film to video, or video to computer disk UNLESS the medium on which the work is stored is obsolete based on the legal definition of "obsolete" AND the work is not available for purchase in a newer medium (with a small exception for some distance learning uses under the TEACH act—see Chapter 8); or*
- *Using a program for recreation or reward without acquiring performance rights.*

Another "home use" issue involves the new DVDs that are encoded to be able to skip language, sex, and violence. The Family Movie Act of 2005 allows home (private) viewers to use this technology, but the law does not state that this is acceptable in public performance. (Family, 2005).

Q: For the days that teachers use videos for nothing but babysitting or "rewards," isn't it a violation to air something on our network that is a home use only tape from a video store such as Blockbuster and is an entertainment video?

A: It makes no difference WHERE the tape is from, for either curricular or reward showings, as long as the source is legal. The only significant concern is whether you have public performance rights for the tape. Blockbuster doesn't sell or rent public performance rights, hence you can only use the tapes in curricular situations. If your library owns the tape, for instance, and you have received or purchased public performance rights with the tape, you can show it for whatever purpose you want. If you don't own public performance rights, however, you can only legally show it in curricular situations. A showing that meets the 5 yes/no tests for video does not require public performance rights.

Figure 5.2 — Audiovisual copyright analysis

Teacher _____ Grade level _____

Subject area _____

Media title _____ Producer _____

Length _____

Objective _____

☐ Yes ☐ No   1. Are you a nonprofit educational institution?

☐ Yes ☐ No   2. Is the showing by and for students and teachers in a regularly scheduled class?

☐ Yes ☐ No   3. Is the showing in a classroom or other instructional place?

☐ Yes ☐ No   4. Is the showing from a legally acquired copy of the work?

How acquired?_____

_____

If taped off air, taping date: _____

☐ Yes ☐ No   5. Is the showing a material part of the lesson you are teaching on that topic?

_____

What is the curriculum to which the showing applies? _____

Signature of instructional leader_____

From Copyright for Schools, 4th Edition 2005

Examples of analysis

Situation: Students exempt from state standardized testing need something to keep them occupied for several hours. Principal decides to show a film.

Analysis:

1) nonprofit educational: YES

2) classroom or other instructional place: YES, he plans to use the cafeteria

3) instructors and pupils in a class: NO, these students are from several different classes

You can end the 5 point analysis here, because you encountered a NO response. A public performance license is required for this showing.

Situation: You want to show a film on the bus as the students in your class are on their way to a choir concert in the state capital.

Analysis:

1) nonprofit educational: YES

2) classroom or other instructional place: NO. It would be difficult to justify the bus as a classroom.

You can end the analysis here, because you encountered a NO response. A public performance license is required for this showing. Check with the bus company. Some have a blanket license that will permit this showing. If you have a license from Movie Licensing USA, check your contract to see if it includes bus showings.

Situation: Teacher shows a video from the library about the Age of Plants as enrichment for a unit on the Age of Reptiles so she can work with students who are behind on their dinosaur reports. Only students in the class will watch the showing.

Analysis:

1) nonprofit educational: YES

2) classroom or other instructional place: YES

3) instructors and teachers in a class: YES, all those viewing the film are students and teachers in this specific class

4) legal copy: YES, the video is owned by the school library

5) face-to-face teaching: NO. This is not part of the standard curriculum. It is being used for enrichment/babysitting/reward for students the teacher needs to keep busy while she does something else.

Off-air taping guidelines

To the average classroom teacher, a videotape is a videotape—you stuff it into a recorder and press "Play." But to the librarian who must sort through the jumble of copyright, a teacher approaching with a videotape in hand may be as welcome as a visit from a werewolf. A video of unknown origin is about as dangerous.

A lot of misinformation floats around about what may be taped and what may be retained. The number one consideration to keep in mind when trying to determine a tape's status is "who taped this and when?" Many court cases have determined that a private individual may tape—for the purposes of "time shifting"—anything broadcast over the public airwaves or from cable channels to which the individual subscribes. The person may then retain the tapes without penalty. But the tape is only for the use of that individual, his or her immediate family, and their circle of friends.

Schools and libraries are not permitted such liberal taping. Taping programs from the television can be simple or highly complicated. The key to knowing what you may tape and what you may not is knowing how the program is getting to your television set. For school use, programs may be freely taped from regular broadcast channels. Broadcast channels are those VHF and UHF channels one can ordinarily receive via a regular television antenna. If a particular channel is simultaneously rebroadcast on cable, the actual tape may be made from the cable transmission. This can be an advantage in instances when the cable signal is better than the broadcast signal, or when the VCR is already hooked up to the cable instead of an antenna.

"Air" vs. cable vs. satellite

But what about all those wonderful cable channels? Disney Channel or Nickelodeon or Discovery or Lifetime? There are no fair use rights for exclusively cable channels. Decisions to tape a particular program must be researched on the basis of granted rights. Since reproduction rights reside with the copyright holder, the ability of a school to tape a program and retain it for any amount of time is wholly at the whim of the copyright holder. Many of these channels offer educators' guides that enumerate the available rights on a program-by-program basis. *Kidsnet, Discovery Networks' Educator Guide,* and *Access Learning* magazines also offer retention rights information and addresses of producers so that permissions and supplemental materials may be requested. See Appendix M for addresses and phone numbers of these reference sources.

Satellite programming will have the same restrictions as cable broadcasts. Programs broadcast by satellite may not be taped for school use without specific permission of the copyright holder. Deliberately de-scrambling encrypted satellite signals is a federal offense.

The location of the taping has no effect on the legality of school use. A teacher or librarian or student may tape programs at school or at home. If a librarian is taping a program, that taping must be at the request of a specific teacher or student. In other words, a librarian cannot tape a program just because she knows someone will ask for it after the fact. We all know a teacher who will come into the library the day after a program airs, saying something like, "Gee, it was so good! You wouldn't happen to have that on tape, would you?" If you have taped the program at the specific request of another teacher you may fulfill the appeal; otherwise, you will have to disappoint. Maybe the next time a program airs, the teacher will be better prepared. (See the section on Taping in anticipation). The librarian or administrator can certainly remind teachers that a potentially useful program is approaching, and if a teacher wishes the library to make a copy the teacher should put in a request.

Q: A teacher has some TV broadcasts taped off-air several years ago. He has not been able to find a source from which we may purchase a copy. How do we determine that it is no longer available for purchase? And, if it is no longer available for purchase and/or broadcast is he able to use his taped version in school?

A: The teacher has not been able to retain those programs after 45 days post-broadcast, so the tapes are illegal for school use (personal use at home doesn't have this restriction). This isn't the same situation ("not available at a reasonable price") as replacing a book that has been damaged. This is part of the off-air taping guidelines. It may be that these tapes have NEVER been available for sale, and that is the prerogative of the copyright owner. If the program is not available for sale, and the tapes are older than 45 days past the broadcast from which they were taped, your only option will be to track down the copyright owner to request permission to use the tapes. What I'm not sure of is how you will explain how you have the tapes to begin with since under the off-air guidelines they should have been erased long ago.

Figure 5.3 — Off-air video log sample

Teacher	Program	Channel	Date	Rts.
Miller	Whale watch	PBS	9/3/05	fair use
Armand	Using a ruler	NBC	9/5/05	fair use
Raney	The Vietnam experience	Life	9/16/05	7 day
Kyser	National Geographic special	PBS	9/17/05	life/tape
Miller	Oprah	NBC	9/20/05	fair use

Figure 5.4 — Off-air video log

Teacher	Program	Channel	Date	Rts.

Copyright for Schools: A Practical Guide. 4th Edition

Copies taped off-air **must** include all copyright information, usually included in the credits at the end of the program. The program need not be shown in its entirety, but the program itself must not be edited or altered from its original content. In other words, using the fast forward button on the VCR is acceptable, but editing or shortening the program tape is not always legal, especially if it removes the copyright information.

As the librarian or technologist accepts taping requests from teachers, keep one requirement in mind: The same teacher may not tape, or request to be taped, the same program multiple times, no matter how many times the program is rebroadcast. A common example would be a teacher's taping a program and showing it to his class. He erases the tape when the 45-day limit expires. The next year the program is rebroadcast and he tapes the program again. This second taping may not be used with students unless specific, written permission is received from the copyright holder.

Is this significant? Certainly. An Arizona school district settled a copyright infringement suit alleging that tapes had been made off-air and had not been erased at the end of the 45-day retention period. The Association for Information Media and Equipment (AIME) vigorously pursued the district, eventually receiving significant monetary damages from the district as well as a commitment to follow copyright regulations strictly in the future (AIME, 1990, p. 1). AIME is known as an industry watchdog, and given the slightest inkling that a district is in violation of copyright, it will intervene on behalf of its member companies.

So how does one protect oneself and the school from inadvertent infringement in this area? The best suggestion would be to create and maintain a log of taping and use requests (Figures 5.3 and 5.4).

This database will contain a history of all off-air tapes used by a particular teacher. While it is possible to manually log tapings, a computer database is the most efficient method of maintaining this type of record. Create fields for teacher, program, channel or network, broadcast date or date taped, and retention rights. When a teacher submits another taping request (or presents a home-taped video), sort the database on the teacher's name and check earlier requests. It will be easy to find a duplication by that teacher. Remember that this database will grow. It isn't a database that can be trashed at the end of each school year. Tapings are cumulative. Once a teacher has taped a particular program (meaning episode or single broadcast), that teacher may not tape the same program again without express permission, even if the program is rebroadcast many months or years later.

Retention. Once a program is taped, when must you use it? The legal restrictions on retention are extremely strict. A taped program may be kept for a maximum of 45 consecutive (calendar) days. Of that 45 days, students may view the program only during the first 10 school days. (Note that student use considers school days, but total time counts consecutive days, including weekends and holidays.) Even those first 10 days are prescribed: once for

---

Q: A teacher is teaching a unit on science fiction. She would like to use short clips from several science fiction movies. Can this be handled in a legal manner?

A: The answer is "it depends." If she has the clips cued up on the tapes, and she punches play, runs the clips then pops out the tape and does the same to the next one, sure. If she wants to make a new tape with just the clips in question, then answer is NO—that is considered making an anthology and is not permitted. HOWEVER, if she will make a multimedia program (PowerPoint, etc.) she can use up to 3 minute clips of video in that presentation, but she will need to check the multimedia guidelines for the specific limits, retention times, reuse limits, etc.

Q: As librarian, I like to have materials on hand I know my teachers will want. I know they will ask for a tape of a particular TV program the day after it airs, so can I tape the program knowing they will ask for it?

A: Taping "in anticipation" of request is not permitted. You can, however, notify the teachers in advance and suggest they fill out a taping request so you can have the tape for them when they need it.

Figure 5.5 — Off-air recording verification

This tape _____

was recorded off-air _____ *by me / for me* _____ on channel _____

on (date) _____. The 10th consecutive school day from the

recording date is _____. I may use this recording only once in

relevant teaching activities. I may repeat the showing only once for reinforcement.

The 45th day after the recording date will be _____. Between the 11th

and the 45th day, this tape may be used for teacher evaluation only. It will not be shown to students during

this period unless permission has been received from the copyright owner.

I made _____copies of this recording. Each copy is accompanied by this statement.

This recording will be erased/destroyed no later than the 45th day indicated above.

Teacher _____

Library staff _____

Date _____

Signature indicates the statement above has been read and understood.

instruction, once for reinforcement. No other viewings are possible under the fair use guidelines. During the remaining 35 days of the 45-day period, the program may be used only for evaluation of the program by teachers. The program may be retained beyond the 45-day period only if explicit, written permission has been received from the copyright holders. Lacking such permission, the tape must be erased or destroyed at the end of the 45-day period.

Note that these so-called "fair use" rules apply only to programs taped off regular broadcast channels. Cable or satellite programs that permit limited school use may impose specific retention restrictions that may be more liberal or narrower than the standard 10/45-day fair use, e.g. three days, one year, or life-of-tape. Check program guides and cable-in-education periodicals for specific details on each program.

There are, of course, "special" situations that must be dealt with vis-a-vis copyright. What about a student who was ill and missed an in-class showing? Could another showing be arranged for that student? Probably. Since the library is a place for instruction, and the librarian is certainly an instructor or one directed by the regular instructor, the librarian could arrange a make-up showing of the tape to the student, but only during the first 10 days after the program is taped. The fair use guidelines still apply to the 10-day play limit. If the student does not return until after the 10-day limit has expired, the student will have to rely on other methods to get the information presented in the program.

Home taping. As long as a program is taped and housed in the library, the librarian can be assured that the tape will be properly logged and it will be erased at the end of the 45-day period. But what about home-taped programs brought to school by teachers and students? It makes no difference where the program was taped. What affects school use of taped television programming is the source of the broadcast (broadcast, cable, or satellite) and the date of the taping. The 10/45-day rules apply to tapes from regular broadcast channels, no matter who makes the tape or where it is taped. In other words, if a teacher tapes a program in December, but wants to show it in May, such a showing would not be permitted under fair use, and specific, written permission from the copyright holder would be required. The location of the physical taping makes no difference at all. A tape from a cable or satellite channel would be governed solely by the retention and use periods allocated by the copyright owner, if any.

So how does the librarian or technologist know the specific details of tapes brought into the building by teachers and students? While it is certainly possible to follow a "don't ask, don't tell" policy concerning outside video, there would be no documentation should a tape ever be challenged. The best alternative is to require a signed affidavit stating the date and channel on which the program was taped (Figure 5.5).

Copies of off-air recordings. In some cases, one program might be appropriate for more than one class at a time; for example, a documentary might be suitable for all the American history classes to view. Not all school buildings are fortunate enough to have a centralized video distribution system that allows a single tape to flow to multiple classrooms. In such an instance, the school may make copies of the off-air taping, one for each classroom that would need to view the program at the same time. Each copy must have the same off-air taping notices and copyright information attached, and each copy is subject to the same time restrictions as the original. For example, if a tape were made on Sunday, the third day of the month, and the copies of the original recording were made on Tuesday, the fifth, all showings to students from all of the tapes would have to be counted as if all the tapes were made on Sunday the third. The 45-day requirement would also apply to all of the copies, counted from the date of the original recording.

Taping in anticipation

Persons in authority may not forecast that teachers will request copies of a particular resource and cause that item to be copied so it will be available on the chance that a teacher might ask for it. This type of situation frequently occurs when a principal or librarian notices that there is a television program scheduled to air that would relate to some curriculum. The educator decides to copy the program in expectation that teachers will ask for the program after the fact. In order to comply with the fair use guidelines, the request for taping must come from the teacher who wishes to use the program. This is often described as a "bottom up" rule: The person at the point of use (the classroom) is the one who must make the request for copying.

Public performance rights

Since many audiovisual materials may be purchased with public performance rights, wise librarians track which of their materials have such rights. Entries in the shelf list or catalog, stickers on individual items, and log books all successfully inform library patrons of the items for which rights have been purchased. A notation on how the rights were acquired would be helpful, as well as the duration of the rights, e.g., "via catalog," "life-of-tape," or "on P.O. #123456, 2 years (exp. 11-15-07)."

Q: Administrators ask the library staff to put videos (from the library collection) into the media distribution system so students can view them on two large screen TVs in the cafeteria during the 5 lunch periods. Isn't this in violation of copyright—public performance?

A: This is likely a violation. This showing doesn't meet the requirement for face to face instruction. You may, however, show videos for which you own public performance rights. Check http://courses.unt.edu/csimpson/cright/ppr.htm for producers that routinely sell public performance rights with videos sold to schools and public libraries.

Figure 5.6 — Sample Purchase Order

PURCHASE ORDER #12345123
SMALLVILLE INDEPENDENT SCHOOL DISTRICT
4321 S. Front Street
Middletown, USA

To: Video Supplier
     1234 Main Street
     Hollywood, CA

Please accept our order for the following:

Quantity	Title	Price
1	Copyright and you (VHS)	$25.00
1	A school librarian's view of copyright (VHS)	$50.00
	shipping	$ 5.00

Note: All videos will include public performance rights. If additional charges are required confirmation must be received before shipment.

TOTAL $80.00

A file of performance rights documentation would also be a good idea. A few suppliers, especially video producers, provide blanket public performance rights in the prices of all videos in their catalogs. A photocopy of this statement from the catalog attached to the purchase order for the videos should be sufficient documentation. Another supplier includes a statement on the order envelope stating, "The video cassettes you purchase from XYZ Company are sold for school and library use. Broadcast rights are not included. Programs may not be reproduced, copied, or transmitted without written permission." An extra-thorough method of ensuring a complete understanding would be to include a line on the purchase order stating: "All materials to include public performance rights" (or archival rights). Acceptance of the order with this statement included would contractually obligate the supplier to provide public performance rights as well (Figure 5.6).

Caveat: Be certain that you are sending the order to a company that is able to broker such licenses. Some AV jobbers will supply the tapes on the purchase order even though they are not able to broker the performance rights.

The sale of public performance rights is a contractual obligation, so the purchaser and the copyright owner (usually through a supplier or distributor) can negotiate whatever rights package the owner would like to sell and the purchaser can afford. Don't be afraid to propose the type of performance rights you need. The worst the copyright owner can do is say "no." Just make sure you prepare your proposal far in advance of your anticipated performance date. The educational fair use exemptions don't apply to public performances and if you have not acquired the necessary rights before your public performance, you are on extremely hazardous ground.

Examples of acceptable performances

A teacher shows a library-owned filmstrip to his sixth-grade science class to demonstrate the effects of water pollution as part of a lesson on ecology. This use is protected under the educational exemption because it meets all of the previous criteria: It is presented for enrolled students by an instructor in face-to-face teaching in a classroom; the copy is legally owned by the library (or at least the teacher has no reason to think it is not legally acquired.).

An English teacher's classes have been studying Romeo and Juliet. To conclude the unit, the teacher shows the English department's tape of the Franco Zefferelli version of the play in class, spreading the program over three class days. This use is also protected under the educational exemption. The teacher is showing the program; it is an integral portion of the lesson; the performance is taking place in the classroom; and the copy has been purchased by the English department.

An elementary school music teacher plays a recording of a performance of John Philip Sousa's "Stars and Stripes Forever" as part of a unit on patriotic music for third graders. The recording accompanied the music text. While the medium has changed, the guidelines remain the same. This is a performance in class, by a teacher, within a lesson plan, with a legally acquired copy.

Examples of unacceptable performances

The PTA shows a library-owned copy of *The Little Mermaid* to the children of members in a classroom while the officers have a meeting in the library. The copy is legally acquired, the performance takes place in a classroom, and the performance may be presented by a teacher or pupil, but this performance is not a part of face-to-face teaching activities. This would be considered entertainment or reward, and as such is not permitted without public performance rights. This example would require payment of royalties for the performance. Renting a copy of the video would have no effect on the legality of the performance, and the school may be liable for providing equipment for an infringing performance. The same prohibition would apply to movies or recordings used to reward classes for good grades, commendable behavior, or perfect attendance.

On the last day of the semester, the American history teacher decides to play for his class a record on the Cuban missile crisis so he can calculate grades while the students are occupied. The class is not currently studying that portion of the curriculum. This use is not acceptable because the face-to-face teaching requirement is not met. While a weak case can be made for the fact that the topic will eventually be covered, this topic is not under the current lesson plan. Public performance rights would be recommended in this case.

Because the drama teacher gives such hard tests, a group of drama students decides to rent a video of a play they have been studying and show it in the drama room after school to review for the

Q: Is it a violation of copyright to show just a clip of a movie?

A: As long as the clip doesn't constitute the "essence" of the work (basically conveys the whole message of the film in that scene or clip—like the final scene in *Bonnie & Clyde)* you should be OK. Of course, if this clip meets all the requirements of the AV guidelines, you are OK with a clip or the whole film.

Q: The orchestra director would like to have a concert using movie theme songs. We would like to play video of the movie while the orchestra is playing. Our question is, how can we use the video without breaking any copyright laws?

A: This isn't face-to-face instruction, and simply answering "no" to that qualifying question means that you don't qualify for an automatic fair use exemption. You can, however, go through the four tests of fair use to see if you qualify on those grounds.

Q: I have some very expensive videos in my library collection and I'm afraid to circulate them for fear that something might happen to them. May I make an archival copy of the video as I do with the computer diskettes we circulate?

A: No, you can't make backup or archival copies without specific permission to do so. Copyright laws give express permission to make archival copies of computer software only. No other medium is granted such permission. However, if the video is on Betatape (now obsolete) and not for sale in newer formats, the DMCA allows you to transfer the tape to a current technology (VHS or digital).

Q: I remember hearing from some source several years ago that it was OK to purchase a videotape, make a copy, and circulate the copy while keeping the original in an archive. Is this true?

A: Since 1976 it has been legal to make backup copies of computer diskettes. There is not now and never has been permission to make backup copies of videos, audiocassettes, phonograph records, or laserdiscs.

upcoming exam. Several of the students plan to bring friends to watch the movie with them. This would definitely be considered a public performance because non-students (the friends) are involved in the session. This would also not be considered face-to-face teaching because the instructor did not participate in the meeting.

Archiving audiovisual works

Copyright law pertaining to computer software allows the purchaser to make a single backup copy (also called archival copy) of the diskettes in case something unfortunate should happen to the original diskettes. Unfortunately, audiovisual materials do not offer the same archival permission as does computer software. Owners of film, video, or audio may not make backup copies of the works. The usual terms of purchase are similar to that of a book: You may use the material until it wears out or breaks. At that point you may attempt to repair it, but the best alternative is to replace the work. In the case of video and audio, this is called "life of tape". You have the right to use the program as long as the tape works. When the tape wears out, it is time to buy a replacement. The good news is that tape costs are usually quite reasonable, at least for works available from more than one source. Some producers offer lifetime replacements, as well. The Preservation of Orphan Works Act of 2005 allows *libraries* (only) to make copies of out-of-print and unavailable for purchase works in the last 20 years of their term of copyright, but this is unlikely to help schools protect their general collection.

When a film breaks, since backup onto tape is not permitted (as this would be change of format), the only alternatives consistent with copyright law are to splice the film or to purchase replacement footage if the damage is extensive. The same holds true with audio tape. Backups onto other tapes or digital media (compact disc or digital audio storage) are not allowed. This prohibition is waived when a copyrighted work is recorded on a medium that is no longer in popular use, such as Beta format videotape. Because Beta format is obsolete, you may transfer your Beta programs onto VHS tape or digital storage without specific permission for each program. The DMCA defines obsolete as "if the machine or device necessary to render perceptible a work stored in that format is no longer manufactured or is no longer reasonably available in the commercial marketplace." So if you can no longer buy a Beta format VCR, you can transfer your work onto DVD or VHS tape. But if you can still buy a VHS player at a "reasonable price," you may not legally transfer your programs to the streaming server or to DVD. Note that if the work is available for sale in a modern format, the law demands purchase rather than copying.

Closed captioning

There has been much discussion of the legality of adding closed captions to existing video. Some experts argue that adding the special digital coding required for this feature results in a "derivative work" (Sinofsky, 1993; Kruppenbacher, 1993). Such a derivative work would not be in compliance with copyright. Kruppenbacher, ITV program coordinator at the National Technical Institute for the Deaf, argues that, in order to make a closed-captioned copy, one must make a working copy to which one adds the necessary encoding. He contends that the working copy is, in itself, a violation of copyright. However, Congressman Robert Kastenmeier stated during congressional arguments on the Copyright Revision Act of 1976 that the legislative intent of the law would specifically allow the making of a working copy with closed captioning in an institution serving the hearing impaired, as long as the copy stayed within the institution requiring it. The copy must necessarily be restricted from general use, but it might be shared among other institutions serving hearing-impaired populations (Official Fair Use Guidelines, 1987, p.17).

Such diverse opinions put use of this technology in the gray area. If your building has a population of hearing-impaired patrons, you would probably be safe in closed-captioning your videos that aren't already so encoded. Keep in mind the guidelines Congressman Kastenmeier set forth as parameters and you will probably not be challenged. If still in doubt, consult a copyright attorney.

Video distribution

Video distribution is a type of closed-circuit network in which a classroom teacher (usually) controls video being sent from centralized equipment in the building. Videos are loaded into centrally housed players and are either started at a pre-determined time or are started by the particular teacher requesting the program. The advantage of the technology is that one doesn't have to roll equipment all over a building, and there is some control over the amount and type of video being used in a building. Additionally, the software that controls the players can track and record usage and generate reports of which tapes and players were used most often, and which tapes were played by which teachers. The primary disadvantage is that since the librarian (usually) is the person loading and perhaps starting the videos, the librarian becomes a part of the copyright compliance loop.

According to Mary Brandt Jensen, law librarian and law professor, the library or librarian can be considered a contributory infringer if "the library caused, assisted, encouraged, or authorized the patron to do the infringing act or was in a position to control the use of the copyrighted work by the patron" (Jensen, 1992, p. 150). Obviously, if the library is the site of a video being infringed, the library would have to produce considerable evidence that it was unaware of the nature of the video in order to be held blameless.

The author solved the problem of questionable videotapes in the video distribution system by requesting certain documents from teachers before the tapes were played:

- *If the tape to be played is owned by the library, all the teacher need submit is a copy of the lesson plan showing the link between the lesson and the video. Since the building librarian is familiar with the curriculum of the various grades and classes, it is obvious if someone is showing video that is outside their assigned curriculum. The librarian could be extra vigilant in these circumstances, perhaps requesting the assistance of the administrative staff in assessing the appropriateness of the showing.*

Q: If we have a situation that otherwise meets the conditions of fair use, and we have three separate classrooms that need to see the same video, can we stick a home-use video into our media distribution system and send it out to the 3 rooms simultaneously?

A: This is likely a fair use. Providing all the classes are studying the same topic, and teachers and students are present, this type of showing is not significantly different from hooking three TV monitors to one VCR—a use which is generally accepted to be fair.

Q: Our district is looking at a system for videotape delivery. To make this work, every videotape must be transferred to a new, digital format and stored on a server. Not only will this be changing format, but also by putting the video on the server multiple users can then use the video. The district people and sales people are saying they think it's legal because we would only be transferring the image of tapes we have bought.

A: Just because you own the tapes doesn't mean you can do anything with them you choose. You have no inherent right to make a copy of the videotape in VHS format, much less in digital format. Note that often you will see a prohibition about "storage in any digital retrieval system." This proposed use potentially violates the right of duplication, the right of adaptation and the right of distribution. Depending on the audience for the showings of these tapes, you may also violate the right of public performance. Remember: a sales person wants to sell you an expensive new toy, not necessarily to advise you that the use of that toy might be illegal. Get permission to digitize those tapes.

- *If the tape to be shown was rented from a local video store, the teacher still must meet the fair use requirements of the law in order to use the tape in class.*
- *If the tape was taped off-air, the teacher must submit a verification of fair use compliance.*

Taping off-air, in contrast to taping from cable, is permissible within strict fair-use guidelines. Those guidelines were discussed in the section on off-air taping. Programs taped by the library staff at the request of teachers should be clearly labeled as copyrighted material, and both the record date and erase date explicitly noted on the tape. Presenting a home-taped video to be played in the video distribution system places the librarian's legal life in the hands of another. To assume that all tapes brought to the library are within the legal limits for fair use is naive. If the teacher were to play an illegal tape and be caught, the copyright owner would have a potential case against the librarian as a contributory infringer since the librarian assisted in the illegal display.

Educators can make a modest effort to protect themselves and their schools by requesting disclosure forms from persons wishing to play video through the centralized system. With such verification on file, the school should have a modicum of protection if the tape is later found to be out of compliance. (Figure 5.7)

Additionally, a copy of the teacher's lesson plan showing direct correlation of the film to the day's lesson is a good idea.

Digital video servers

This technology is so new that everyone employing it is a pioneer—and a potential test case. Few know how this technology will be interpreted by the courts, but here is a casual assessment of the technology. When converting analog (tape) videos into digital (hard disk) storage, one must first convert the format of the video. Format conversion is an adaptation, creating a derivative work. This is a violation of one of the rights of the copyright holder. In addition, the purpose of the conversion is to distribute the video, another right of the copyright holder. Naturally, you have also made a copy of the work, and you have copied all of it. The work is creative, and you have done the copying to avoid paying for a digital copy of the work. So a fair use assessment here doesn't look good either. Use extreme caution in making these conversions.

Sound recordings

Sound recordings, as used in this section, will include phonograph records, cassette tapes in analog and digital formats, compact discs, reel-to-reel tape, and hard disk-based recordings. These are distinct from the section on music because music also includes the print music notation, as well as performance of the printed music. This section will only deal with recorded aspects of music, but will also include all other types of recordings, such as spoken word.

Figure 5.7 — Video release form

Video Release for Middletown High School

I hereby grant permission to _____

to use these videotapes_____

_____

at Middletown High School. It is agreed by myself, as owner of these tapes, and the teacher, as representative of Middletown High School, that the tapes will be shown only for direct instruction, and will not be copied or altered in any way. Neither Middletown High School nor the teacher will charge any fees to any person to view any of the tapes listed above. The teacher named above will be singly responsible for any damage incurred in the use of the above described tapes.

Owner _____

Date_____ Teacher _____

     All the formats listed above can be and are copyrighted. Even if you do not see a copyright symbol on the item itself, you must assume all materials to be copyrighted unless specifically shown otherwise because the law no longer requires notice of copyright. Some recordings use the special symbol assigned to phonorecords—
a 'p' in a circle, similar to the 'c' in a circle commonly understood to be the symbol designating copyrighted print materials. Remember that neither symbol is required.

     In earlier times when a sound recording was played publicly, the composer of the music was entitled to a royalty but the performer of the music was not. The performers did receive royalties from sales of recordings, but not from public performances of the recordings. The reasoning here was that sound recordings did not have public performance rights. However, jazz recordings, and some blues recordings, are performances that have always been covered by copyright. These styles of music rely heavily on improvisation. Since the work is "fixed" only at the time of recording, there is a dual copyright—that of the composer who wrote the basic song, and that of the performer who improvised a section of the performance. However, since February 15, 1972, sound recordings now carry a dual copyright: for the composer and for the performer. This expansion of the earlier rights explains why you see a copyright notice on a recording of a public domain work, such as classical music.

     Recordings fixed prior to February 15, 1972 may have had some copyright protection under state copyright laws, but such protection is highly variable. Since the Internet has become an active medium in the transmission of sound recordings, and because many people are substituting Internet transmissions of performances for the purchase of CDs or tapes, in 1995 Congress granted public performance rights to "digital audio performances." Web pages that deliver recordings on the request of the viewer may be in violation of the new right (17 USC §§ 114(d-f)). The No Electronic Theft (NET) Act (P.L. 105-147) provides criminal penalties for those who violate copyright of sound recordings via the Internet, even if the violator makes no profit from the exchange (Recording Industry Association of America, 2003).

     Sound recordings have the same requirements and permissions as do all audiovisual

Q: Our assistant principal wants to purchase a high-speed cassette duplicating machine. He wants to get recordings of various types and pick songs or stories from them to make a collection. He will copy all these cassettes so that teachers can have them in their classrooms. Isn't this an anthology?

A: Not only is this making an anthology, it is reproduction (a protected right) and distribution (yet another protected right). None of these suggested uses say anything about curriculum, classroom teaching or any of the other triggers that might bring in a discussion of fair use. Of course, at the scope suggested, fair use would likely be out the window anyway.

Playing the original recordings in the classroom, as long as they are directly tied to the lesson at hand in that specific classroom at the time,

AND the teacher is the one to make the decision to use the tapes (remember — a bottom up copying scheme)

AND the only ones to hear the tape are the students and teachers in the class

AND you are in a nonprofit educational institution

AND you are working with a legally acquired (i.e. bought) copy of the work should be OK. The problem here is that under the AV guidelines (basically summarized above) you must comply with ALL of the provisions. If you say "no" to any of the conditions, you don't qualify for fair use.

materials. See the section on the four tests of fair use for the specific details. Sound recordings of music add an extra onus to the mix. A work may involve three copyrights: one for the music itself, a second for the recording, and a third on the arrangement. For example, a current hit record may have music and lyrics copyrighted by the author, while the actual recording of the performance of that music and lyrics may be covered by an entirely different copyright. In order to receive permission to use the recording in any derivative work, videotape, or public performance, you must get permission from all copyright holders. Occasionally a teacher will ask students to perform music and record the performance to use as background music for a multimedia presentation. Even if the music is in the public domain, the arrangement of the music may not be. Additionally, the students now own the copyright to their own performance of the music. Clearance will be required for any use beyond use by the students involved.

Two organizations do most of the copyright clearances for professional music recordings: American Society of Composers, Authors and Publishers (ASCAP) and Broadcast Music Inc. (BMI). You can contact these organizations at:

ASCAP
One Lincoln Plaza
New York, NY 10023
212/621-6000
or on the Internet at: http://www.ascap.com

BMI (Broadcast Music, Inc.)
320 W. 57th St.
New York, NY 10019
212/586-2000
or on the Internet at: http://www.bmi.com

As with all audiovisual materials, the owner of a copy of a sound recording may not make any copies of the original, even archival copies. Some tapes may be purchased with duplication rights, especially foreign language tapes. Be sure to retain the paperwork granting the duplication rights and any restrictions that may accompany them, e.g., duplication of one copy per student or one copy per textbook purchased. If such numerical restrictions apply, create and maintain a log of duplications (Figures 5.8 and 5.9).

A bit of extra time spent in the process can save many hours of research compiling records at a later date, should you be challenged on compliance.

Figure 5.8 — Sample duplicate log

Date	Tape	Copies	Comments
7/22	Un jour en France	15	Dubonet – 235 remain
8/15	Un jour en France	10	Martin – 225 remain
8/16	Habla espanol	13	Spanish 4 1/student

Figure 5.9 — Audio tape duplicate log

Date	Tape	Copies	Comments

Sampling

The amazing capabilities of digital editing equipment make all sorts of creative work with audio not only possible but also simple. This equipment is so sophisticated that individual wave forms can be edited, copied, modified, or erased. The technology is called "sampling." Several lawsuits have been filed and won as a result of one party extracting selected sounds from a copyrighted work and inserting them into a new, derivative work. How were they caught? Does it make any difference? They were caught, found guilty in an expensive trial, and paid the appropriate penalties. But if you need ammunition to convince crafty audiophiles, there are certain digital "signatures" that enable audio to be quite simply identified (with the necessary equipment and expertise).

How much sampling is "too much" in a fair use assessment? A copyright attorney posted on CNI-COPYRIGHT that if a consumer can recognize a snippet of a song as being from the original, that is too much. When you think of game shows like *Name That Tune*, where contestants could name a song from 3 or 4 notes, you realize that it doesn't take a lot of song before you have run into the "significant amount" issue.

Sampling tips:

Sample from your own recordings (ones recorded by you or your students.) You will still need permission from music publishers if you are sampling from recorded music, voices or environmental sounds. One federal circuit (6th Circuit covering Michigan, Ohio, Kentucky and Tennessee) holds that no amount of sampling is legal without permission (*Bridgeport Music v. Dimension Films*, 383 F.3d 390 (6th Cir. 2004)).

Remember (and remind students and colleagues) that there is a difference between "can" and "supposed to." You can sample from virtually any audio source. You are not supposed to do so without permission.

The MP3 dilemma

As the Napster case (*A&M Records, Inc. v. Napster, Inc.*, 284 F.3d 1091 (C.A.9 (Cal.), 2002)) has shown, some trading of copyright-protected material via file sharing networks is illegal. Schools will want to watch for packets associated with various file sharing software packages since the Recording Industry Association of America (RIAA) has declared its intent to sue educational institutions for contributory and/or vicarious infringement if shared files are traced back to those organizations. The RIAA declares: "A copyright is infringed when a song is made available to the public by uploading it to an Internet site for other people to download, sending it through an e-mail or chat service, or otherwise reproducing or distributing copies without authorization from the copyright owner. In civil cases copyright infringement can occur whether or not money was exchanged for the music, and in criminal cases there only needs to be a possibility of financial loss to the copyright holder or financial gain to the infringer. The NET Act sets penalties for willful copyright infringement" (RIAA, 2003).

The NET Act imposes criminal penalties of up to 5 years in prison, and fines up to $250,000 in statutory fines if the infringement included an expectation of financial gain. That expectation could be as little as expecting another file in return, as is the case with file sharing.

The Electronic Frontier Foundation has a page of tips to minimize the danger of fle sharing software. EEF, 2004.

Related cases

A&M Records, Inc. v. Napster, Inc., 284 F.3d 1091 (C.A.9 (Cal.), 2002).
Internet service that allowed users to share digital audio files (mostly music) was found to infringe the copyright of the works' owners. Schools may be accused of vicarious or contributory liability if file-sharing software is installed on school computers and subsequently used to share files.

Encyclopedia Britannica Educational Corp. v. Crooks, 542 F. Supp. 1156 (W.D.N.Y. 1982).
Regional educational agency converted films to videotape and distributed them to member districts. The agency remains under a permanent injunction preventing them from making copies of programs.

Columbia Pictures Industries v. Redd Horne, 749 F.2d 154 (3rd Cir. 1984)
The Redd Horne company was found guilty of copyright infringement by charging patrons to perform copyright protected videos. Officers of the company were found liable for contributory infringement. The case showed that even performances in closed rooms may be considered to be public under the definition of the law. The court said, "A defendant is not immune from liability for copyright infringement simply because the technologies are of recent origin or are being applied to innovative uses."

Works cited

A&M Records, Inc. v. Napster, Inc., 284 F.3d 1091 (C.A.9 (Cal.), 2002).

Association for Information Media and Equipment. 1990. *Press release.* Elkader, IA: AIME.

Bridgeport Music v. Dimension Films, 383 F.3d 390 (6th Cir. 2004).

Columbia Pictures Industries v. Redd Horne, 749 F.2d 154 (3rd Cir. 1984).

Electronic Frontier Foundation. 2004. *How not to get sued by the RIAA for file-sharing.* Retrieved December 30, 2004 from http://www.eff.org/IP/P2P/howto-notgetsued.php.

Family Entertainment and Copyright Act of 2005, Pub. L. No. 109-9, (effective Apr. 27, 2005).

Jensen, M.B. (1992, Winter). I'm not my brother's keeper: Why libraries shouldn't worry too much about what patrons do with library materials at home. *The Bookmark,* 50, 150-4.

Kruppenbacher, F. (14 June 1993). Re: CC and copyright. Discussion on the addition of closed captioning to commercial videotapes. Message posted to CNI-COPYRIGHT electronic mailing list.

Official fair-use guidelines: complete texts of four official documents arranged for use by educators. (1985, 1987). (4th ed.). Friday Harbor, WA: Copyright Information Services.

Recording Industry Association of America. 2002. *RIAA Releases Mid-Year Snapshot of Music Industry.* Retrieved January 7, 2005 from http://www.riaa.com/news/newsletter/082602.asp.

Recording Industry Association of America. 2003. *Downloading and uploading.* Retrieved December 30, 2004 from http://www.riaa.com/issues/music/downup.asp.

Reed, M. H. 1989. *Videotapes: copyright and licensing considerations for schools and libraries.* Syracuse, NY: ERIC Clearinghouse on Information Resources. (ERIC Document Reproduction Service No. ED 308 855).

Sinofsky, E. (14 June 1993). Re: Closed-caption videotape conversion. Discussion on the addition of closed captioning to commercial videotapes. Message posted to CNI-

Chapter 6

Music Materials in Schools *(Print and Recorded)*

Music, as with most of the other media, has its own set of guidelines. Music, in the context used here, means sheet music, not sound recordings. However, making sound recordings of sheet music will fall under these guidelines in certain circumstances.

What typical activities are covered?

Typical activities in schools include reproduction and performance to some extent. Keep in mind that printed music is always covered by the print guidelines. However, certain uses of music in education are exempt from the print requirements in ways that uses of standard prose are not.

Reproduction of sheet music—issues

Sheet music publishers make their livelihood from selling copies of sheet music. They are highly protective of their one product. With photocopiers able to make fast, high-quality copies, this method of piracy is a serious threat to music publishers.

Typical activities involving reproduction of sheet music include:
- *Elementary music teacher finds a song in a book. She makes enough copies for her entire choir, and saves the copies for use in future years.*
- *High school band director buys one copy of music for each type of instrument in the band, e.g. one trumpet part, one flute part, one drum part, etc. He duplicates enough copies of the music for each person in the band to have the appropriate music.*
- *The choir director purchased a set of music for his choir. A set includes 8 of each part:*

soprano, alto, tenor, baritone. However, this year he has 12 sopranos, but only 3 altos.
He would like to make 4 extra soprano parts to make up for the alto parts he won't be using.

Performances of sheet music—issues

Even if students are expected to memorize music before performance, the music being played originated with sheet music. Performances of music beyond the classroom are public performances. However, for non-dramatic performances in school where there is no admission charged, or where all of the admission proceeds go to the educational institution, most use is permitted unless the copyright owner objects at least 7 days in advance.

Typical performances of sheet music include:
- *The band will be performing copyright protected sheet music as it marches in the homecoming parade. The use is not in school, and not part of a class.*
- *The choir performs copyright protected sheet music as it sings holiday songs at a local nursing home.*
- *The Junior/Senior class musical is not a classroom activity, but it does use copyright protected sheet music. The classes charge admission to raise money for the Junior/Senior Prom.*

Reproduction of recorded music—issues

Occasionally music teachers need to make copies of recorded music for their students. This type of situation occurs more frequently at the college level, but if you have a music theory class, or a history of music class, similar things may happen at a high school. Teachers may make copies of complete works or portions of works, and may make anthologies of such excerpts for the purpose of conducting "aural exercises or examinations."

Typical reproductions of recorded music might include:
- *The band has a concert, and the assistant principal records the performance. To raise money for new band instruments, the band makes copies of the recording and sells it to band members and their parents.*
- *The music teacher wants to demonstrate syncopation to his class. He makes copies of several examples of the technique from differing decades to show how different composers treated it.*
- *The band director wants to make copies of a recording of the work the band will play in the next concert, so the students may practice at home with a full ensemble.*

Performances of recorded music—issues

Performing recorded, copyright-protected sheet music is a common occurrence. Most of these issues are addressed in the chapter on audiovisual materials under the section on sound recording. However, some additional

Q: *We want to take a popular song and rewrite the lyrics to honor our retiring principal. The choir would perform this song at the principal's retirement celebration. Is this legal?*

A: Based on the Guidelines for Educational Uses of Music, this is not permitted under fair use. Copies of purchased music may be simplified (arranged for young learners) but lyrics may not be changed or added.

Q: *The music appreciation class wants to take portions of recordings and make "listening tests." Since this is an anthology, is this permitted?*

A: According to the Guidelines for Educational Uses of Music, taking excerpts of school-owned recordings for "aural examinations" is permitted.

topics come into play. Non-instructional public performances of recorded music always require a license. The difficulty is in getting a license for a secondary or elementary school.

Typical recording performance issues include:
- *The communications director wishes to put the videotape of the recent band concert on the local cable public access channel that is available to every home in the district and beyond.*
- *The principal wishes to play recorded music over the PA system during passing period, lunchtime, and during the closed circuit announcements.*
- *The district technology director decides she wants "music on hold" over the telephone system.*
- *A fifth grade teacher wishes to play relaxing music in the background while her students work on projects. The music does not relate to the instructional goal; it just provides a tranquil environment for productive work.*

Adaptation of sheet music—issues

All adaptations are within the rights of the copyright owner. However, schools do have some limited exemptions to create adapted works within an educational context.

Typical music adaptation issues in schools include:
- *The choir teacher purchased music for a female duet, but would like to adapt the music to include two male parts. The publisher sells a 4 part version of this piece, but the teacher has no budget to purchase new music, so he writes the two needed parts.*
- *The marching band director wants to have an innovative performance for the regional contest, so he writes an arrangement of a new off-Broadway musical.*
- *An arrangement of a Beethoven sonata for modern instruments is too difficult for the beginning orchestra to play, so the middle school director simplifies the piece.*

Q: Our high school recently staged a musical and legitimately purchased the production rights for this event. A parent videotaped the performance and now would like to make copies of the videotape to sell to parents of cast members at exactly the cost of making the copies. These tapes would be used only for the enjoyment of the students' families. Will this violate copyright law?

A: Unless the school (or the parent) also purchased rights to distribute the production, this use would likely be a violation of copyright. The law doesn't address this specific situation but it does address performances of music. A school may make a single tape of a musical performance, but that copy can be used only in class to critique the performance.

What guidelines affect music?

There is no section of current copyright law that identifies specific guidelines for permitted educational uses of music, either printed or recorded. However, several groups collaborated to draw up a set of guidelines that address the unique aspects of using music in schools. In 1976, at the same time Congress was developing the Fair Use Guidelines, several music industry groups and music educators developed the Guidelines for Educational Uses of Music. The groups participating included Music Publishers' Association of the United States, Inc., the National Music Publishers' Association, Inc., the Music Teachers National Association, the Music Educators National Conference, the National Association of Schools of Music, and the Ad Hoc Committee on Copyright Law Revision. Since these guidelines aren't law, they are more of a "gentlemen's agreement" than believing

Q: *The music teacher wants to copy an old music workbook because the work is now out of print and she cannot locate the publisher. Since the work is not available for purchase, is this permitted?*

A: The Guidelines for Educational Uses of Music state that copying of consumables is never fair.

that the uses described are acceptable by all parties. Staying within these guidelines is a sensible fair practice. Someone might be able to make a case for slight extensions of the limits detailed here, but just as in speeding, the more one exceeds the limits the more one is at risk of penalty.

In addition, standard tests of fair use always apply, as do the print guidelines, audiovisual guidelines, TEACH act, and multimedia guidelines. Always look at all aspects of a given situation to assess all the possible angles before making a determination if a use is fair or not.

There are actually three sets of guidelines covering educational use of music. The longer lived of the guidelines, The Guidelines for Educational Uses of Music, are generally accepted. Following guidelines promulgated by such a collaborative group (composed of copyright owners and end users) forms a reasonable basis to make decisions on what types of use are appropriate. Beyond what these guidelines offer, the Music Publisher's Association has some additional guidelines, as does the National Association for Music Education. Both these supplemental guidelines expand on the original set of rules, and add supplemental information on new technologies that were not available when the original guidelines were written in 1976. The expansions are not endorsed by copyright owner groups, however, so use caution in their application.

Print music

The types of copying of printed music that are acceptable include:

- *Emergency copying when purchased copies have not arrived in time for a performance, with the understanding that the emergency copies will be replaced with purchased copies.*

- *For non-performance classroom purposes, the teacher may make one or more copies of portions of works, as long as the parts are not a part that would constitute a "performable unit such as a section, movement or aria." The copied portion may not exceed 10 percent of the whole work. You may only make one copy per pupil.*

- *If the school buys sufficient copies of printed music, those copies may be edited or simplified as long as the fundamental character of the work is not changed (e.g. jazz stays jazz), or the lyrics are not altered or added if none exist.*

According to the Guidelines, there are several prohibited types of music copying:

- *Any copying that substitutes for purchasing a collection, anthology, or collection of music.*

- *Any copying of "consumable" materials such as workbooks, tests, exercises, etc.*

- *Copying music for performance, except as explained in the first permission above.*

- *Copying with the intention of not purchasing music, except as explained in the first and second permissions above.*

- *Copying without including the copyright notice that appears on the printed copy.*

Recorded music

Under certain circumstances school users may make copies of recorded music. Those circumstances include:

- *You may make a single copy of recordings of performances by students but it may only be used for evaluation or rehearsal. This recording may be kept by the school or individual teacher.*

- *You may make a single copy of a sound recording of copyrighted music (as long as the recording is owned by the school or an individual teacher) for the purpose of constructing "aural exercises or examinations." This derivative recording may be retained by the school or teacher. (This permission pertains only to the copyright of the printed music and not to any copyright which may exist in the sound recording.)*

What rules/laws are different about recordings?

Recordings are treated no differently if they are music than if they are spoken word. The 5 yes/no tests still apply to using copyrighted recordings of music in the classroom. The direct teaching aspect will be an essential element of the fair use assessment, so entertainment, ambience, or enrichment are not sufficient to get the nod on the face-to-face teaching question. The bad news about using sound recordings is that two copyrights apply to sound recordings created after February 1, 1972. Prior to 1972, there was no copyright in the actual recording, so a recording of public domain music (such as much of classical music) would be in the public domain. After 1972, however, there is a copyright in the underlying composition (sheet music) plus a copyright in the recorded performance. For that reason, recent recordings of Bach, Beethoven and the great masters (in fact, any music published before 1923 as long as it is in the original form) are protected by copyright even though the underlying work is long in the public domain.

A hot topic in the recording industry today involves peer-to-peer file sharing. Individual users, for private use, may make copies of works they lawfully own. So someone might copy a song from a compact disc to an MP3 player in a completely lawful manner. However, schools are not individual users, and making copies of recordings must follow the requirements set forth above. Sharing digital files with others who do not own legal copies of recordings is not legal, for both individual users and schools. In addition, the RIAA announced

---

Q: At the sports awards banquets, the coaches want to have a slide show of team photos with music from a CD. Even though PowerPoint allows this option, is it within copyright guidelines? This is for entertainment purposes. Is it legal to play a CD on a boom box while the slide show plays (rather than adding the songs to the slide show on the computer)?

A: It makes no difference if the performance runs through PowerPoint or a boom box for the purposes of determining that this is a public performance. They are both copyright problems. Copyright allows plenty of permissions for using materials IN CLASS to TEACH CONTENT to ENROLLED STUDENTS. However, once you extend beyond those limits, copyright permissions drop back to the very limited fair use that is allowed for you, me, and the man-on-the-street. The fairly liberal multimedia guidelines would permit some music in a PowerPoint, but only for private use of students, staff development, or classroom assignments. This use wouldn't qualify. The standard fair use tests wouldn't give the needed permission here because the work being used is creative, you are using all of it, and the use is to avoid purchasing a license for performance. You have a public performance and need permission or a license. HOWEVER, if that banquet is taking place at the local country club, or some venue that has an ASCAP/BMI license, your performance would be covered under the venue license.

its intention to sue those who enable users to share software. (ITVibe, 2004). If peer-to-peer file sharing software is installed on school computers, and users distribute a significant amount of music, the host and the individual may be named in suits.

Music in performance

Performing music can happen in a classroom setting, or it can happen in a public performance such as a concert, sports event, talent show, dance recital, musical or other event. Some key questions to ask when assessing potential for liability in music performance include:

- *Is the work a musical, opera, operetta, or other dramatic work? Dramatic works have no exemptions under the guidelines, and permission from a rights holder or broker is always required, even for no-charge performances. Ordinarily one gets the rights at the time one purchases the scripts, scores, etc. If you wish to tape and sell copies of the performance, be sure to negotiate those rights at the same time.*

- *Is the performance part of face-to-face teaching? Following the audiovisual guidelines, the five yes/no tests give guidance in the appropriate setting to use music. Enrichment, reward, general cultural value ("Every student should know this piece of music!") and entertainment are not qualifying situations for performance of copyrighted music.*

- *Is the performance live, with no commercial advantage? This strange phrase means that no performers, promoters, or organizers get any money from the event, and that there is no direct or indirect admission charge. (Althouse, 1999, p. 75). There is a small exception for this rule, however. If all proceeds go to educational, religious, or charitable purposes, an admission fee is acceptable. However, making copies of the performance to sell would not be within the limits since it is beyond a live performance. Note that the copyright owner of any works to be performed can object to the performance and prevent use of their work(s) if the objection is registered 7 days in advance. Such an event isn't likely, however, since unless you advertise the program the copyright owner probably will never know you are using the work. Note that this exemption only applies to non-dramatic works. Plays, musicals, operas, etc. don't count, so a play by the third grade before the PTA may need permission or license. Check with the publisher. A performance by a DJ at a school dance, or by a live band, would not meet this exemption because the performers are paid.*

Performance rights organizations

Suppose you have determined that you need permission or license to copy or arrange music, to have a dance with a DJ, or to perform music where the performers are paid though the proceeds will go to the booster club or the PTA. A performing rights organization will be a convenient place to get those rights. Virtually every night club, honky tonk, city stadium, theatre, coliseum or other venue where music might be performed for commercial purposes can obtain a venue license to cover performances in that location from one of the performing rights organizations. The two primary sources for performance rights are ASCAP and BMI: (see Appendix D for contact information). Though many performances in schools are exempt, there are entertainment performances that require a performance license. While colleges and universities have been able to get affordable campus licensing for performances, elementary and secondary schools do not have that option. None of the major rights organizations offer a campus or district license for K-12 education. With such a license a school would be able to play music on the telephone, offer background music in the lunchroom, perform music at athletic events, and hire a local band to perform for the student dance.

A blanket license that covers everything on the campus is not the only way to comply with the law, however. For example, if the band boosters should decide to hire a local band to perform a concert to raise money for new band instruments, a school would need to contact one of the organizations for a single performance license in order to be within the limitations of the law. (Althouse, 1999, 83).

Permissions

Getting permission to make new arrangements of music, to translate or adapt music, to perform music in a broadcast setting or any of the many other times that exemptions do not cover the activities in a school, one should contact either the rights broker or the copyright owner for permission. When requesting permission, it is important to be explicit in what you plan to do, how many times, how many copies, what use will be made of the resulting material. The publisher or copyright owner is not required to reply to your request. If the answer is no or you do not get a response, you have the same result: don't use the work. Some copyright owners will allow use of out-of-print works at no charge, but others feel a responsibility to exploit works to their maximum. They are the ones in the driver's seat in this situation.

Depending on what you want to do will depend on the type of license or permission you need. Public performances and copying sheet music need permissions from ASCAP or BMI. If you plan to record sheet music (such as making copies of a band or choir performance), you need what is known as a "mechanical license" from the Harry Fox Agency (see Appendix D for contact information) (Music Publisher's Association, 2004). The Music Publisher's Association has several useful forms for requesting permission or license to copy or perform music.

Resources for understanding

Columbia Law School Music Plagiarism Project—
http://www.ccnmtl.columbia.edu/projects/law/library/entrance.html
Includes hundreds of documents (texts, scores, audio, and video) about music copyright
infringement cases in the U.S. from 1845 forward.

Music Library Association. (2004). Copyright for Music Librarians—
http://www.lib.jmu.edu/Org/MLA/
A complete source for all the guidelines that affect music, from copying to library archives. Not just
for librarians.

Music Publisher's Association Copyright Resource Center—
http://www.mpa.org/copyright/copyresc.html
Includes forms and other tips on working with music publishers to get hard-to-find music.

Related cases

***A&M Records, Inc. v. Napster, Inc.*, 284 F.3d 1091 (C.A.9 (Cal.), 2002).**
Internet service that allowed users to share digital audio files (mostly music) was found to infringe
the copyright of the works' owners. Schools may be accused of vicarious or contributory liability if
file-sharing software is installed on school computers and subsequently used to share files.

Works cited

Althouse, J. (1999). *Copyright: the complete guide for music educators.* (2d ed.). Van
    Nuys, CA: Alfred.

I.T. Vibe. (1 May 2004). *RIAA sue another 477 music sharers.* Retrieved January 8, 2005
    from http://itvibe.com/news/2501/.

Music Publisher's Association. (2004). *Making a Record: Do I Have To Obtain a Mechanical*

Chapter 7

Multimedia in Schools

M ultimedia was invented after the latest revision of copyright law. There are no definitive court cases in this arena, but thanks to the hard work of a group of media producers, publishers, and media consumers, a set of clear-cut guidelines on the use of multimedia in education was approved late in 1996 and published shortly there after.

What typical activities are covered?

In creating a multimedia presentation the user is likely to deal with copyrights on all aspects of the production that aren't actually originated by the author: video, graphics, music or other sound recording, and computer software. Here are some typical things that happen in a school that would fall under the class of activities known as "multimedia":

- *teacher prepares a PowerPoint™ presentation using graphics from a disk of clip art.*
- *students create a KidPix™ presentation using video clips downloaded from the Internet*

Student multimedia projects—issues

- *students play a current popular song in its entirety as background on their PowerPoint project*
- *students find popular cartoon images online, and they wish to include them in a Hyperstudio™ project that they will display for the PTA.*
- *students create a project in Hypercard™, and they wish to mount the project on the school Web site.*
- *student wishes to attach an award-winning PowerPoint project from Freshman English to his college application*

Teacher multimedia projects—issues

- *teacher wishes to create a PowerPoint presentation on the play, Hamlet, using multiple clips from Mel Gibson's and Laurence Olivier's films.*
- *teacher plans to retain for the foreseeable future a well executed instructional multimedia program he created that includes graphics harvested from the Internet, and use the program.*
- *teacher wishes to post an instructional multimedia program on the class Web site, for*

students to access at any time during the semester. The program includes images scanned from several supplemental texts.

What rights are affected?

Reproduction

Any work included in a multimedia program must be copied in order to be included. Because multimedia programs are, by definition, computer driven, the works must be digital. Copyright owners are, as a rule, nervous about digital reproduction because all copies are identical in every detail to the original and can be reproduced indefinitely.

Adaptation

Adaptation would include editing, cropping, excerpting from complete works. Including something in a multimedia work creates a derivative work, which is an adaptation. Copyright owners are cautious about their works being used as the basis for other works over which they might have no control.

Distribution

Multimedia works may be distributed by disk, CD, or file transfer. Mounting a multimedia program on the Web also distributes the work to the world, or to all those who have access.

Public performance

Because a school is a public place, any performance of a multimedia program is a public performance. Using the copyrighted works of others in a multimedia program performs those works whenever the multimedia work is performed.

Public display

For works of art and other copyrighted static images, display occurs any time the program is viewed.

Digital transmission

Mounting multimedia with audio on the Web means that any accompanying audio will be transmitted digitally. Copyright owners are highly suspicious of digital transmissions of audio.

What guidelines affect multimedia?

Standard fair use applies to use of copyright protected materials by anyone, so even if the following educational guidelines don't provide enough use for a specific application, one can always fall back on the four tests of fair use to determine possible permitted use. The Fair Use Guidelines for Educational Multimedia appeared in 1997, and provided a set of rules that were specific to this emerging technology. However, in reading the specific requirements below, never fail to remember that standard fair use tests may also apply. Because the multimedia guidelines are easier to interpret, apply them first. If those don't meet your needs, you can fall back on the general fair use tests.

Multimedia guidelines

When multimedia first emerged as an educational medium, there were no copyright rules that addressed the types of uses required for the technology. Falling back on the print guidelines or the audiovisual guidelines just didn't address the unique needs of this technology. In order to create a multimedia work, virtually all the relevant material must be transferred to digital format, either disk, laser disk, or CD-ROM. Music, video or still images, and graphics all have different copyrights. And while you may own a CD recording, for example, all you really own is the right to listen to the music until the disk breaks or wears out. You don't own the rights to convert any of that material into another format such as tape or computer disk. The Audio Home Recording Act of 1992 permits such actions for your personal use at home, but use in school doesn't fall under that legislation. Even some material that might be considered to be in the public domain may have restrictions. Many movie stars made films promoting war bonds, for example. And those films are in the public domain—but only for the purpose of selling war bonds. To use the likeness of any of the stars, you would need to get permission from whoever owns the rights to the likeness (Schneider, 1992, p. 33).

In order to clarify exactly what uses of traditional media would be considered "fair" in this new technology, the Conference on Fair Use (CONFU) set about to gather potential stakeholders to negotiate fair use guidelines for several different areas of electronic access, including multimedia. Few of the other groups achieved guidelines to be agreed upon, but the multimedia group at least gained a goodly consensus of opinion that the guidelines drafted are fair (Office of General Counsel, 2004). One notable group, the American Library Association, refused to endorse the guidelines because they felt the guidelines were not liberal enough. So while they don't accept the limits imposed by the guidelines as maximums, they do accept them as fair.

These guidelines outline the limits of acceptable use of copyrighted materials in fair use situations. The guidelines are not law, just as the classroom guidelines are not law. The guidelines are simply an agreement between those who own the copyrights and those who wish to use the copyrighted materials on what will be permitted under a claim of fair use. Compliance under the guidelines doesn't mean the use is "legal." It means that the copyright holder agrees not to sue someone who uses their materials within these limits. As with all claims of fair use, the claim is an affirmative defense to infringement. The use being defended is an infringement of one or more of the 6 rights of the copyright holder, but the claim of fair use is a permissible defense to that infringement. Since the guidelines are not actually part of the law, an infringer would point to the guidelines as evidence of reasonableness in use of material in an educational context.

The agreement on Fair Use Guidelines for Educational Multimedia provides concrete limits on the types and amounts of material that may be included in works created by teachers and students. One of the first notations in the guidelines is that all materials used in derivative works should be properly cited as being taken from the works of others. The guidelines also state that multimedia works made from the copyrighted materials of others may be used only in support of the education of students in nonprofit educational institutions.

Special definitions for multimedia

Educational institutions: "nonprofit organizations whose primary focus is supporting research and instructional activities of educators and students for noncommercial purposes" (Educational Multimedia Fair Use Guidelines Development Committee, 1997).

Educational multimedia projects programs that "incorporate students' or educators' original material, such as course notes or commentary, together with various copyrighted media formats including but not limited to, motion media, music, text material, graphics, illustrations, photographs and digital software which are combined into an integrated presentation" (Educational Multimedia Fair Use Guidelines Development Committee, 1997).

Educational purposes: "systematic learning activities including use in connection with noncommercial curriculum-based learning and teaching activities by educators to students enrolled in courses at nonprofit educational institutions" (Educational Multimedia Fair Use Guidelines Development Committee, 1997).

Educators: "faculty, teachers, instructors, and others who engage in scholarly, research and instructional activities for educational institutions" (Educational Multimedia Fair Use Guidelines Development Committee, 1997).

Lawfully acquired: "obtained by the institution or individual through lawful means such as purchase, gift or license agreement but not pirated copies" (Educational Multimedia Fair Use Guidelines Development Committee, 1997).

Multimedia: "Material is stored so that it may be retrieved in a nonlinear fashion, depending on the needs or interests of learners" (Educational Multimedia Fair Use Guidelines Development Committee, 1997).

Multimedia—covered or not?

All references to multimedia works are to productions that include copyrighted materials. Obviously, any multimedia production in which the teacher or student creates all the text, data, sounds, and graphics would be totally under the control of the creator. The guidelines permit multimedia works made by students to be used in the class for which they were created, and also retained in portfolios maintained by the student for job interviews, college applications, and other purposes. Teachers may use the multimedia presentations they create in face-to-face instruction, or they may assign students to view the presentations on their own. Repeatedly in the guidelines, you see the phrase "Educator Use for Curriculum-Based Instruction." The guidelines are very much in the same vein as the audiovisual guidelines and the print guidelines in that they support direct teaching but not the supplemental, extracurricular activities so often seen in schools.

Retention and access

Teachers may display their own multimedia programs at conferences and workshops, and they may retain the programs they create in portfolios for job interviews, evaluations, and other uses. There is a finite limit to an educator's right to keep a work created from copyrighted material, however. While a student may keep a work indefinitely, a teacher may keep a work for only two years from the time of its first use with a class. Beyond the two-year window, permission to retain or use the material is required for EACH portion of copyrighted material used in the presentation. In other words, for teachers, after two years there is no more fair use of the material used in that particular production.

If a multimedia work is to be used over a network for students at a distant location, several factors come into play. To ensure that only students enrolled in the course may see the program, some type of security is required. Students must log in or provide some other evidence of identity. In addition, the network over which the program is transmitted must have in place a means to prohibit copying of the program. If there is no such safeguard, the program

---

Q: Can I take a student's multimedia project to a teacher's workshop outside the school district to use as an example if I obtain the student's and parent's permission?

A: If the student did all the work on the project—there is no copyrighted material included in the project that the student did not create—the permission of the student and parent is all that is required. If, however, the project includes copyrighted material used by the student under the multimedia fair use guidelines, only the student may use the project for workshops. The teacher may not retain copies of the work for any reason. Teachers may use projects they create themselves for workshops per the guidelines, however.

may be used on the network for only 15 days. After that time, the program disk may be checked out to students, but only with a warning that the program may not be copied.

Secure network

A secure network meets two requirements. It requires a login or PIN to access the resources, and it restricts copying of the materials held therein.

Insecure network

A network that requires a login or PIN, but does not have the ability to prevent copying of materials posted there.

Typical scenarios to illustrate the retention guidelines:

> *A teacher creates a multimedia presentation to illustrate a point of his curriculum. The production uses some copyrighted sounds and graphics. The presentation is so successful that the teacher wishes to demonstrate his work at a national conference of teachers. Such a use is within the guidelines, provided that the display is within two years of the teacher's first use of this production for his classes.*

> *A student creates a multimedia work utilizing copyrighted materials. The presentation is such an excellent example of student work on this topic that the teacher would like to put the presentation up on the school's network for other students to view in the future for reference, and as an example of how a presentation should be made. This use is permitted only if the audience for this presentation is limited to students enrolled in the class. Some type of network security (passwords, access restrictions) must be in place to prevent access by students outside the class.*

> *A teacher wishes to display at an open house, technology fair, or science fair an exemplary student multimedia production that incorporates some copyrighted material. Use of copyrighted materials is permitted for class use only. The guidelines do not allow public performances of materials under fair use.*

Quantity limits

The guidelines specify the amounts of different types of copyrighted materials from a single source that may be used in all multimedia projects created in the course of a term. In other words, from any one video, recording, or database, a specific limit is assigned that a student or teacher may not exceed in a single year or term. Should a teacher reach this theoretical limit, any additional material in a presentation would require permission. Students, especially students in grades K-6, are granted more leeway in their use of copyrighted material. A concrete example of this rule would be the teacher who uses several images from a library book to create a multimedia presentation for his class. The number of images used reaches the limit assigned in the guidelines for this type of material. Before the term is finished, the teacher wishes to use additional materials from the same book for another multimedia presentation to his students. Any use of materials in a single term beyond the limits will require specific permission for each item. The teacher will need to request permission in advance before he may use the additional images.

> **Q:** *The principal in my school would like to use a popular "top 40-type" song, along with a PowerPoint presentation. Do we need special permission?*
>
> **A:** Basically, your principal can use up to 30 seconds of the song without permission. He may retain the presentation for two years from the date of its first use. He MUST have, as the first slide in his presentation, a statement similar to "This presentation contains copyrighted material used under the educational fair use exemption to U.S. Copyright law. Further use is prohibited." (or words to that effect). The LAST slide(s) of the program must include a mediagraphy that includes the copyright information (copyright date and copyright holder) for each piece of copyrighted material used in the presentation.

The limits are:

Motion media (film, video, television): Up to 10 percent or three minutes, whichever is less, of an individual program.

Text (prose, poetry, drama): Up to 10 percent or 1000 words, whichever is less, of a novel, story, play, or long poem. Short poems less than 250 words may be used in their entirety. Only three poems by one poet or five poems by different poets from an anthology may be used. For poems longer than 250 words, only three excerpts from one poet or five from works by different poets in an anthology are permitted.

Music, lyrics, and music video: Up to 10 percent but not more than 30 seconds from a single work (or combined from separate extracts of a work). It makes no difference if the work is being used as a musical work on its own or is an incidental accompaniment to some visual material. If a video clip has music in the background and you can't separate the music from the visual material, you will be restricted by the 30-second limitation for music. If the music is altered in any way, the fundamental melody must be maintained and the basic character of the work should be preserved.

Illustrations, cartoons, and photographs: A work may be used in its entirety but only if no more than five images from a single artist or photographer are used in a multimedia work. In addition, if images are taken from a single collective work, no more than 10 percent or 15 images may be used.

Numerical data sets (computer databases or spreadsheets): Up to 10 percent or 2,500 fields or cells, whichever is less, may be used from a copyrighted database.

How many copies?

An educator or student may make only two copies (including the original) of the multimedia work. An additional copy may be made if one of the copies is lost, stolen, or damaged. If more than one person creates the multimedia work, each may have one copy of the work. Each copy may be retained as long as is permitted for the type of author (student or teacher). See the section on retention and access for the specific lengths of time.

Other restrictions

The opening screen of the multimedia work and any accompanying printed materials must contain a notice that the work contains copyrighted materials which have been used under the fair use exemption of the U.S. Copyright Law. While teachers and students may make alterations to copyrighted material if the purpose is to support specific educational objectives, the author must clearly indicate that such alterations have been made. While the guidelines don't specify the wording of the notice, something like the following would appear to meet the requirement:

NOTICE: The following presentation contains copyrighted materials used under the Multimedia Guidelines and Fair Use exemptions of U.S. Copyright law. Further use is prohibited.

However, because this required notice applies to all users, even 2nd graders who are creating KidPix™ presentations would need to have something similar. Obviously a second grader wouldn't understand anything like the sample notice above. However, a notice like the following would both meet the guideline requirement AND be understandable to young students:

NOTICE: I borrowed other people's stuff to create my project. I followed the rules. Please don't copy my project.

Attribution

The guidelines, and academic integrity, require complete attribution and acknowledgement of all copyright protected materials used in a multimedia presentation. How to document images and sounds in a multimedia presentation is sometimes a quandary.

Consider the analogy of a documented research paper. In addition to the bibliography or mediagraphy at the end of the paper, the author documents each item used at the point of use in the paper. The in-text documentation usually takes the form of a short parenthetical reference to the complete information found in the works cited section of the paper. A multimedia project is no different.

In a multimedia presentation, at the point of insertion of some external, copyright protected work (video, image, audio, etc.) include a shorthand reference to that item as listed in the complete works cited section. The type of reference can be consistent with whatever style sheet governs the project. See figure 7.1.

In Figure 7.1, the slide has a simple text box added to the page, and placed near the location of the copyrighted item. The text need not be large, or distracting;

Figure 7.1

Sample Documentation

- Indicate first word to locate in Works Cited
- Include date.

Simpson, 2003

in fact, the text in the sample was made larger than would normally be used so it would be easier to read in this book. But small text (though not miniscule) would certainly be acceptable.

In addition to the in-text attribution, the multimedia guidelines require specific information in the entries in the works cited section. The guidelines specify the type of information that must be listed, but not the order, so the required information may be arranged in whatever format the assigned style sheet specifies. The items that must be included are:

- *author*
- *title*
- *publisher*

- *date of publication*
- *copyright symbol (©)*
- *year of first publication*
- *name of the copyright holder*

• place of publication

A sample bibliography entry for the work shown in Figure 7.1 might look like this:

Simpson, C. 2003. The White Temple. Lewisville, Tex.: self-published. © 2003, Carol Simpson.

Keeping track of the copyright owners is a good idea, even if the guidelines didn't require that. For teachers, especially, fair use only covers 2 years of use. Retention after that time requires permission of the copyright holder. Since material may disappear, or be destroyed, in the interim, having all that information recorded with the item is essential. You also have it at hand if the presentation becomes commercially viable, or you want to extend use beyond what is granted in the guidelines. Additionally, the copyright owner is not always the same as the publisher or the author.

Multimedia tips

The power of multimedia and the computer applications that support it also provide powerful liability for the users. While you have the capability to grab a frame from a film or extract a single face from a photograph or isolate an instrument from the accompaniment of a popular song, you may not exceed the limits imposed in the multimedia guidelines without permission from whoever owns the rights to those items.

Guidelines to remember when creating multimedia presentations:

- *Students and teachers may use copyrighted material in multimedia presentations if quantity limits are observed.*
- *Students and teachers may use copyrighted material in multimedia presentations if they support direct instruction.*
- *Students and teachers may keep the multimedia presentations they create for class, though teachers face a two-year limit.*
- *Specific limits are established for the amount of material that may be used in multimedia presentations, based on the original medium.*
- *All copyrighted work must be acknowledged with a specific format of bibliography or mediagraphy.*

Best Advice: Invest in clip art, music, and video sold expressly for multimedia productions, or create your own. The multimedia collections are always copyright cleared for such applications. Clip art books would fall under the "illustrations" portion of the guidelines, since one would have to scan or otherwise digitize the images to include them in a multimedia presentation.

Resources for understanding

Fair Use Guidelines for Educational Multimedia
http://www.utsystem.edu/OGC/IntellectualProperty/ccmcguid.htm
This is the full text of the guidelines. Because the guidelines were written by educators and producers, they are written in readable English, not legalese.

Works cited

Educational Multimedia Fair Use Guidelines Development Committee. (1997). [online] http://www.utsystem.edu/OGC/IntellectualProperty/ccmcguid.htm [accessed 1-1-05].

Office of General Counsel, University of Texas System. (2004, December 22). *CONFU: the Conference on Fair Use*. Retrieved January 4, 2005 from http://www.utsystem.edu/OGC/IntellectualProperty/confu.htm.

Schneider, B. (1992, December). Practice safe multimedia: wear a copyright. *Newmedia, 33.*

Chapter 8

Distance Learning in Schools

Distance learning has been a black eye for copyright advocates for a long time. A significant reason is that Congress has a hard time keeping up with the pace of technological change. Add to that the age of most Congressmen and Senators, and you realize that they just don't understand how distance learning works, much less how the use of copyrighted material is just as essential to the success of distance learning as it is to face-to-face instruction. Consider it a generation gap of the educational kind.

History of distance learning and copyright

The 1976 version of the law made transmission of any audiovisual work a violation of the law. Though only radio and limited video teaching existed at that time, they could not be used to send copyright protected materials. So while using recordings, videos, films, and other audiovisual works in face to face settings was perfectly legitimate, using those same items in the same quantity to the same students who happened to be in a location apart from their teacher was considered to be an infringement. How were they to reconcile this seemingly odd disparity of regulations?

Enter the new millennium. Entire courses are delivered via satellite, or videoconference, or Internet. Web pages for teachers have become a primary channel of communication and distribution of exercises, homework assignments, and other supplementary materials. Producers are concerned that their works might be compromised by video, audio, or Internet transmission. These new capabilities didn't mesh with the distance learning provisions of the 1976 Act.

When the Digital Millennium Copyright Act was passed, a provision called for the Register of Copyrights to hold hearings on the best way to develop fair use guidelines for distance learning. The resulting report was turned into legislation that eventually emerged as the T.E.A.C.H. Act (Technology, Education and Copyright Harmonization Act). The bill was signed into law by President George W. Bush on Nov. 3, 2002, and it went into effect immediately. It provides guidelines on how copyright protected materials can be used in distance education. The TEACH Act completely revises section 110(2) of U.S. copyright law.

TEACH Act guidelines

The TEACH Act provides considerable support for using copyright protected audio and video materials in online and video distributed courses as long as they are used in support of direct instruction. The act requires several conditions to be met before the protections of the act are available. Following the lead of the audiovisual guidelines, the TEACH Act requires:

- *that there be a direct connection to the current curriculum.*
- *that only officially registered students may view the materials.*
- *that both the transmitting and receiving ends of a transmission must see that transient copies of works are removed quickly (by flushing the cache, etc.)*
- *that the transmitting body is responsible to protect the copyright of any materials it transmits. (This means the school is ultimately responsible for protecting any copyrighted materials it transmits in distance learning.)*

In order to make the law as forward-looking as possible, the act isn't restricted to the types of distance learning that existed at the time of the passage. Rather, the teaching activity as a whole must meet the definition of "distance education" as defined in the law.

- *Must occur in discrete installments*
- *Must occur within a confined span of time (undefined)*
- *Parts must integrate into a "lecture-like" whole*
- *"Mediated instructional activities" must resemble traditional classroom sessions.*

Despite the fact that constructivist teaching methods are promoted for face-to-face classrooms (the guide on the side, not the sage on the stage), only more traditional teaching activities, teacher-directed, will qualify for the TEACH Act exemptions. Some pundits have likened the act's provisions as an attempt to make distance learning resemble Beaver and Miss Landers. But whatever else the act did, it acknowledged distance learning and distance supported face-to-face learning as valid educational activities that deserved to use copyrighted materials under a fair use defense just as traditional classrooms had done for so long.

However, every silver lining must have its cloud. These activities are expressly prohibited by the TEACH act:

- *Scanning or uploading complete or long works*
- *Storing works on open Web sites (no login/password)*
- *Allowing student access at will (such as supplemental material, or material with no specific, limited time frame)*

Three groups share statutory responsibility for complying with the requirements of the TEACH Act: Policymakers, Information Technology staff, and Instructors/Developers. Each group has specific tasks assigned, and unless all three groups do their part, the protections of the act fall away. Compliance must be a carefully considered, well-orchestrated activity.

Policy makers

Policy makers are, in most instances, the Board of Education. This group must be able to verify nonprofit educational status. Generally the state education agency can certify a district's status, but other methods are possible. The Board must have an adopted copyright policy. Most states' education agency or School Board Association has a set of boilerplate policies that Boards can adopt. A copyright policy must be adopted to take advantage of the TEACH Act provisions.

Faculty, students, and staff must be trained on copyright compliance. Being trained means more than putting a copy of this book in the library. Just as with sexual harassment training or asbestos abatement, sign-off training documents each individual's attendance and demonstrates the Board takes the training seriously. Similarly, students must be informed that teaching materials may be protected by copyright. An administrative expectation of compliance by all parties is the key.

Finally, the policy makers must order that access to distance learning materials is limited to enrolled students only. Restricting access to enrolled students resembles the audiovisual guidelines' directive that only students and teachers in a class be present when copyrighted audiovisuals are shown under a fair use defense. In the case of distance learning, restricting materials to enrolled students means using passwords or other access limitation measures. Some districts offer self-enrollment for community education classes, etc., and such access would prohibit the use of materials under the protections of TEACH.

Information technology staff

The information technology (IT) staff bears a significant part of the burden of compliance with TEACH act provisions. They must assure that only registered students can access course materials. They must prevent students from capturing material for longer than a class session. Preventing capture may mean encrypting materials, in some cases. The IT staff must prevent student redistribution of copyrighted material. Preventing redistribution may go hand-in-hand with preventing capture, if streaming technologies are used.

IT staff must protect digital rights management information, which can include verifying that materials have not been cropped or edited to remove copyright notices, and that all audiovisual materials include credits and copyright statements. They must make sure only "intended recipients" can access any transmissions. This requirement will require working with internetwork hosts, if any, to see that access to files and data streams are secure.

Finally, the IT staff must make long term retention out of student reach. Copyrighted works may be retained from term to term, for example, but they must be stored in access areas that are not available to students or others. This requirement is particularly important for programs where online or broadcast courses are hosted on remote servers or through remote transmission facilities. The IT staff must see that the courses are taken offline, and stored where the staff at the hosting facility can't access the copyright protected materials.

Instructors/developers

Instructors and developers of courses and course materials bear the biggest burden in TEACH Act compliance. Regarding copyrighted materials they may include in a course, they may read stories, poems, essays, etc. They may play nondramatic music (not musicals or operas). An instructor may show "reasonable and limited" portions of dramatic audiovisual works (movies and operas). The term "reasonable and limited" is given no specific time period, however in a face-to-face class a teacher may show an entire film, if that film meets the audiovisual guidelines tests. The act goes on to state that the teacher may use other works typical of a classroom session.

An instructor may not (under fair use) use any work marketed for online learning, such as digital curriculum, electronic databases, or learning systems. All online learning materials are licensed for online learning, and using these materials under fair use would deprive the copyright owner of a sale of a license for these materials. In addition, an instructor or developer may not use anything that is from an illegal copy if he had any reason to think the copy might be illegal. So using a DVD that was purchased from a video supplier, and that comes in an appropriate looking case, would not raise any suspicions that the product was manufactured in the far East in a pirate facility. The user would likely be exempt from liability in such a situation.

An instructor must:

> a. Plan and conduct all use of copyrighted materials
>
> b. Insure that all use is part of regular, systematic instruction
>
> c. Insure that all use is directly related to teaching content
>
> d. Insure that all use is not entertainment, reward, or enrichment

An instructor or designer may digitize materials if the use meets portion limitations. In addition, the instructor must verify that no digital version of the work is available or that the work is inaccessible because of a protection scheme.

Finally, the instructor may not digitize textbooks, books, workbooks, etc. Students or schools are expected to purchase books and workbooks in the traditional manner. Some occasional handouts are likely OK in the manner of the original print guidelines.

Many school activities will fall under the TEACH Act's provisions even if it isn't teaching complete courses online. Many teachers use a Web site for course support, or to mount today's homework worksheet in case it "gets lost" on the way home. School or library web pages may use copyright protected materials in pursuit of their educational goals, but don't qualify for the special exemptions permitted under TEACH. A careful analysis of the situation will determine if the TEACH Act provisions may be relied upon for a given situation.

Resources for understanding

TEACH Act—
http://thomas.loc.gov/cgi-bin/cpquery/?&dbname=cp107&maxdocs=100&report=
hr685.107&sel=TOC_507516&
The full text of the Act itself.

Copyright & digital distance education—
http://www.copyright.gov/disted/
An explanation from the U.S. Copyright Office.

Distance Education and the TEACH Act—
http://www.ala.org/ala/washoff/WOissues/copyrightb/distanceed/Default3685.htm
Prepared by Kenneth Crews, lawyer and librarian, regarding provisions of the Act.

Checklist to Help Institutions/Governmental Bodies Comply with the Distance Education Exemption—
http://www.menc.org/information/copyright/copyr.html#appendixf
A condensed, point-by-point review of the requirements of the TEACH Act.

Chapter 9

Internet in Schools

Internet is the new communication medium. Resources come to the school in that manner. Student work is published online. It is only natural that this would be a widely used communications channel in schools. However, on the Internet you are on your own, copyright wise. There are no Internet-specific guidelines to regulate our activities.

What typical activities are covered?

Because the Internet is so broad in its coverage and style, the types of activities that fall into this area is huge.

Printing pages—issues

Printing pages from the Internet falls under similar rules to those of the print guidelines. Look to those for how many copies one may make and what one may do with them. Typical activities that would be governed by these rules include:

- *A teacher finds a Web page that clearly explains a concept that the class is studying. She makes a copy and duplicates it for each student.*

- *A student locates a poem online for a poetry notebook he is creating. He prints off the copy to include in his notebook.*

- *A librarian finds an image of all the book covers from the nominees for the state reading incentive. She prints multiple copies of the image to broadcast around the school to increase interest in the program.*

- *The PE teacher uses an online catalog to find sports equipment for his upcoming order. He prints copies of the various items he wishes to purchase so he can comparison shop.*

- *The school webmaster finds a Web site whose style he finds attractive and user-friendly. He prints the entire site so he can use the design as he reworks the school's web page.*

Bookmarks—issues

Bookmarks are files of links to frequently visited, or not-to-be-forgotten Web pages. Making bookmarks is similar to writing down an address. Addresses are facts, and are not protectable by copyright. Typical activities that would involve bookmarks include:

- *A group of students is working on a WebQuest. They bookmark a group of sites that have relevant information for their final project.*
- *A principal bookmarks sites that have information about a grant program he plans to apply for.*
- *The librarian bookmarks sites that the class coming tomorrow for research will need. Having the sites pre-identified keeps the students on task and away from surfing potentially off-topic sites.*

Links—issues

Links are similar to bookmarks, in that they are Web page addresses. Links can be problematic when the Web page owner objects to your link to their page. The primary reason the owner might object is that they feel you are capitalizing on their site without appropriate attribution or payment. Using frames to access a Web site hides the true origin of a Web page (the URL doesn't show in the address bar) and the actual Web site from which the content is displayed may get no acknowledgement.

While individual links may be public domain facts, collections of links, especially those collections with significant organization or annotation, gain what is called a "compilation copyright" over the selection, annotation, and organization of those links.
Typical activities that would involve links include:

- *Librarian finds another library's list of links on a reference topic. A class will be studying that topic shortly, so she copies all the links and puts them on the school library's Web resource page for this class.*
- *A principal links from the school's Web page to the district's Web page and that of the feeder schools in their vertical path.*
- *The school webmaster finds some online resources that support the school curriculum. He embeds the resources into frames on the school's Web page so that no one has to know where they come from.*

Copying pages to local servers — issues

Especially when Internet access is slow, or a large number of students must access the same material at once, it is sometimes easier to copy a Web page or Web site and put the information on a local server rather than bringing the page across the net every time a student must get information. Some software will allow you to copy an entire site at once, even collecting outside pages or sites to which the first page is linked. Going through a fair use assessment doesn't provide much support that copying this extensively and then redistributing would be a fair use.

Typical activities involving copying pages include:

- *Teacher uses Web page harvesting software to collect several Web sites that will be important for an upcoming research project. She specifies that she wishes to go four layers deep into the site to be sure to get the necessary information.*
- *The music teacher copies 200 pages of sheet music from a subscription database. She stores the pages on her local computer, and prints copies when her classes need new music.*
- *The principal pays for a single subscription to a Web site that has worksheets for math remediation. He copies the pages using a special harvesting program, and installs the copies in the Resource room. Students from several grade levels use these pages to practice for the upcoming standardized tests.*

Redistributing pages—issues

Copying a page is not the only potential troublespot for appropriating Web material. Sometimes teachers or students not only copy material from a Web page, but they also incorporate that material into a new page. Once the new page has been mounted on the web, it has been distributed to the world.

Typical activities involving redistributed pages include:

- *A teacher finds a WebQuest that is perfect for the unit the class is about to begin. Rather than use the posted site, the teacher copies the pages and mounts them within her own Web site so she is in control of the pages.*
- *A district webmaster locates several pages on teen suicide that are particularly appropriate to the situation in that district. To make the pages consistent with the design of the pages on the local Web site, the webmaster reposts the pages using cascading style sheets so they will look like the rest of the site.*

E-mail—issues

E-mail is probably the most abused Internet property. It is forwarded, edited, copied and reprinted, sometimes to the point that the original author is long lost. E-mail, as with other written material, is the intellectual property of its author if the contents of the e-mail are minimally creative. Because an e-mail is not published (it is a private communication, just as a letter is), protection for e-mail is much stronger than for typical published materials. The recipient may retain his one copy of the e-mail, but he may not redistribute it, adapt it, or make additional copies of the e-mail without permission.

Typical activities involving e-mail include:

- *Student receives a message from an unwelcome admirer in e-mail and forwards it to 25 friends in the band.*
- *Librarian sees a post on a mailing list identifying resources for a commonly taught topic. He forwards the message to all the teachers in the relevant department, asking if they would like him to create a Web page with links to those items.*
- *Principal receives an angry e-mail from a parent. He forwards the e-mail to teachers who have that person's children in class.*

Chat and IM—issues

Chat and instant message applications are blocked in many schools; but for those who allow the practice, the communications in both those applications are usually ephemeral—they exist only briefly and are not saved "in tangible form." When a work is not fixed in tangible form, no copyright exists. However, if the chat is logged or archived, each participant would own the rights to his respective contributions.

Typical activities involving chat and IM include:

- *A 4th grade class has a chat with the author of a book they have been reading. The chat log is retained as a record of the experience.*

- *A teacher has an IM discussion with the parents of a problem student. They agree to keep copies of the log in the student's file.*

What rights are affected?

Virtually all possible rights of a copyright holder are affected by the Internet.

Reproduction

Because the Internet is digital, unlimited perfect copies are possible of any work transmitted by this medium. For that reason, copyright owners are exceptionally sensitive to having their work posted on the Internet without permission.

Adaptation

Capturing digital content makes editing with powerful digital tools a simple process. Copyright owners fear that their work will be appropriated and repurposed against their will or without compensation.

Distribution

Distribution on the Internet is worldwide, instantaneous, and free. Whereas with print distribution, costs and logistics come into play, and distribution may be so minor as to be a non-issue, distribution via the open Internet can be immensely harmful to the value of a work or the market for that work. Why buy it when you can download it for free? Many copyright owners are horrified at the prospect of wide Internet distribution of their work.

Public performance

Video or audio programs broadcast across the Internet may be public performances if they meet the criteria for that designation. Copyright owners are just as concerned about Internet performances as face-to-face ones—perhaps more so since the medium can be played almost indefinitely, and to a vast number of persons.

Public display

Public display is the sister right to public performance, and the same concerns apply.

Digital transmission

Performing sound recordings via the Internet is a huge concern for the owners of copyrights in these recordings. Since the recording can be captured in its pure digital form, the person recording from an Internet transmission has a perfect copy of the original. Why buy a CD when you can capture the one track you like directly from the Internet radio station or other source? Copyright owners have suffered huge losses in revenue because of this practice, and take extraordinary steps to stop any such use without permission or royalty payment.

The difference between an AUP and copyright

An acceptable use policy (actually an acceptable use agreement) is a document that sets the rules by which an end user accesses the Internet through their Internet service provider. Copyright is federal law, and its requirements supersede any rules established by the service provider. An AUP may or may not have any stipulations about copyright among its provisions and rules. Even if the AUP is silent on copyright, the law still applies and must be obeyed.

Special rules for Internet

The Digital Millennium Copyright Act established some forms of protection from liability that may effect schools. Detailed in Section 512, the many specific requirements to be eligible for protection under this section are quite complex. Essentially, the law states that if an Internet (or online) service provider (ISP or OSP) registers with the Copyright Office, and if they comply with a long string of action items—such as agreeing to remove potentially infringing material once it is brought to their attention—the copyright infringement exposure of the OSP is limited. Schools, because they provide Internet access to their staff and students, are probably OSPs or ISPs. The protection offered by the DMCA only extends to the school or district, not to the individuals who may have committed the infringements.

Registered agent

The designation of someone to be the copyright agent for notification of claims of copyright infringement is one step that schools can easily take. The school designates a single person who will respond to claims of copyright infringement and registers that person with the Copyright Office (**http://www.copyright.gov/onlinesp/**). The school posts complete contact information for this person on the school Web site. If someone should find infringing material on a Web page, he notifies the copyright agent, who will then take down or disable access to the material in question.

Q: Must I have permission to put a link to another Web page on my own page?

A: Links have been likened to cross references in a library card catalog. They are facts (just like street addresses) and cannot be protected by copyright, so making links should be acceptable. Some sites don't like you to "deep link" (linking deeper into the site than the main page) because you might miss advertising, disclaimer, or conditions of use posted there. These sites may object, but it shouldn't be on copyright grounds. If you use frames, remember that the referred site will appear to be on your server. Some sites may object to the implied relationship.

Why is this important?

By complying with the requirements of the Digital Millennium Copyright Act OSP provisions, the school is protected against liability for infringements that may happen as a result of students or teachers posting infringing materials on a school Web site. When might that happen? Based on reports to the author, it happens more often than you might imagine. Gifted and Talented students are in GT classes because they write well (among other reasons). When a GT student turns in a marvelous essay or poem or short story, the teacher praises the student, reads the work to the class, and asks to post the work on the school Web site or online literary magazine. If a student in remedial English had written the same essay or poem or short story, the teacher would have immediately accused the student of plagiarism. But because the GT students are exemplary students, the teacher accepts the paper at face value and posts the work online. About three months later the real author contacts the school district, threatening to sue for copyright infringement. Having a registered agent, and following the appropriate take down provisions, the school is protected from a lawsuit (though the busted student is now in the hot seat).

What guidelines affect Internet?

Unlike print works, music, audiovisuals, multimedia, computer software, and distance learning, there are no set copyright guidelines for the Internet. Partly because the Internet is composed of print, music, audiovisuals, multimedia, and computer software, none of the established guidelines fit perfectly, but ALL of the established guidelines may apply to some extent. For that reason, it is often easier to fall back on the standard four tests of fair use to determine if the use of material taken from the Internet is fair. Also remember that access to many of the works on the Internet is through license. Articles from online databases and Web sites that require registration predicate access to those items on terms of the license agreement rather than through fair use. Whatever terms you accept through the license are binding, even if those terms are more restrictive than those of fair use or agreed guidelines. The key to knowing what to use is knowing what items on the Internet are protected by copyright.

Suppose you write a document on a word processor. Perhaps it is a poem or a chapter of a book. As soon as you save the file on the hard disk, your work is protected under copyright. You can send the chapter to your publisher, you can ask other writers to read the manuscript and give suggestions, and you can pass out copies at workshops. The work is still protected under copyright law. Should one of those people take your manuscript and misuse it, you could sue with a reasonable likelihood of success. You may register your work with the Copyright Office if you like, but registration isn't required. Registration does, however, confer a number of important advantages for enforcement.

Now suppose you put that very same manuscript on your Internet home page. Have you just abandoned the copyright to that work? Not at all. You still own five rights, assuming this isn't a sound recording of a copyright holder: reproduction, distribution, adaptation, public performance, and public display. And so does every other creator of materials available via the Internet.

Every creator? Yes. Every person who writes a document published on the Internet, who creates a graphic or icon, who scans his own photograph or records his own voice into a digital file, who sends an electronic mail message, who creates a document for a newsgroup or who designs a Web page owns the copyright to his creative work unless barred by law. And because the United States is a signatory to the Berne Convention, no notice of copyright is required on ANY item in order for the item to be protected by copyright law.

As the creator, that person can decide exactly how he wishes that material to be used. Obviously the creator has decided to permit display of this work via the Internet since he included it on a Web page, sent it via e-mail, or posted it to a newsgroup. The fact that the copyright holder elected to share his work in this manner, however, does not mean that anyone can freely appropriate that material for other uses.

As a friend likes to point out, "there is a difference between 'can't' and 'not supposed to.'" The technology exists for someone to view a document or graphic and, by clicking on the appropriate button or menu, grab that item in a pure digital form. From that point it is quite simple to adapt, modify, resend, forward, copy, or display the item. Someone could certainly do those things, but one is not supposed to. Why not? Because the rights to do all those things are reserved for the copyright holder. All the copyright holder permits when an item is displayed on the Internet is to allow you to view the item as you navigate around the network (Bender, 1996, p. 1).

Certainly there are some documents that state that they have been dedicated to the public domain, or that use for nonprofit purposes is permitted by the copyright holder. Naturally these situations are apart from the average item located on the Internet. And a case may be made for "fair use" of Internet materials, just as one may make a claim of fair use for print and audiovisual materials. Similar situations must apply before a claim of fair use may be considered valid. Since there are to this point virtually no significant cases dealing with fair use of Internet materials, one must analyze and evaluate every use in the light of the general guidelines. Remember that each of the four tests of fair use must be weighed against every claim:

The purpose of the use. Is the use for nonprofit educational purposes? Displaying a Web page or making a transparency of some information for the purposes of teaching a lesson at a public or nonprofit private school would likely be looked upon favorably.

The character of the use. What type of material is going to be used? Factual material placed on the Internet has little protection of copyright since facts can't be copyrighted. If you are using lists of common facts such as the 10 longest rivers, or population figures, you have much more latitude to use the material. Highly creative material, such as art work, videos, or Web page design would be much more highly protected.

The amount of material copied (also called the extent). How much of the material are you going to use? If you plan to copy the entire item (whole text file, complete graphic, entire Web page) you'd best have good answers to the other three qualifying questions. The more of an item you plan to use, the less leeway you are permitted. This factor has significant impact on software that can capture entire Web sites for use in an offline situation.

Q: One of our teachers has created a beautiful Web site which he has enhanced with 30 seconds of music from the movie JAWS. Is it permissible for him to "loop" that 30 seconds on his site, or must he obtain permission or a license from the copyright holder in order to do so?

A: While it is possible to use 30 seconds of music from a movie in a PowerPoint program (thanks to the multimedia guidelines) the right to digitally transmit a sound recording is still reserved to the copyright holder. If your teacher had this stream behind a password protection scheme and met the other guidelines of the TEACH act, he might have more leeway, but as it is, this doesn't look very good.

The effect of the use on the market for the work. What effect would your type of use have if everyone made similar use of the material? For example, if everyone were to download the whole Web page, do you think anyone would want to visit the site? Probably not. When you consider that some sites have advertising or other agendas on their sites, they wouldn't want someone to miss seeing those friendly notices. By downloading the page to an offline machine one would miss the constantly changing variety of advertisements that the sponsor of the page spends lots of money for you to see. Missing those advertisements would potentially deprive the sponsor of revenue. As far as copyright goes, that is a no-no. What if the page is put up by a nonprofit individual or organization? The same reasoning applies. Perhaps the author of the document will one day develop that information into a book or magazine article. Would the market for the book be as great if everyone were to capture the material from the Internet? Maybe the nonprofit organization wants Internet explorers to see the wealth of material their members can assemble, and if one captures a document there would be no point in returning to this site again. Or the information is quickly dated and the organization feels it would be harmed if it were identified with outdated material. There could be many ways that financial harm might affect the copyright holder of an Internet document or file.

Keep in mind that each classroom use of material retrieved from the Internet must be weighed against the four factors listed earlier in this chapter and several other places in this book. Imagine a scale, and each of the factors coming onto the scale on either the side for you or the side against you. Some of the factors weigh more than others. The fourth factor, for example, usually weighs much more than all the others. Consider that when making your analysis.

Special considerations for different Internet services

The Internet has several unique services that require analysis for appropriate use in a copyright context. E-mail, news and discussion groups, file transfer (including peer to peer file sharing), and the Web all require specific types of analysis.

E-mail

The author of an e-mail message owns the content of that message. You, as the recipient, may not make copies of that message, or distribute it without the consent of the original author. This impacts messages you may forward to third parties without the express consent of the original author. There would probably be allowances to reprint some or all of the message in a reply to the sender. You might also paraphrase the message in the reply. Since you are sending that information back to the copyright holder, there would likely be no problem. One of the critical questions asked in determining if a use of a copyrighted work is fair is "has the work been published?" Typically, private e-mail has never been published in such a way that many people would likely have seen this particular work. Since the work has not been published, there is very little likelihood that the work could ever fall into a situation covered by fair use. In addition, if the e-mail is created at work under the scope of employment, there is the possibility that the e-mail is a work for hire (Fishman, 2000, p.14/9). Are there any court cases to support this? Not yet.

For safe parameters, keep private e-mail private unless you have express permission of the original writer. Don't forward it to newsgroups or listservs, don't include it in a message to a third party, and don't post it on your Web page, unless you receive permission. It's good manners; it's good practice.

Newsgroup and discussion list information

When someone posts a message to a newsgroup or a discussion list, he or she makes an implied decision to "publish" the work. Once a work is published there is much more latitude to use portions of that work within the fair use exemption. One may, however, negate that implied license simply by noting in the posting that you request the material not be distributed beyond the list. Again, there are no significant court cases to support these assumptions. These are rules derived from the world of print and extrapolated into cyberspace.

For a safe guideline, you can probably copy a few sentences or paragraphs of a newsgroup or discussion list posting since it was published, as long as you aren't going to use it for a money-making purpose. You can also probably repost the article or message to another newsgroup unless the original author states that isn't permitted. It is always good manners (and safe legal practice) to ask permission to repost.

Use of Web page information

When deciding how to use a Web page, make your analysis similar to a print document or an audiovisual item (depending on what you will be using from the Web.) Keep in mind the four tests of fair use. The nonprofit educational use is a given, but what about the character of the material used and the extent of the material used? The more creative the site (i.e., the less factual) the less of the site may be used without prior permission. As a matter of good teaching, one would want to make the best use of teaching resources. One doesn't use more of a video than is necessary to make a point. Teaching time is too valuable. So one would make optimum use of Web-based resources, as well. Use what is necessary, then get on to other things.

Using any Web page involves a display of the material. Display is the right of the copyright holder. While a display to an individual is expected, display to a public group (your class) isn't. Material located shortly before use—before permission could normally be expected, say a week before anticipated use, since most webmasters can be reached electronically—could be used for a single lesson. Beyond that use, request permission. Any repeat use ALWAYS needs permission, whether this re-use is in the same term or in subsequent terms.

Beware of programs that allow you to "capture" an entire Web site or portion of a site for use offline. While this is a boon to teachers with unreliable Web connections, downloading and storing Web pages or sites for public display in a classroom involve several problematic events. The author(s) and copyright holders design Web pages to be interactive and responsive. Many have ever-changing sponsorships and real-time data that is designed to be viewed in an active, not a static, environment. The owners of these sites have the authority to decide if they feel that your proposed collection of their work fits into their plans. Remember that under the fair use tests, one of the significant questions is how much of the item will be used. If one captures the entire site, one is taking 100 percent. Since Web pages are ordinarily highly creative in design and content (the character of the use), the likelihood for a ruling of fair use declines significantly.

In a discussion of this topic on the Internet newsgroup LM_NET, Stephen Collins, webmaster of Web66, commented:

> Not only is [copying Web pages] very probably a violation of copyright law, it is certainly unethical, and to your students it models a lack of respect for other people's property. It also has very concrete consequences. I run Web66, which is funded by grant monies and by the University of Minnesota. They provide funding in large part based on the popularity of Web66. If I can only show a few accesses because you've all [duplicated] your own copies, then I won't be able to get funding to continue Web66. If you all access it directly, and I can show that it gets 40,000 hits per day from 2,000 different organizations and 25 different countries, then I won't have any trouble getting funding. Most "free" sites are in the same position. When you [copy] them, you're killing off your own resources.

He makes a powerful argument, which reinforces the old saying "There ain't no free lunch."

In creating Web pages, one must have concerns about using copyrighted materials on those pages since the pages are distributed to the world. One must make copies to put a page on the web, and frequently one must also convert materials from an analog format to digital to get the information on the Internet. Music, multimedia elements and other copyrighted information, once mounted on a Web page, are not only copied but they are distributed and performed publicly. All these conditions are cause for concern. In the interest of copyright compliance, some rights brokers have established a "click-through" license for quick, efficient licensing (ASCAP, BMI). Note that there is no automatic fair use for these types of elements on Web pages. Each individual use must be subjected to a fair use analysis.

Chat

Chat is as spontaneous as face-to-face conversation. However, few people record (or "fix") conversation. There is no case law regarding the ownership of chat conversations. Extrapolating from other media one might be able to say that chat is ephemeral, not being "fixed." In such a case, no copyright is vested in a communication that is not fixed in a tangible medium of expression. If the chat is captured, however, fixation automatically generates a copyright for the author of each communication. So each "send" might be construed as a separate "work" protected by copyright, or a series of posts might be taken as a long, possibly disjointed, document.

Copying internet code

While it is possible to download a site's HTML code and adapt the design into your own page, remember that the creative work that went into the design is also copyrighted. Just as copying a drawing or painting requires permission, if you admire the design work of a Web page, ask the creator before you appropriate the result.

Resources for understanding

Web-based material is copyrighted just as print and audiovisual materials are, and notification of copyright status is not required. Small portions of Web documents may be used by teachers in class if there is not sufficient time to secure permission, just as with print materials. Large chunks of images, documents, and Web sites should not be taken without prior consent. Watch for Web pages granting permission for use in educational situations. There are many.

Since there is greater latitude for student use of copyrighted materials, they may also use modest portions of Web documents as long as the copies they make belong to them. Teachers may not keep copies or originals of works made by students in which they incorporate materials copied from the Internet. The copies made from the Internet must reside with the student.

Remember that showing a Web document to a class constitutes a public performance or display of that page. Copyright law and its associated guidelines don't speak of the Internet, but common sense can gauge how closely a given use meets the fair use test. And, as always, permission can override any limitations imposed by the law or guidelines. The good news is that the persons responsible for many Web pages have e-mail links built right into the pages, so contacting the proper party for permission is a lot simpler than tracking down print or video copyright holders.

When putting up your own Web page, make sure you have the proper rights for the graphics, designs, logos, and photos you use. Photos are especially touchy. You need permission not only from the photographer, but also from any recognizable person in the photograph. When requesting permission, as in all cases of permissions, verify that you are getting rights from the person authorized to grant such rights.

Works cited

Bender, I. (1996). The Internet—It's not free and never was. *AIME News.* Summer, 1996.

Fishman, S. (2000). *The copyright handbook.* (5th ed.). Berkeley, CA: NOLO.

Chapter 10

Computer Software in Schools

When the present version of the copyright law was adopted in 1976, computers were huge machines in refrigerated rooms. Few but the most visionary foresaw the emergence of computers as a household or personal appliance—certainly not the Congress as they moved through their deliberations. The 1976 copyright law offered protection to computer programs only as a new form of literary work. By 1980, however, computer programs received expanded protection under Section 117 of the newly revised statute. Making unauthorized copies of computer software has risen in seriousness in recent years. A revision of the law passed in 1992 brought software piracy to felony status, with fines up to $250,000 for systematic violations. The "No Electronic Theft" (Net) Act, passed in 1997, eliminated a loophole for those who provide infringing copies of software via the Internet and other networks. Those who willfully infringe more than $2500 worth of software are liable for infringement, whether or not a profit is made.

What typical activities are covered?

School personnel who knowingly lend computer software to persons who intend to copy it, and school personnel who knowingly lend the necessary equipment to copy software may also be charged with copyright infringement. This situation is known as contributory infringement. Prosecution under this aspect of the law is uncommon, but not impossible. An example of such an act would be a video store selling tapes it knew to be in violation of copyright. They did not make the infringing copies, but they profited by the sale of copies they knew to be illegally made (Berman, 1993). A school whose educators use videos they know to be improperly made would be at risk of some sort of enforcement action.

Similarly, a principal who had been notified that an employee was violating copyright but who took no action could be charged with vicarious infringement if the employee knew the actions violated the law. Naturally, any of these cases would have a vigorous defense on several grounds, but the fact remains that one does not actually have to make the copy to be held liable. One must decide for oneself if the risk of suit is worth the activity. Here are some common computer software copyright situations and their legal implications:

- *A teacher comes to the library to ask to install her personal copy of a word processing program on one of the school computers. She will be using the program at home in the evenings and at school during the day, so only one copy will be in use at a time.*

  In the absence of a license provision permitting such uses, having the same software loaded on two computers even if they are not in use at the same time is not permitted.

- *The technology coordinator wants to save some money on the new building-wide network. In order to avoid the expense of a CD-ROM tower, he proposes to copy the library's CD-ROM discs onto a large hard disk for access.*

  Copying CD-ROMs onto hard disks for active use is not permitted under the standard software copyright provisions. Many software companies will, however, grant permission to access CD-ROM data in this fashion if asked.

- *A student accesses the Internet from the library, and downloads a shareware game from a Web site. He proceeds to give copies of the game to all his friends.*

  Shareware is a type of copyrighted software which may be freely distributed. The user of the software must pay a fee if he or she decides to keep the software after trying it. Anyone may give copies of shareware software to others. The ultimate user is the person who is obligated to pay the license fee.

Multiple installs—issues

Computer software is so very tempting. It will easily install as many times as you need, and will run on all the computers on which you install it. Unfortunately, each installation requires a license.

Typical activities involving multiple installs include:

- *Student computer assistants tire of checking out CD-ROMs to students in the library, so they install the program on each library computer. The program only comes with a license for one installation.*

- *A teacher buys a program at home that helps him create interactive tests for his students. Because it is so helpful, the teacher also installs the program on his laptop and his computer at school. The program allows installation on one desktop machine and that user's laptop.*

- *The industrial arts teacher is required to teach technical drawing. The state urges them to use Computer-Assisted Design (CAD) software. The district has had financial difficulties, and can only afford 3 copies of the software. There are 6 computers in the lab. The teacher installs the program on the other three computers so more students can work at once.*

Q: I want to install software I use at work on my computer at home so I can transfer data back and forth. Can I rely on the 80/20 rule to install this software?

A: There is no such thing as an 80/20 rule. Some software licenses allow you to install software from a work computer onto a laptop or a computer at home, but the provisions of the individual software license will determine if such installations are acceptable.

Networking—issues

Putting software on a network can result in distribution of the software beyond the limits allowed by the license. With broad access permitted by internetworked computers, access to site-licensed software can be from anywhere.

Typical activities involving networking include:

- *The computer technician put a single user copy of software on the district Web server where anyone with rights to the server could access it. The software does not have technological means to prevent more than one person from running the software at the same time.*

- *The webmaster puts a link to the school's contracted periodical database on a public Web page so students could access from home. The database license specifically states that only access from school is permitted.*

Checking out software—issues

Why would someone want to borrow software? The answer is simple. You need to print one poster, and don't want to spend a lot of money for a program to print that one. So, you borrow the software, install it, print the poster, install the software, then return it. It is legal to circulate software, with some detailed caveats.

Typical issues involving circulating software include:

- *A teacher borrows a crossword puzzle making program to create a puzzle with this week's vocabulary words. She enjoys the program so much, she doesn't uninstall the program when she returns the software.*

- *A school secretary borrows a graphics program from the library. As she is walking out, she tells the librarian, "I'm so glad you had this! My pastor has wanted it for the church for a long time. I'll go install it there, and have this back by Monday morning!"*

Clip art—issues

Electronic clip art is the panacea for those who cannot draw a straight line. It is also a huge pit of potential copyright infringement. Because clip art is protected by copyright the moment the file is saved to disk by the original artist, very little clip art is in the public domain. Yet the ease of copying digital files tempts even the most honest computer user.

Typical actions involving clip art include:

- *Computer teacher collects clip art files and mounts them on a Web page for ease of access for his students*

- *Elementary teacher prefers her students not surf the Internet for images, so she finds a dozen or two appropriate images and mounts them to the class Web page so students working from home can access the images.*

- *Cheerleaders need clip art for posters, so they find an image of a famous cartoon character. With digital editing software, they put the cartoon character into the school basketball uniform for use on the posters.*

Q: *I never know what computer will be available when a student asks to use a particular CD-ROM program. Can I install the program on all my computers so it will work on whatever computer is free? The program will not work without the CD in the drive.*

A: This isn't a recommended practice. If your license indicates you may only install the software on one machine, that is specific. If you were to be audited, the audit program would tally each installation of the program. You would have to produce a license for each installation.

Q: *Since single-user CD-ROM programs may not be partially installed on more than one computer even though the CD must be in the computer for actual usage, could the CD-ROM programs be used in this manner if we received permission from the producer/publisher of the CD?*

A: The conditions I describe are those allowed under fair use WITH NO PERMISSION. If you get permission or a license that gives greater rights, you are limited to what the license will (or will not) allow.

Types of infringement

Infringement actions similar to those that can occur in the realm of print can also occur with computer software. The Software and Information Industry Association defines several types of software copying to which it objects. These types of copying would be ones that the SIIA would be willing to prosecute. Here are their definitions of the types of activities of which to be wary:

Direct Infringement

"Anyone who violates any of the exclusive rights of the copyright owner [reproduction, adaptation, distribution to the public, public performance, public display, rental for commercial advantage or importation] is an infringer of the copyright or the right of the author" Section 501(a)

- *downloading software*
- *uploading software*
- *making software available for download*
- *transmitting software files*

Remember that you need not be the one actually making the illegal copies to be held liable for copyright infringement. Those who knowledgeably control the means necessary to make copies, or those who cause others to actually make the copies are contributorily or vicariously liable as well.

Indirect Infringement

Contributory Infringement. Anyone who knows or should have known that he or she is assisting, inducing, or materially contributing to infringement of any of the exclusive rights by another person is liable for contributory infringement.

- *posting of serial numbers*
- *posting of cracker utilities*
- *linking to FTP [file transfer protocol] sites were software may be unlawfully obtained*
- *informing others of FTP sites were software may be unlawfully obtained*
- *aiding others in locating or using unauthorized software*
- *supporting sites upon which the above information may be obtained*
- *allowing sites where the above information may be obtained to exist on a server*

Vicarious Liability for Infringement by Another Person. Anyone who has the authority and ability to control another person who infringes any of the exclusive rights and who derives a financial benefit therefore is vicariously liable for the infringement of another person.

- *ISPs [Internet service providers] who have warez [proprietary software with copy protection removed illegally] or pirate sites on their system*
- *ISPs who have pirates for customers*
- *sys admins for newsgroups or IRC [Internet Relay Chat] where pirate activity takes place (Software and Information Industry Association, http://siia.net/piracy/pubs/DirectIndirectCopyrightInfringement.pdf)*

What rights are affected?

Computer software issues can affect almost all of the rights reserved to the copyright holder.

Reproduction

Copyright owners are especially concerned about reproduction of software because all copies are identical to the original. Software is expensive to develop, and each copy duplicated illegally is a significant amount of profit/cost recovery.

Adaptation

Digital adaptation is easy and may be undetectable. Copyright owners worry about essential portions of their underlying code being stolen and reproduced in competition.

Distribution

Distribution of software is fast, simple, and inexpensive compared to the costs involved in print distribution, for example. A digital work can be available around the world in a matter of seconds.

Public performance

Performance of digital works can reduce demand for legitimate copies of the work.

Public display

Public display is less possible for computer software, but digital images and other digital works such as Web pages are also displayed.

Special rules that affect computer software

Computer software is unique in many aspects. Because it is digital, copyright owners have developed different forms of distribution and different terms of sale than other, more traditional media. Software can be highly lucrative, and it begins at a high price point. Those who want to be cool want to have the latest toys, but the high price only makes them that much more determined to get the software without benefit to the copyright owner. As a result, software has suffered more piracy than most other media. Copyright owners responded with their own volleys, and the war was on. Various selling methods and distribution channels emerged to address these scuffles.

License vs. copyright

While most software (even "shareware") is copyrighted, the purchase of software is usually governed by a license agreement as well as by copyright law. When purchasing a book, the purchaser does not own the book but merely the paper, the ink and binding, and the right to read the words until that copy of the book wears out. The same holds true with software. The purchaser does not own the software, but rather the right to use the software in a manner described in a license agreement, usually included in the documentation of the software package. Reading and understanding the license agreement is an important part of acquiring a new package. Once accepted, these restrictions govern all use of the software.

There are several forms of license agreements: signed agreements, usually on some sort of warranty registration; implied licenses; and so-called "shrink-wrap" licenses. Implied licenses are included in the software packaging, usually as a part of the documentation or as a separate sheet. These licenses usually say something like "use of the software after reading the license terms implies acceptance." If you don't care for the terms of the license, the manufacturer will usually allow return of the package for a refund. Shrink-wrap licenses are often visible through a plastic overwrap on the software package. A similar type of license is called "click wrap" because the license appears when the software is installed. The user must click on an acknowledgement of the license to complete the software installation. The wording of both of these licenses will state that the user is bound by the conditions of the license if the shrink-wrap is opened or the accept button is clicked. There is a degree of controversy about such default contracts. Some courts indicate that if one is given the opportunity to return software once the details of the license are known, the license may be valid. Know your rights in your state.

If the signed license agreement is returned to the software company, or if you click on the "I agree" button, you will be legally bound by the restrictions imposed therein. This license agreement may supersede some standard rights under copyright. It may also grant some extra privileges, such as the ability for the person on whose computer certain software is installed to also install the software on a laptop or home computer. This permission is by no means a right, but a gracious offer on the part of the software company. Read the fine print to determine if you have permission to make any additional installations, and what permissions you may have.

Some license agreements grant the purchaser the right to duplicate a specified number of copies—commonly called a limited site license. The software producer allows a discount on the software price, and in return the purchaser uses his own diskettes and labor to make copies. Site licenses are generally specified on purchase orders, hence are legal and binding contracts between the purchaser and the producer. Because the deal involves a contract, producers may be able to work out the exact type of license you desire, even if those particular terms may not be listed on the producer's price sheet. If the producer suspects the purchaser has violated the license agreement, the legal action is more likely to be based on contract law than on copyright, but damages could still be significant if the purchaser is found guilty.

Legitimate copying vs. piracy

Illegal copying of computer software is called "piracy." For teachers and students who have computers at home that are compatible with the equipment at school, the temptation is strong to bring home a copy of the school's software so that work can be transferred back and forth. The rules on making copies of computer programs allow only two instances in which copies may be made of programs outside the scope of a valid license agreement.

A copy or adaptation may be made if such a copy is an essential part of the operation of the computer program. For example, if the program must be copied to the hard disk of the computer, that copying is acceptable. Since most, if not all, computer programs require the program to copy itself into the computer's memory in order to run, such an "ephemeral" copy is also permitted under this portion of the law. The program erases itself when the program is finished. In addition, modifications such as installing a printer driver or other customizations allowed by the software itself are also within the acceptable limits of adaptation.

A copy or adaptation for archival purposes may be made if the archival copy is not used. This copy can be on disk, diskette, backup CD, or tape. The archival or "backup" copy should be destroyed if the program is sold or transferred. You may use the backup copy of the software and put the original away for safekeeping, or vice versa. Either is acceptable as long as both copies are not used at the same time. This provision is only for "owners" of software, however, not for licensees, so determine which you are before you make your backups.

Don't forget that the Digital Millennium Copyright Act requires that one not remove copyright management information from protected works, including computer software. A license agreement may contain the copyright management information for a specific software package, so be wary about discarding all that fine print.

Software for free?

Two forms of software may be freely copied without any licenses or agreements. The first type is known as "public domain" software. Public domain software is a computer program that has been released by the author to be freely copied by whomever would like to use it. Such software is often found on Internet Web sites dedicated to the public domain, and from computer users' groups and clubs. The title screen of the program or the documentation will indicate the public domain status of the program.

The other form of software that may be freely copied isn't exactly free. Known as "shareware," this software is copyright protected. The author or copyright holder has elected to distribute the software through a try-it-before-you-buy-it method. Shareware software is available through the same channels as public domain software; but once the software has been used and evaluated, the user is expected to register the software and pay a fee for the program—anything from a voluntary donation (sometimes to a charitable organization) up to $100 or so. Some authors give a time frame for this trial period. The software may or may not continue to work at the end of the stated period. Others just say "if you like it, send money." It's the honor system at its most fragile. If users of shareware fail to register and pay for the software that they retain and use, this method of software distribution may disappear.

Lending software

In 1990 Congress responded to the complaints of computer software producers that lending and renting of computer software were eroding the market for their products. The Copyright Software Rental Amendments Act was the result. In essence, the act granted to copyright owners (of computer software only) the right to control rental, lease, or lending of their software. However, the law did provide an exemption for nonprofit libraries provided that a warning of copyright is affixed to each package. The Federal Register specified the exact wording of the notice:

> **Notice: Warning of copyright restrictions**
> **The copyright law of the United States (Title 17, United States Code) governs the reproduction, distribution, adaptation, public performance, and public display of copyrighted material. Under certain conditions specified in law, nonprofit libraries are authorized to lend, lease, or rent copies of computer programs to patrons on a nonprofit basis and for nonprofit purposes. Any person who makes an unauthorized copy or adaptation of the computer program, or redistributes the loan copy, or publicly performs or displays the computer program, except as permitted by Title 17 of the United States Code, may be liable for copyright infringement. This institution reserves the right to refuse to fulfill a loan request if, in its judgment, fulfillment of the request would lead to violation of the copyright law.**

The Register further states that this notice must be "durably attached" to the package that is loaned to patrons. Some library supply houses sell stickers that make this required statement. As a final note, remember that this exemption for lending software is allowed for libraries only. Academic departments, administrators, or computer or technology directors may not make such loans because they do not qualify for this exemption.

Single-user programs

A common act of software piracy in schools is that of purchasing a single-user copy of a program and then installing it on multiple machines. The program may be a grade book, a database manager, a word processor, or an integrated software package. The program may even be as basic as the disk operating system (Windows or OS X) itself! Teachers and administrators rationalize the decision by saying that they aren't making any profit on the deal, and the school certainly can't afford all those single copies. Unfortunately, the end doesn't justify the means. And making more than 10 copies of a program immediately raises the penalty for infringement to up to $250,000 in fines and up to five years in prison on felony charges (Marshall, 1993, p. 441).

If such multiple loads currently reside on programs in a district, often software producers will sell school districts licenses only for software at a greatly reduced price. The license includes no disks or documentation, but it legitimizes copies currently residing on the computers.

Some CD-ROMs require that a portion of the program be installed to the local hard disk in order to speed access to the CD. With such an installation, at the time of use one needs only to slip the CD-ROM into the drive and the program will work. Unfortunately, loading even a portion of the program on multiple computers without specific exemption is technically a violation of the single-use license, and software audits will show each installation of the program "kernel" on the hard drive as an installation requiring a license.

Networking

If the hardware will support it, network options allow multiple computers to share one copy of the software. However, networking software is not covered under fair use. All network and site licenses are contracts negotiated with the sellers—not a right under fair use. The fact that a particular piece of software can operate in a networked environment is immaterial. Networking a piece of computer software always requires a license. And get it in writing!

Some software, particularly CD-ROMs, will permit unlimited networking within a single building. "Building" can be defined as an organizational campus—a group of students who have a separate administrative head. Many schools, such as a high school, will have multiple buildings comprising their physical plant. There may be a central building, a field house, an annex or portable buildings, or a separate gymnasium or auditorium. As long as those buildings comprise the physical plant of that organizational unit, any computer in those buildings could qualify to access the CD-ROM under the network site license.

Some school-owned plots of land house two schools, however. An elementary school and a high school might be on the same plot of land. They might even share network components. But for license purposes, those are probably two separate schools. If the two schools have separate names, and perhaps if they have separate administrators, the software people would be able to make an excellent case for their being two entities. It is best to be up-front with the software producer when purchasing a license in such out-of-the-ordinary circumstances.

The software police

While the dreaded software police don't actually exist, the FBI can, and does, investigate and enforce suspected copyright violations as part of its general responsibilities. Since computer software piracy is now punishable as a felony (Marshall, 1993, p. 441), prosecution is pursued much more seriously. One of the schools in a district where I worked was, in fact, visited by representatives of a software publishing firm. They asked courteously but firmly to see verification that legitimate copies of their software had been purchased. When the original packages and documentation were produced for their inspection, they thanked the librarian politely and left. They declined to say why they had selected this building for an inspection. Other districts have suffered large fines and public humiliation for lax computer software license enforcement (Business Software Alliance, 1999.)

Schools and districts are advised by organizations such as the Business Software Alliance (BSA) and the Software and Information Industry Association (SIIA) to conduct software audits. Essentially this puts someone in the building and district in the position of software policeman. The Software and Information Industry Association even offers a school policy recommendation that outlines steps for maintaining records of legitimate copies of software. The SIIA also recommends several software programs that conduct a software audit by logging installed applications into a printed record. Most work across a network and across operating systems.

In addition to locating pirated software, a software audit makes employees who put personal software on institutional machines subject to further investigation to determine if such use is within the applicable software licenses. With few exceptions, people may not load copies of software installed at home on school machines as well (under the same license). Vigorous application of a copyright compliance policy could subject employees to disciplinary procedures if they are found in violation of the copyright laws during such an audit.

Two school districts in Texas do surprise software audits of one another. Armed with an audit program, officials from one district appear at a selected school of the other district, acting in the manner of federal marshals. They run the audit program on all computers. The program produces a printout of all the installed programs. The owner must then produce authentication that each program is legitimate. An official of one of the districts recounted that one individual had many questionable programs on the computer's hard disk. When this employee had not accounted for programs on the computer a month later, an official letter of reprimand went into the person's file. This reciprocal checking is helping to keep both districts in compliance and out of court.

Checking is a good thing. The SIIA offers sizable monetary rewards (up to $50,000) for those who report software and content pirates, including corporate infringers. Some software producers attempt to enforce their own contract terms by selling software that can count the number of users in a network environment. For example, if the school has paid for a four-user license, the software will allow only that number of concurrent users and no more. Other makers disable or limit features of the software, such as being able to copy information to floppy disk, so that wholesale portions of the copyrighted database cannot be incorporated into someone else's work. These features or limitations should be spelled out in the license agreement and software documentation before the purchase is concluded so that both the producer and the purchaser understand the requirements and limits of the program and its data.

The Digital Millennium Copyright Act put some teeth into the law about circumventing technical protections. In other words, if software has a password or copy protection scheme, it is now a violation to circumvent or bypass these protections. There are some complicated exceptions for libraries, but mostly these exceptions are in place so that libraries can inspect items prior to purchasing them. In most instances, evaluation copies are available to make sound purchase decisions, so this is less of a bonus than it might appear.

Negotiated online database licenses are just as binding as computer software licenses. The databases that are so attractive may not be legally shared with other schools or to students at home if the license states "no remote access." This contract supersedes the Section 108 rights of libraries to provide information to anyone who requests it. In essence, by accepting the software license, the purchaser waives other rights under copyright, just as with regular computer software.

Copyright infringement vs. plagiarism

A question arises concerning students who download or capture information from a database, CD-ROM, or other electronic sources. As in most student situations, students may use all sorts of information for personal research. The fact that the student has used electronic means to put the information into the product rather than hand-typing is irrelevant. The problem here is not copyright infringement, but plagiarism. The student may be operating within fair use to use the copyright protected materials, but his failure to cite the sources is plagiarism. For someone attempting to prove plagiarism, having information in electronic format is actually a blessing. In pre-electronic days, the teacher had to scan printed works hoping to stumble upon the exact suspected text. Now the teacher need only do a simple text search of the source to find all instances of the wording in question.

A specific instance of plagiarism is likely a copyright violation, because in the absence of attribution, the student isn't likely to be covered by the fair use exemption. In dealing with ethical issues such as copyright law compliance and plagiarism, it is important for teachers and librarians to emphasize high expectations. Adherence to copyright law and rules against plagiarism should be fully detailed in student codes of conduct, with specific penalties for violations.

Software management tips

Maintain copyright and license records on all programs in the building. If a site license or network copy was ordered, retain a copy of the purchase order as proof of the contract.

Make one archival copy of each program and store it off-site. Do not use or circulate the archival copy. One archival copy of software documentation is allowed. More than one requires permission.

Don't install non-network software on a network. Installing software on a network requires a network license.

Don't lend equipment that would facilitate copying software. Don't own programs whose sole purpose is to "crack" software protection schemes.

Refuse to lend software to library patrons who indicate they plan to make infringing copies. At minimum, inform them that the software is protected by copyright and their use of the software is governed by the notice affixed to the package.

Place appropriate copyright warning stickers on all software circulated from the library. Register shareware.

Enforce multi-user limitations. Install software metering programs or use network operating system security options to monitor licenses.

Monitor use of computer scanners and digitizers. Encourage use of public domain and royalty-free graphics.

Resources for understanding

The Software and Information Industry Association offers an anti-piracy hotline at 1-800-388-7478. Find them online at http://siia.com. The Business Software Alliance also has an anti-piracy hotline at 1-888-NOPIRACY. Their web address is http://www.bsa.org

Works cited

Berman, D. (13 May 1993). *Re: Questionable videotapes: Discussion on liability in the use of copyrighted videotapes.* Message posted to CNI-COPYRIGHT electronic mailing list.

Business Software Alliance. (24 February 1999). *Five Southern California Organizations Settle Software Copyright Claims.* Retrieved January 5, 2004 from http://www.bsa.org/usa/press/newsreleases/Five-Southern-California-Organizations-Settle-Software-Copyright-Claims.cfm.

Marshall, P.G. (21 May 1993). Software piracy. *CQ Researcher.* Retrieved on April 30, 2005.

Chapter 11

School Library Exemptions

Just as schools have special exemptions for their nonprofit educational mission, libraries were given special protections to enable them to carry out their missions, as well. While the rules were identified primarily for public libraries, the rules identified for libraries also apply to the various activities that go on within the school library.

Library exemptions

School libraries have the best of all possible worlds when it comes to copyright exemptions because they get both the school and the library exemptions. The down side of this bonus is that libraries must keep track of twice as many sets of regulations. Section 108 provides an assortment of special exceptions for libraries including copying for interlibrary loan, copying at the request of patrons for their personal use, and copying for preservation. Aside from the regulations discussed below, to qualify for the library exemptions the library must be open to the public (or to researchers in a field). Most school libraries would meet this requirement based on the definition of "public" discussed earlier. A second requirement of the library exemptions is that all copies made must be made "without any purpose of direct or indirect commercial advantage." All copies made must contain a notice of copyright; and copying must be of single copies on "isolated and unrelated" occasions. A key phrase in the law states that "systematic reproduction or distribution of single or multiple copies" is always prohibited.

Put a dozen librarians in a room and you will come up with two dozen plans to economize while providing exemplary library service. (All good librarians have a backup plan!) Providing outstanding service can be problematic if the library doesn't have all, or enough, of the items the patrons seek. Many creative ideas have been proposed to provide extra copies of materials, secure materials that libraries don't own, and get materials quickly to patrons who need information immediately. But as with all innovative solutions, new outcomes will be measured against traditional laws. Lawmakers are notoriously slow to adapt current laws to new technologies, and until they do so, one must use the old laws and attempt to extrapolate the legal requirements.

There are other exceptions for libraries. For example, if a library owns a copy of a book, and a page is damaged beyond use, it is within the library uses granted under Section 108 of the copyright law to photocopy and tip in the missing page from another copy. In fact, it is within the rights granted libraries to copy an entire book when the original is lost, damaged, or deteriorated beyond use if an unused replacement cannot be purchased at a reasonable price.

Preservation

The Digital Millennium Copyright Act added some positive permissions for libraries dealing with deteriorating, damaged or obsolete materials. If a work has been damaged or defaced, and an "unused replacement" cannot be purchased at a reasonable cost, the library may make the copies necessary to repair or replace the item. Laura Gasaway, in a presentation to the Texas Library Association in April 2000, explained that if you own a set of encyclopedias, and someone steals or destroys a single volume, and if the publisher will not sell you a single replacement volume, you may assume that an unused replacement is not available at a reasonable price. In such an instance, she recommends making the copies necessary to repair or replace the item.

The subsection on preservation (c) permits copies of any material if a) that material cannot be replaced at a reasonable cost, or b) if the format in which the material is stored is obsolete. The law defines obsolete to be "if the machine or device necessary to render perceptible a work stored in that format is no longer manufactured or is no longer reasonably available in the commercial marketplace." Preservation copies can even be digital copies if the copies are not made available to the public outside the library holding the original item. This section would permit a library, for example, to copy Beta-format videotapes into VHS or DVD format because the necessary equipment is no longer available on the general market. However, if that item is available on the market in a modern format, you must purchase rather than convert. Phonograph records are not as fortunate as Beta-format videos because turntables are still readily available.

When copying unpublished materials (diaries, family photographs, historical documents, etc.) the copying must a) be for preservation, security, or deposit at a different library (a good insurance against fire or other disaster); and b) be of an original owned by the copying library. The key to the permission is that a digital copy cannot be accessed from beyond the library walls. The library may make the digital copy available only on the local network (within the library, not the entire school) or on disc, and certainly not via the Internet. This rule was designed to help academic libraries and archives preserve and make available for researchers works that are too fragile to be handled. This rule will seldom come into play in school libraries.

Interlibrary loan

Common sense tells us that by pooling resources, several libraries can share expensive or seldom-used materials. Interlibrary loan has served that function for many years. As library budgets get tighter, librarians look for creative ways to make the budget dollars stretch a little further. One oft-suggested idea is to spread periodical subscriptions around, each cooperating library taking a portion of the lesser-used, but still important, titles. When a patron needs something from one of the titles subscribed to by one of the sharing partners, a simple interlibrary loan request will rush the information to the patron. With a fax machine, access to remote documents is almost instantaneous. Sound too good to be true? It is.

At this point in our plan we run afoul of the copyright law. One of the principal tenets of the law is that copying should not affect the market for or value of the copyrighted work. Does securing a needed article or book from a remote site deprive the copyright holder of a sale? Would the patron or the library have bought the title just to have access to that particular article? Does rapid document delivery affect sales of periodical titles? Good questions, and ones that the congressional committee considered when they discussed fair use in the areas of photocopying and resource sharing.

Items available for interlibrary loan would include books, periodicals, and any other work that the library chooses to release from its premises. Copying for interlibrary loan, however, picks up an extensive list of restrictions. Thanks to the Digital Millennium Copyright Act, libraries may not copy a musical work; a picture, sculpture, or graphic (unless those items are included as illustrations in a textual item); or a movie or audiovisual work. Text may be copied for interlibrary loan (subject to the CONTU guidelines, below) as may sound recordings. Audiovisual works dealing with news may also be copied for interlibrary loan.

> **Q:** Are there any copyright restrictions on lending an entire bound periodical volume to another school?
>
> **A:** If you are talking about physically sending the magazine to another school, there are no restrictions on that form of inter-library loan (ILL) The ILL guidelines are for ILL copying.

The copying requirements for interlibrary loan are essentially the same as the library copying requirements listed above. Because the 1976 law allowed libraries to participate in interlibrary loan (ILL) arrangements as long as "aggregate quantities" of articles or items received did not substitute for a periodical subscription or other purchase, a group known as the National Commission on New Technological Uses of Copyrighted Works (a.k.a. CONTU) developed a set of guidelines that were adopted as fair and reasonable. Known universally as the CONTU Guidelines, these rules establish operational procedures that should be followed in interlibrary loan copying to assure compliance with the copyright law. The rules are not intended to apply to every situation, but Congress itself declared that they would "provide guidance in the most commonly encountered interlibrary photocopying situations" (Copyright Office, Circular R21, 1998, p. 18-19). Keep in mind that the CONTU guidelines govern *inter*library loan of periodicals and other works. *Intra*library loan is an entirely different animal. The difference? Primarily funding. The guidelines point to "common funding" as the key element in determining if libraries are part of the same system (Ensign, 1992, p. 126). For example, all the schools in a school district would be considered part of a common system and therefore loans among them would be intralibrary loans. Loans between school districts would be *inter*library loans.

In dealing with intralibrary loan, sending a photocopy of an article is handled exactly the same as if the copy were being made in the patron's library by library personnel. Section 108 of the copyright law allows not-for-profit libraries to make single copies of material for patrons as long as there is no commercial advantage, the library is open to the public, and each reproduction includes a notice of copyright.

Caveat: The law, however, has a very specific prohibition against "systematic" copying. One of the illustrations given in the guidelines as an example of systematic copying is this: "Several branches of a library system agree that one branch will subscribe to particular journals in lieu of each branch purchasing its own subscriptions, and the one subscribing branch will reproduce copies of articles from the publication for users of other branches." This budget-stretching plan to share periodical subscriptions or reference books among campuses within or without a school district (or perhaps between the schools and the public library) is not in compliance with the copyright law in any case.

Q: *How many articles from each issue of a periodical can a library copy for interlibrary loan?*

A: *The providing library may make any copies requested by other organizations since it is the requesting library's responsibility to maintain copyright compliance according to the CONTU guidelines.*

Following the CONTU Guidelines gives a librarian a set of conservative, baseline rules on acceptable copying for inter- or intralibrary loan copies. These guidelines are mandatory for interlibrary loans. Since maintaining two sets of ILL rules would boggle even the clearest mind, applying those rules to intralibrary loan gives a safe level of ILL practice and consistent operational procedures. The guidelines are very specific and, once implemented, relatively easy to follow. They apply to interlibrary loan *copying*, not interlibrary loans in which the original material is mailed or delivered to the requesting library.

The BORROWING LIBRARY must post a "display warning of copyright" at the place interlibrary loan orders are accepted. The size and wording of this notice are specified by law. Copies are sold by library supply houses. See Appendix E for exact requirements.

Only one copy of the requested material may be sent, and the copy must become the property of the requesting patron. This will have impact when using fax delivery. It is also significant for libraries that would like to retain the copy for the vertical file.

The BORROWING LIBRARY must abide by the "Rule of Five." (Explanation of this rule follows.)

The BORROWING LIBRARY must keep records of CONTU-governed loan requests. The records must be kept for the current year and the three previous calendar years, i.e., on Jan. 1, 2004, the records for 2000 may be discarded. A database, loose-leaf notebook, or card-based record-keeping system can track requests. See examples of forms later in this chapter.

The BORROWING LIBRARY must verify copyright compliance on the ILL request. Most stock ILL forms have a section for copyright compliance, indicating CCL ("complies with Copyright Law," i.e., fair use) or CCG (complies with CONTU Guidelines, i.e., Rule of Five).

The LENDING LIBRARY must mark on each copy that the "request was made in conformity with these guidelines." In general, that means the copy should be stamped with the standard Notice: This material may be protected by Copyright Law (Title 17 U.S. Code).

Rule of five

The Rule of five was designed to guide librarians in tracking appropriate levels of interlibrary loan copying. The rules seem complex at first, but once you grasp the five year window, calculating the limits is very simple.

Periodicals

The CONTU Guidelines pertain to periodical titles (as opposed to individual issues) published within five years from the date of the request. Copying older materials may be considered to be fair use on the part of the requesting library. The borrowing library may receive five photocopied articles per periodical title (not per issue) covered under the CONTU Guidelines per calendar year. On the standard ILL form, these first five copies may be marked as CCG since they are permitted under the CONTU Guidelines. To give a specific example, in a single year, a library that does not subscribe to *Library Media Connection* could, within these guidelines, request five single articles published within the past five years. Some exemptions apply to the numerical requirement:

> • *A title "on order." If you have entered an order for a periodical title, you may request unlimited copies from the title under CONTU. The Rule of Five does not apply.*

- *A title at the bindery. If you own the title and you have sent the issues to the bindery, you may request unlimited copies from those issues under CONTU.*

- *Missing issues in an owned volume. If you already own a volume of a periodical, and need to request an interlibrary photocopy to supplement a missing issue, you may make the request under CONTU. Those requests will not count in your five.*

- *Such exceptions need not be logged under CONTU, and CCG compliance may be claimed on the ILL form. Issues older than five years are not governed by CONTU, so CCL is the correct choice on the ILL form.*

Other print materials

This rule applies to materials in books, mostly. Only five copies may be requested from any single work (including collective works) per year, during the entire time a work falls under copyright protection. To illustrate this requirement, imagine there is a book of poetry called *School Days*. Suppose that the school library has an index that lists all the poems in this book and many others. The library doesn't own *School Days*, but teachers use the index to find poems to use with their classes. The public library owns a copy of the *School Days* book and they will supply the school library with photocopies of material from the volume. Four teachers so far this calendar year have requested copies of poems from this work. The school librarian may request one more copy of a poem from this work in this calendar year under the Rule of Five. After that request, the school must pay royalties on copies or purchase its own copy of the book. If the librarian places an order for the book, and the copy is not yet received, he or she may request other copies of poems from the book under fair use since the book has been purchased, but not received. This requirement holds true even if the book is out of print. Out-of-print status is not the same as being out of copyright.

Keeping ILL forms on file is the best method of keeping interlibrary loan records. While one must keep the loan records for non-periodical requests for only a calendar year, keeping a history of requests can be helpful for collection development purposes.

Examples and explanations

A library may not retain photocopies of articles ordered for patrons through interlibrary loan. Photocopies for patrons are legal only when made for specific, individual users. Including such copies in the vertical file or a ready reference file would not be within the guidelines for such copying. Similarly, a librarian may not request copies of articles for library purposes, no matter how relevant the article might be to the library's patrons. Such ordering would deprive the publisher of a sale of an issue or a reprint and hence does not fall within the fair use exemption (Dukelow, 1992, p.36).

Note: For all these transactions, assume today's date to be June 2, 2005.

Patron requests an article from periodical XYZ, issue dated December 5, seven years ago. This is the first request for an article from this periodical this year. This request is considered fair use and need not be logged under CONTU because the periodical issue requested is over five years old.

Q: For interlibrary loan, can a library request five articles from each issue of a given periodical?

A: The Rule of Five states that during the current calendar year you may request up to five copies of articles from the last four calendar years of a periodical title. It makes no difference from whom you request the articles.

Q: I need to make copies of an entire book because I can't find it— the book is out of print. Is this fair use?

A: Out of print is not the same as out of copyright. Check out of print dealers such as Bibliofind.com, Bookrescue.com, and BookCloseOuts.com.

Patron requests an article from periodical ABC, issue dated December 5 three years ago. This is the third request for this periodical this year. This request would be filled under CONTU guidelines and should be logged as request number three on this periodical title.

Patron requests six poems be copied from a single collective work. No other items have been requested from this collection this year. Only five of the poems may be requested via ILL from this particular title. Perhaps one of the poems could be found in another collection, or the Copyright Clearance Center could be contacted for the cost to reproduce the item. Copies of the ILL request forms for the five permitted reproductions should be retained by the requesting library for one year to track requests per title.

Patron requests an article from the January 4, 2005, issue of journal PQR because the copy is missing from the library's shelves. This request may be filled under CONTU since the requesting library subscribes to the journal. The request does not fall under the Rule of Five, however, because the library owns this title.

Patron requests an article from the September 15, 2001, issue of journal NOP. The library has already requested five articles from this journal from a single library this calendar year. Perhaps another library would be a source for five more copies? The requesting library is permitted five requests per calendar year from a single journal title. The library that supplies the requests is not considered in counting the five. All five requests may come from one library, or all five may come from different libraries. The total of five remains the same. This request would fall outside the Rule of Five, and royalties would have to be paid on the sixth request.

Keep in mind that the burden of assuring compliance with the CONTU Guidelines falls to the requesting library (Jackson, 1991, p. 87). It is the requesting library that must determine the fair use (CCL) or CONTU Guidelines (CCG) applicability and also maintain the necessary records. If a request should come into a library, that library may fulfill the request without question since the requesting library will have taken care of the copyright compliance.

In summary, while the CONTU Guidelines may have initially been intended to deal with interlibrary loan, they do provide a conservative set of guidelines for intralibrary loans. And while some stretching of the CONTU limits might be overlooked, beware of anything that might smack of "systematic copying." For more information on copying for interlibrary loan, see this Web site: **http://www.utsystem.edu/OGC/IntellectualProperty/l-108g.htm**.

Photocopying

If a library makes copies of magazine articles or other parts of larger works for patrons to use in personal research, the library must attend to several points of operation. The copies must become the property of the user. Libraries may not make a copy for a user then retain the copy once the user is finished. The library must not know that a copy will be used for other than personal research. The library must display the "display warning of copyright" at the point where the requests for copies are made. If the patron requests a complete work, the library may make the copies if a) the library can determine that a copy for purchase is not available at a fair price; b) the user will keep the complete copy to be made; c) the library has no information that the copy will be used for anything beyond personal research; and d) the library has an appropriate "display warning of copyright" where copying orders are placed. In addition, the works copied cannot be pictures or graphics unless those are illustrations or diagrams in other works.

When the library staff becomes involved in actually making copies of copyright protected materials for patrons, additional requirements arise. Since notice of copyright can be an important factor in determining responsibility for willful infringement, the Digital Millennium Copyright Act included strict new regulations regarding removal of what the Act calls "copyright management information." Such information can include the actual copyright notice affixed, but also might include the names of the author and copyright holder, performers, writers, title, etc. Removal of copyright information will be especially important in cases of library photocopying. Under previous iterations of the law, a simple notice of possible copyright was sufficient to protect a library from complicity in copy infringements. Most libraries used a basic ALA-approved stamp stating "NOTICE: This material may be protected by Copyright Law (Title 17 U.S. Code)." Under DMCA, this warning would no longer be sufficient. If a work's copyright notice can be found, the entire notice must be included (either photocopied or hand written) with the copies. If you can find no copyright notice on the work, the former stamp would be sufficient.

Unattended copiers

Librarians want to share information with everyone. They have made photocopiers available for patrons so they may make copies of whatever information they desire. Copyright law even says that a person may make a single copy of certain information for one's personal research and education. But what if the photocopier is located in the library, and the patron exceeds the limits of the law? Does that make the library responsible for any infringements committed there? Libraries (though not other copiers in the school) have certain protections against being sued for copyright infringement when infringing copies are made on unsupervised copiers in the library. "Unsupervised" could be construed to mean those coin-operated or free copiers available for public use in the library. The library staff has no responsibility for the making of copies on these machines other than perhaps stocking the machine with paper and occasionally unjamming the works.

The key to the answer lies in the location of the copier. The law specifies that libraries are not held accountable for copyright infringements on "unsupervised" copiers. What is considered to be "supervised?" "Supervised" isn't defined, but there are some common sense guidelines one can follow. If the library staff makes the copies, certainly that would mean they are supervising the making of copies and the library would be liable for any infringements made there. A copier beside the circulation desk or reference desk could also be considered "supervised" in some instances. A self-service copier across the room from the staff, however, would be independent, even if the library staff maintain the paper and toner in the machine.

Library staff are not held liable for copies made on "unsupervised" copiers if there is an appropriate notice on the copier informing the patron that some materials may be protected by U.S. copyright law. This notice is most often placed on the lid of the copier, where the patron is sure to see it as the original is placed on the machine for copying. Many library supply houses have signs or adhesive notices just for the purpose of informing patrons of their responsibilities under the law. The statute does not specify wording in this instance, but the American Library Association suggests the following:

> **Notice: The copyright law of the United States (Title 17 U.S. Code) governs the making of photocopies or other reproductions of copyrighted material. The person using this equipment is liable for any infringement.**

Q: I am putting up a Web page and want to post images of Cezanne and Van Gogh's paintings. If I take a photograph of a painting, can I use this?

A: If you can get the museum to allow you to take a photo of the original (which is long out of copyright), you can post it. If you scan a professional photo of an old master painting (published before 1923), you have not violated the copyright of the photographer or the museum, because the work is now in the public domain.

This notice should be affixed to all equipment capable of making infringing copies: photocopiers, overhead projectors, opaque projectors, computers, videocassette recorders, scanners, audio cassette recorders, fax machines, and any other equipment that can be used to copy video, sound, or print. Placing such a notice in a prominent position on copy-producing equipment can lessen (though never eliminate) the library's and the librarian's exposure to copyright suit if the library's equipment is used by patrons to make infringing copies. Keep in mind that this exemption in the law applies only to libraries. School-owned copiers in the office, workroom, or department do not have this exemption, so school staff must be especially vigilant about unauthorized copies on all machines.

Copying orders

If the library copier is unsupervised, i.e., users make their own copies on a coin- or card- or even honor-system-operated machine without intervention or supervision by the library staff, a library is not liable for copyright violations. If the school staff makes the copies, or the library staff is consulted in the making of copies, the copier is considered to be supervised and the school will likely be held accountable for the illegal copies. The term "supervised" would also include any copies made by library staff for patrons or school staff, regardless of the location of the copier. Copies made by library staff must include the ENTIRE original statement of copyright as printed on the item being reproduced. This may be manually transcribed, or it may be a photocopy of the copyright statement on the item. If the item being copied has no statement of copyright, one cannot easily determine if the item is or is not protected by copyright. In such an instance the copies should be stamped with a notice indicating that the material copied may be covered by copyright, and that appropriate use of copyrighted material is the responsibility of the patron. While no specific wording is specified by law, many libraries use wording like this:

Notice: This material may be protected by copyright law (Title 17 U.S. Code).

stamped on copies in a conspicuous color. It is especially important to be diligent about including the copyright statement on school- or library-made copies if one wishes to protect the building and the personnel against infringement actions. The removal or omission of the copyright statement violates the DMCA.

Copies for vertical file or item repair

Vertical files may be a foreign term to many librarians. Vertical files are also called pamphlet files or clipping files. In a vertical file the librarian stores small, easily lost materials that are valuable for student papers and reports. Typical items include brochures from foundations that support research on genetic diseases, government pamphlets, or short "how it works" sheets on specific technologies. Each topic has a file folder, and in that topical folder the library staff collects articles and pamphlets related to that topic. The term "vertical" applies to the way file folders are stored.

Often a librarian will find an article in a magazine or newspaper that would be appropriate for inclusion in the vertical file. Perhaps the magazine title is bound, and the librarian would like to avoid mutilating the bound copy to include the article in the vertical file. Or the article is on the online encyclopedia, and by having a few copies in the vertical file each student doesn't have to print out a copy of the same article to free the computer for the next searcher. Such use is not within the scope of the library-permissible

Q: Can a library include in its vertical file magazine articles or pictures cut out of magazines?

A: As long as the items are CUT from the magazines, there is no problem. What is illegal is making copies and putting them in the vertical file.

sections of the copyright law. However, if the library owns an item that is deteriorating or mutilated, lost or stolen, and a replacement cannot be obtained "at a fair price," the librarian may make a replacement copy of the damaged work. The librarian may also make replacement pages for pages defaced or destroyed in materials the library already owns, but these copies are to replace the damaged sections of the magazines, not for the vertical file.

Facsimile

The most common technology used with ILL is telefacsimile, commonly known as the fax. While it may simplify and speed up the ILL process, fax creates an unforeseen copyright complication. Since most periodicals aren't loose-leaf, the sending library usually must photocopy the required pages before transmitting them via fax. This creates complications. The relevant section of the copyright law provides for interlibrary loan under the premise that one copy be made of the requested information and that the single copy become the property of the patron requesting it. In a fax situation, the sending library creates a photocopy, then faxes it to the requesting library. At that instant, two copies of the information now exist—the original photocopy and the fax copy.

While in a literal sense there has been a technical violation of copyright, if the sending library destroys the photocopy when the transmission is complete and confirmed, the cumulative effect is the same as one copy. Libraries intending to use fax as a means for sending or receiving ILL transactions should be aware of the possible violation of copyright and have written policies and procedures to address the problem (Ensign, 1992, p. 126). One certain violation is the plan to keep the original photocopy in a ready-reference collection or vertical file. The first copy of the faxed ILL document MUST be destroyed to comply with the CONTU guidelines.

Reserves

Any library materials, or those of faculty members, may be put on reserve at any time. Such use has no impact on copyright at all. Making copies for reserve, however, enters into an entirely different arena. While there is no specific discussion of this procedure in the law, the American Library Association has written a model policy targeted to college and university libraries that takes into account various portions of the law that might impact copying for reserve. And while the policy is targeted to college and university libraries, the extension of these rational guidelines to school libraries is not unreasonable.

The document *Model Policy Concerning College and University Photocopying for Classroom Research and Library Reserve Use* permits single copies of a book chapter, an entire periodical article, or a single poem. For multiple copies to fall within the policy, they must be:

- *Of a reasonable amount considering the nature of the course, its subject matter and level, and the amount of material usually assigned for a single class term;*
- *The number of copies should be "less than six," unless enrollment in that course and others which will use the same material would dictate that six is insufficient to meet anticipated demand;*
- *Each copy must contain notice of copyright; and*
- *The effect of the copying should not diminish the market for the original. The policy strongly recommends that the library own a copy of the original (ALA, 1982, p.6).*

Figure 11.1 — Sample CONTU card system

Periodical Title					
Year	Issue	Requested	Received	CCL	CCG

Copies for interlibrary loan

The CONTU guidelines deal with interlibrary loan of copies of periodical articles and portions of books, and the rules they spell out are very specific. Keep in mind when dealing with these rules that all periodical transactions may not be governed by CONTU.

A simple 3x5 card system such as pictured in Figure 11.1 would provide all the documentation needed for CONTU compliance. A computer database could also maintain the same type of records. Remember that the library maintains this type of record only on their requests, not on those ILL orders they fill. Whatever record-keeping method you choose, you need to keep records of periodical requests for only four years—the current year plus the three previous years. Records of requests for materials in books should be kept for four years also, but you need consider only the current year in determining if a particular request exceeds the Rule of Five.

What to do when you can't meet CONTU requirements

If you have more requests for articles from a certain periodical title than you can legally request under the CONTU Guidelines, what do you do? You have several options:

- *You can purchase a subscription to the periodical. Because the law and the guidelines aren't specific about how far back the subscription must go, purchasing a subscription to the current volume has been used as justification for CCG requests for back issues. This is a gray area you will have to wrestle with, assisted by legal counsel.*

- *You can borrow issues from other libraries. Sometimes you have demand only during a particular part of the school year. A public library might lend you its bound volume for a short time. Your patrons can then make their own copies without CONTU implications.*

- *Advise your patrons of other libraries in the area that either subscribe to the periodical or would make an ILL request.*

- *Request a copyright-cleared copy of the material from a document delivery service. These organizations pay royalties on each copy supplied. However, remember that a copy purchased from one of these sources is not cleared for multiple copies, except as under fair use. (Copyright Clearance Center does clear course pack requests.)*

- *Write to the copyright holder for permission. (See section on permissions for sample forms.)*

- *Join the Copyright Clearance Center. This organization acts as a clearinghouse for copyright permissions and, while it doesn't supply the articles themselves, it does collect fees for copies and distributes them to copyright holders. (See chapter on permissions for more information.)*

- *Purchase back issues from the publisher, if available. Sometimes brokers of back issues can also supply individual issues (Jackson, 1991, p. 87).*

In summary, interlibrary loan may not be the panacea to shrinking library budgets. The CONTU guidelines place strict limits on the number of articles a library may request from a periodical title during a calendar year. Articles more than five years old are exempt from the guidelines, but for those covered, a library may request only five articles from a given title during a calendar year. The requesting library must also follow strict record-keeping requirements.

These guidelines help publishers know that they can sell adequate copies of their periodicals to stay profitable. They also assure libraries that their patrons will be able to access infrequently requested periodical titles. CONTU also governs photocopies from books in a similar manner (complies with CONTU Guidelines).

While ILL copying between library systems is always governed by CONTU, lending within a system is not. However, the law specifies that "systematic copying" is not acceptable in any circumstance, especially when such copying would take the place of the purchase of materials. The CONTU wording was intended to spell out exactly what "systematic copying" was, so the CONTU guidelines may be considered reasonable limits on ILL requests between schools in the same district.

Electronic reserves

Some libraries are trying a new system of putting materials on reserve. Rather than making photocopies of materials, or putting the originals in an area behind the circulation desk, these libraries are scanning the materials and making them available to patrons via a computer network. Making copies electronically is similar to making photocopies as far as reserves are concerned, as long as you can meet the four tests of fair use. But electronic reserves touch more than just the copying provisions of the law. Each time a user pulls up the image on his screen, a display of the image takes place. If the work has video or audio accompaniment, there is a performance. Sending the image over the computer network is a transmission. There is no case law to guide us here.

The CONTU working group assigned to develop electronic reserves guidelines could not muster widespread support for the guidelines it drafted. However, reliance on the guidelines may be an affirmative defense of good faith if challenged. The guidelines cover only copyrighted materials, and do not include materials for which libraries have other license agreements in place, such as full-text periodical databases. The guidelines state that an article, or book chapter, may be scanned into an electronic retrieval system for the purpose of electronic reserve, subject to some conditions. (Office of General Counsel, 2001)

- *The course instructor must request the material be placed on reserve.*

- *The school must own a lawful copy of the work.*

- *The amount of material assigned under reserve must be a relatively small part of the total assigned reading for the course.*

- *The reserve system must include on the opening screen a notice similar to that placed on copy machines, adding that further electronic distribution is prohibited.*

- *Each copy in the electronic reserve system must bear a notice of copyright in a prominent place, indicating "Copyright [date], [copyright owner]."*

- *Each copy must have appropriate attribution or citation of source.*

- *Only teachers and students enrolled in the course for which the materials are on reserve may have access to the reserve material. (The guidelines offer several suggestions to limit access.)*

- *Students may not be charged for access.*

- *After one term on reserve, permission is required for repeat use. Items may be retained in electronic form for up to three years while permission is sought. Students clearing incompletes may continue to have brief electronic access during this time.*

Works cited

American Library Association. (1982). *Model policy concerning college and university photocopying for classroom research and library reserve use.* Chicago: ALA.

American Library Association. (2004). *Fair use and electronic reserves.* Chicago: ALA. Retrieved January 4, 2005 from http://www.ala.org/ala/washoff/WOissues/copyrightb/fairuseandelectronicreserves/ereservesFU.htm.

Copyright Office. (1998). *Circular R21: Reproduction of copyrighted works by educators and librarians.* Washington, D.C.: Library of Congress.

Dukelow, R. H. (1992). *The library copyright guide.* Washington, D.C.: Copyright Information Services, Association for Educational Communications & Technology.

Ensign, D.J. (1992, Winter). Fax—a special case: implications of copyright law for facsimile document delivery. *The Bookmark,* 50, 125-8.

Jackson, M.E. (1991). Library to library: copyright and ILL. *Wilson Library Bulletin.* 66(2), 84-7.

Office of General Counsel, University of Texas System. (2001, November 12). *Fair use guidelines for electronic reserve systems.* Retrieved January 4, 2005 from http://www.utsystem.edu/OGC/IntellectualProperty/rsrvguid.htm.

Office of General Counsel, University of Texas System. (2003, January 30). *Copyright in the library: reserve electronic copies.* Retrieved January 3, 2005 from http://www.utsystem.edu/OGC/IntellectualProperty/l-resele.htm.

Chapter 12

Permissions

As previous chapters have shown, not all use of copyright protected materials in schools may occur without permission or royalty payment. Once an assessment has shown that fair use does not apply, the least expensive option is to get permission for the proposed use from the copyright holder or his agent. Failing permission, the only legal option is to pay for a license or royalty through a broker or directly to the copyright owner.

Copyright vs. contract

The central theme of this book is "if uncertain, ask permission." That sounds simple enough. The difficulty comes first in deciding when to ask permission, and second in knowing how to ask permission.

As discussed in the chapter on fair use, for some applications written permission is not necessary. Fair use guidelines are explicit regarding the instances for which educators need not seek permission. Some of the highly specific fair use guidelines are, effectively, permission in advance as long as certain requirements are met. For print works, the long rules detailed in the chapter on printed materials determine if copies can be considered fair use. For audiovisuals, if the use meets all of the five fair use criteria, permission is granted automatically:

- *The performance occurs in a nonprofit educational institution; and*
- *The performance is used for face-to-face teaching; and*
- *The performance is presented by instructors or pupils; and*
- *The performance takes place in a classroom or similar place for instruction (including the library); and*
- *The performance is of a legally acquired (or legally copied) copy of the work.*

More detailed descriptions of the fair use guidelines are given in the chapters covering various types of materials.

Some materials are covered by copyright but, for a particular reason, the copyright holder has decided to withhold rights for the work. In such an instance, the copyright holder will license the work rather than sell it. This practice is quite common in the computer software area, where publishers wish licensees to have very specific, restricted rights.

Copyright law allows a copyright holder to modify the blanket copyright provisions via contract. In essence, that means that you may sign your fair use rights away and not even know it if you send in a product registration card or license agreement or even fill out an order blank without reading the fine print. It is possible to modify the license or contract by simply marking out and initialing the portions of the license agreement or order form conditions that you wish to change, when you send it in. The copyright owner may, or may not, agree to your modifications. If the owner refuses to accept your modifications, you may either reconsider your position or elect to purchase other materials that you may license or purchase with the rights you require.

Several years ago some innovative software publishers and computer manufacturers tried to sneak this little-noticed feature past the buying public via so-called "shrink-wrap" licenses. *ProCD, Inc. v. Zeidenberg*, 86 F.3d 1447 (7th Cir. 1996); The main thrust of the shrink-wrap license was to bind the purchaser to a lengthy and technical set of license restrictions in a negative fashion. The purchaser was to read the provisions of the contract in super-fine print through the shrink wrap on the package, for once the shrink wrap was broken, the purchaser would be bound by the contract provisions. Some of the restrictions could be extreme; they included a prohibition against disposing of the software and, in the case of libraries, a prohibition against lending the software. Many licenses conveyed usage rights only; the software itself remained the property of the copyright holder.

Consumers were outraged. Several consumer protection agencies tackled the problem, even taking the shrink-wrap contract to several court challenges. Results varied from state to state. Some upheld the copyright owner's right to limit the sale of rights with the software; others ruled the contract null and void. Check with experts in your own state to see what rights bind you in software shrink-wrap contracts.

While shrink-wrap licenses and publishers' restrictive statements may seem discouraging, the good news is that the "home use only" stickers often found on videos are not binding on schools in any way, unless a statement agreeing to such use is part of the purchase contract. This unfortunate bit of wording only serves to explain that this particular copy of the video does not come with public performance rights. Public performance rights are not required for qualifying curricular performances, so home use only tapes may be used in instructional situations. Home use only videos may not be used for reward, entertainment, or time-filling situations without permission or royalty payment. Rental videos may be restricted to home use only if the membership agreement you signed when you got the video membership specified that there were to be no public performances of the films rented from the video store. In such a case a permission is required—not from the copyright holder, since performance in a school is permissible under fair use—but from the video store! This is a contract problem, not a copyright issue. Few video stores make customers sign rental agreements any more, so this issue is mostly moot.

Some nonprofit commercial activities. Schools, while being nonprofit organizations, often partake in a bit of fund raising. Video and audio are a favorite form of money-making. Booster clubs often sell recordings (audio or video) of athletic or band performances; drama clubs may offer a video of the class play; the journalism class may put together a video yearbook; PTA may offer parents videos of their children in the spring field day. Any or all of these may have a bit of music to accompany the action. Unfortunately, there are some copyright liabilities that need to accompany the process as well. Carol Ruth Shepherd remarked on the Internet mailing list CNI-COPYRIGHT that in order to sell videos, organizations must get permission from the persons in the performance, get performance and distribution rights for any musical or dramatic works included, and get sync rights for any music used to accompany the program (Shepherd, 1996).

Permissions

After checking all the angles, you've discovered that your anticipated use of some material will not be considered fair use. You know you will need permission from the copyright holder to reproduce or use the desired material. How do you obtain this permission? What information will the copyright holder want from you? How much will it cost? How do you even find out who owns the copyright so you can ask them? Good questions, all.

Check the back of the title page (or sometimes the introduction or acknowledgments section) for the name of the copyright holder. If the holder is a publisher, locate the address in *Books in Print, The Literary Marketplace,* or one of several directories of the publishing industry. If the copyright holder is an individual, the publisher may or may not be able to broker the permissions. Be especially alert to the fact that some materials appearing in copyrighted works are quoted with permission of the original copyright holder. Many books dealing with literary topics, such as literary criticism and literary collections and anthologies, will show lengthy copyright acknowledgements. Such items are usually acknowledged in a section on the same page as the copyright information or in a foreword or introduction. If any copies include this material, separate permission must be received from the copyright holders of that additional information.

Be aware that some copyright holders will attempt to abridge your rights under fair use. Their books and periodicals have a notice on the title page (or verso) that states, in some variation on these words, "This material may not be copied for any purpose." A more wordy version of the statement might read, "Infringement occurs when any part of the publication is reproduced to be distributed to anyone, within or outside of the subscriber's organization" (Hoart, 1992). Both of the preceding statements are not in conformance with the fair use guidelines. Even if such statements are published in the book or journal, any use meeting the requirements of fair use may be copied under that exemption unless you have signed as agreement otherwise. Don't let such statements intimidate you from using such material, provided your use complies with all the fair use provisions.

In writing for permission, be sure to give a full citation of the material to be copied (author, title, edition); a description of the material to be copied (amount, page numbers, chapters); the number of copies to be made; how the material will be used; the method of distribution; charge (if any) for the materials; and the method of reproduction.

Tips: There are several points to keep in mind when requesting permissions, no matter if the request is for print, video, or any other copyrighted material.

- *Make your request far enough in advance that the copyright owner has a reasonable chance to respond. A month in advance should be sufficient, but six weeks is better for print materials. For information from the Internet, a week's notice is usually sufficient for a first-time classroom use. For non-classroom use or repeat use, consider that the owner might be on vacation and cannot respond to your electronic request right away. Allow at least a month.*

- *Be specific in your request. Don't say, "Please grant all rights to . . . ." You'll be turned down. Try to be exact: "I would like to request archival rights to XYZ videotape," or "I would like to photocopy pages 4 and 5 of your book for a workshop I will be teaching" are much more likely to receive a favorable response.*

Don't be surprised if there is a fee for the rights you request. Authors and producers make their living selling their products. By making copies, you are using their material without paying for a new copy. They may decide to charge a fee for the permission you request, and they are within their rights to do so. You are free to decline to pay for the permission, but in that case you may not use the material.

Tracking down the copyright owner to ask permission may be the major hurdle. For works created prior to 1978, most copyrighted materials have some indication of copyright ownership, though sometimes that person or company may not be easily found. For works created after January 1, 1978, all works should be considered copyrighted unless proved otherwise. Finding out who owns these copyrights may be a frustrating procedure, especially if the initial publisher has gone out of business or has merged with a company that has again merged.

Fortunately, the United States Copyright Office maintains records of registered copyrights. Those seeking copyright information can go to the office and perform their own searches through the copyright records or pay the library an hourly fee to perform searches for them. Additionally, copyright records are available online through the Library of Congress online information system at **http://www.copyright.gov/records/**. Just remember that a work need not be registered to be copyrighted. The fact that you don't find a registration in the system does not mean the work is unprotected. It may mean you should look for a work whose copyright owner is more accessible.

When writing a letter requesting permission to reproduce or use copyrighted information, keep in mind that you may be addressing this letter to the permissions department of a publishing house. This staff may have to deal with hundreds of titles. To speed your permission approval, help the staff as much as possible by being specific in your request. Include these items in your permission letter:

- *Author or editor, title, date, and edition of the material.*
- *Exact description of the material to be used or copied, including amount, page numbers, scenes or footage, chapters, any other locator information. In the case of a print work, include a photocopy of the material under consideration.*
- *The number of copies to be made.*
- *Purpose of the copies.*
- *How the material will be distributed or used (e.g., in class, closed circuit, modified for a mural, placed in a newsletter).*
- *Cost of the material charged to recipients, if any.*
- *How material will be reproduced, if copied (photocopy, ditto, photographic enlargement, archival copy, or other).*

In a work with included copyright information, you may find multiple copyright dates, and you may find a long list of acknowledgments. Any material covered in the acknowledgments section of the copyright information is covered by separate copyrights. The copyright holder of the primary work cannot grant permission to reproduce material under another's copyright. You will need to apply directly to those rights holders.

Beware of the inclination to send the request for permission to the person or firm from which you purchased the material. This tendency is especially prevalent in the case of video permissions. Distributors may have been designated by the copyright holder as agents who can grant permissions, but this is not generally the case. There are several agencies that do nothing but broker permissions. The Motion Picture Licensing Corporation and Movie Licensing USA handle many of the film and video permissions. ASCAP, BMI, and Harry Fox Agency broker an assortment of music licenses. The Copyright Clearance Center (CCC) offers several types of print permission services. CCC was established after Congress suggested a mechanism be created to facilitate compliance with print reproduction rights, as defined by the copyright law of 1976. They are the "Reproduction Rights Organization" (RRO) for the U.S. Other countries have similar organizations.

Rights holders register their works with CCC and set the royalty fees that CCC collects on their behalf. Users report and pay for their copying either through a license or each time they use a registered work.

CCC offers a number of services, several of which are useful for schools:

- *The Transactional Reporting Service (TRS) provides users with immediate authorization to make photocopies from over 1.75 million publications. By using CCC, educators do not have to make individual fee payments to publishers, but instead pay a combined fee to CCC who distributes it to copyright owners. This service would be useful for duplication of non-academic materials such as parenting resources, counseling information, and community education materials.*

- *The Academic Permissions Service (APS) enables a school to clear documents for academic coursepacks and classroom handouts. The APS provides customers with a catalog of all CCC registered titles and royalty fees. In addition, CCC will seek permission for many titles not covered by pre-authorized agreements. Permissions can be received in as little as 48 hours. This service will be useful for reproduction of documents for which fair use is not an option, such as repeated copying beyond the first term.*

- *The Electronic Course Content Service (ECCS) is similar to APS but applies to materials used in electronic format, such as online courses, electronic reserves, and electronic handouts.*

As well as offering these services, CCC has specialized services for several kinds of reproduction and distribution rights. For more information, contact the Copyright Clearance Center at **http://www.copyright.com**.

Other providers offer delivery of specialized articles. Docdel.net maintains a list of specialized document providers at **http://www.docdel.net/Full-Service_Providers.html**.

If you decide to request permission directly from the copyright owner or publisher, Figures 12.1 and 12.2 will provide a simple, fill-in-the-blanks option. It is not applicable to all situations, but it will cover most requests for print permissions.

On receipt of a permissions request such as this, publishers have three options. They can approve your request as stated. In that instance you will likely receive your letter back, stamped "approved." You might receive a letter in return, stating the terms under which the copyright holder will grant your permission. You will then be asked to sign the attached agreement and perhaps include payment of a stated fee. The last option of the rights holder is to reject your request. Remember, this is their property. They need not offer any reason for refusal.

If you receive permission to use certain material in exchange for some form of payment, and you later elect NOT to use the material, be sure to notify the agency from which you received the permission. In some instances you will be expected to pay the fee unless you notify the rights holder that the use will not take place. These rights brokers assume the use unless they are notified.

You may never hear anything at all from your request. ***No response does not equal no objection.*** There could have been any number of things that prevented the owner from responding, including the fact that they never received your request. Remember that copyright transfers, permissions, etc. must be in writing. You may hear the suggestion to word your permission request like this: "If I don't hear from you by such-and-such date, I will assume I have permission to …" Such wording is not recommended. The copyright owner is not required to respond to requests, and the lack of response should not be construed as permission.

Figure 12.1—Request for permission

Date

Permission Department

Dear Reader:

This letter is a request for permission to duplicate/use for _____

_____ *, the following:*

Title: _____

Copyright: _____

Author(s): _____

Material to be duplicated: _____

_____

_____

_____

Number of copies: _____

Manner of distribution: _____

Type of reproduction: _____

Purpose of use/reproduction: _____

A self-addressed, stamped envelope is enclosed for your convenience. Please respond and notify me of fees, if any, for this permission.

Sincerely,

Name _____

School name _____

School address _____

City _____ *State* _____ *Zip* _____

Permission granted _____

Date _____

Conditions, if any _____

_____

Figure 12.2—Sample request for permission

Date **9 September 1993**

Permission Department

Company name

Street Address

City, St, ZIP

Dear Reader:

This letter is a request for permission to duplicate/use for _____ next semester _____, the following:

Title: **Practical copyright for schools**

Copyright: **Company name, 1978, 1980, 1991**

Author(s): **J. Jones**

Material to be duplicated: **Pages 35, 36, and 37 in chapter one. See enclosed photocopies.**

Number of copies: **143 (1 per student in 5 classes)**

Manner of distribution: **There will be no charge for the materials**

Type of reproduction: **photocopy**

Purpose of use/reproduction: **Library orientation for freshman**

A self-addressed, stamped envelope is enclosed for your convenience. Please respond and notify me of fees, if any, for this permission.

Sincerely,

Name _____

School name _____

School address _____

City _____ *State* _____ *Zip* _____

Permission granted _____

Date _____

Conditions, if any _____

_____

Student and parent permissions

Publishers aren't the only ones who hold copyrights. Your students own the copyrights on their own works. Before you publish original student work, or reproduce it for a workshop or competition, or display it in a gallery, mall, Web site or other public place, you will need permission from the student or his parents. Appendix G provides an example of the type of permission a school or teacher would require to make use of student work. Displaying work in the classroom would likely not require such permission since that use involves students and teachers in the class. Public use beyond the local classroom would require specific permission.

Keep in mind that if a student is a minor, he cannot grant permission himself. Parental approval is required. Make the request for permission specific, in the manner of a request to a publisher. A parent would want to know how the child will be identified with the work, to whom the work will be displayed, and for how long. Don't request or expect blanket permission to be granted for all classroom work. While such a request is easy, it would probably be entirely too vague to be enforceable.

Works cited

Hoart, H. (1992). "Re: Copyright infringement." Letter to Report on Education Research subscribers.

ProCD, Inc. v. Zeidenberg, 86 F.3d 1447 (7th Cir. 1996).

Shepherd, C.R. (24 May 1996). Re: Sales of videotapes. Discussion on permissions required for sale of videotapes of school performances. Message posted to CNI-COPYRIGHT electronic mailing list.

Chapter 13

Managing Copyright in Schools

K nowing the rules that govern copyright is only the tip of the copyright management iceberg when one considers the difficulty of explaining to complacent faculty and administrators that they may be at risk if they continue infringing practices. The person who brings the news that long held beliefs of free use of all materials for educational purposes is not legally compliant may be met with anger, disbelief, or outright hostility.

Issues of managing copyright

The library media specialist is the most likely person in an individual school building to have had some training in copyright. Because the librarian is aware of the risks, and because the librarian sees all aspects of school practice, this professional is the one most apt to broach the subject of infringement. The librarian is also at some level of risk in infringement because much of the infringement-prone equipment is run through the library: computer networks, media distribution systems, overhead and opaque projectors, etc. tie back to the library in many cases. If the librarian might have known that this equipment was being used to violate copyright, the librarian could be named in a copyright infringement action. In a "sue 'em all" scenario, this is a common practice.

Some librarians take it upon themselves to be the "copyright police," perhaps thinking that they are protecting themselves from danger or protecting their schools from legal action. While this is a noble intent, a librarian acting alone in this capacity will probably alienate the faculty with overzealous enforcement activities. Since the librarian must maintain a collegial relationship with virtually all the faculty in order to support a school-wide information literacy program, the librarian would be better suited as a consultant in an overall copyright management program. As the instructional and administrative leader in a building, the principal is best suited to head up the copyright enforcement efforts.

The person who is most at risk in a single school situation is the administrative leader—the principal. In virtually any copyright action against a single building, the principal is most likely to be named as a party to the case. As the instructional leader, the principal is responsible for all activities that occur under his/her purview, so getting this person on board a copyright management program is essential for the building and himself.

Managing copyright in a building really begins at the district level. When districts are cited for copyright infractions, one of the first things they are required to do in reparation is to write and adopt a district copyright policy. A district policy establishes an administrative expectation of copyright compliance on the part of employees and students. Interestingly, employees seem to have more trepidation of violating district policy than they do of violating federal law. A clear, board-approved policy, with supporting staff development, can go a long way to achieving maximum copyright compliance in a district. Chapter 15 and Appendix F provide ample examples and rationale for a strong copyright policy statement. For a building level person to truly gain cooperation for a copyright compliance effort, a district level policy is the best start.

Beyond a policy, there are other issues involved in managing copyright. Both things and people require some degree of modification if a copyright compliance effort is to be successful. By working to maximize both sections of the management dilemma, the administrator, librarian, technology specialist or other copyright officer can reduce (though likely never eliminate) copyright infringements and still maintain collegial relationships.

Managing things

Managing things is a good place to begin because it is easy, and things don't complain. Having all your inanimate objects properly prepared for copyright compliance will also ease the people who must deal with the things into compliance. For those people who are new to an understanding of their obligations under copyright law, the overt and repeated notices will help remind them that each item has a copyright consideration. While the people may not like to see the notices, they are less objectionable than a nagging voice or wagging finger; they are constant; they are visible; they remove all doubts. In short, preparing all the things prepares you to prepare the people. Each type of thing has its own special management requirements.

Print: Books generally have copyright information printed on the back of the title page. Magazines will usually list copyright information on the masthead page. Making copyright control notations in the catalog record (MARC tag 540) and/or on the protective cover for each title will facilitate inquiries. Plays are controlled under the print guidelines, but the most common abuse of the copyright of plays is performance of all or part of the play to a public audience. Keep a record of any performance rights purchased with the scripts (either in the library or the department in which the play resides). Maintain these records as long as the scripts are held in the district. Poetry is also controlled by the print guidelines. Watch the back of the title page for copyright control information. Many collections combine copyright protected materials from many sources. Know who is the copyright owner of the materials you use. Images are also protected under the print and/or multimedia guidelines. Individual images usually have some notice of copyright attached to the print, or listed in the credits section if published in book form. Public display of images on Web pages is an up-and-coming problem of which to be aware.

Video/film: Video will require tracking both incoming and outgoing. Know what performance rights were purchased with the tape. Public performance rights are required for non-curricular showings. Stickers on the tapes themselves make public performance tapes easy to identify to browsers when they need a video right away for rainy day recess or a teacher who must attend a conference or leave school unexpectedly. (Purchase copyright compliance stickers from library or office supply houses, or from Sudanco — see Appendix E). Off-air video tapes made in-house should have a prominent notice stating the expiration date of off-air rights (which may vary anywhere from the standard 10/45 day period to life-of-tape rights granted by certain producers to educational users). Any off-air tapes brought in from students or teachers should have a certification of eligibility signed before use. Prepare this form in advance and have it handy.

Audio, including music: Audio requirements are similar to video. Using music as background for multimedia productions will likely be the largest demand. Playing audio in public performances such as graduations, dances, school news broadcasts, etc. may also be problematic. Providing a collection of royalty-free music clips and links to royalty-free clip sites on the Internet are ways to ease the transition to compliance.

Computer software: For software that is checked out of libraries, specific copyright notice is required. Stickers to notify borrowers of their copyright obligations are available from the suppliers listed in Appendix E. If the library is alerted that a patron plans to violate copyright, the library staff should remind the patron of the copyright responsibilities. If the patron still indicates plans to violate copyright, the loan should be refused. Home software that is installed on school computers should "live" at school. The box, documentation, license, etc. should be at the computer where the software is installed. The home is unlikely to be audited; the school is much more at risk. Retain license documents and purchase orders of all school-owned software, including operating systems. Retain the base license when software is upgraded, since often the upgrade license doesn't qualify as a base license. This is especially true for upgraded operating systems. If you owned DOS computers that were upgraded to Windows, you must have both a license for DOS and a license for the Windows upgrade. Machines that started with Windows will have a complete Windows license, not an upgrade license. There are cases reported in the press of schools audited for software copyright infringement who were caught because they couldn't produce either the base license or old purchase orders for operating systems.

Hardware: Many common pieces of AV hardware in a school are capable of being used to violate copyright. Just as unattended copy machines must have copyright notices attached to protect the host library, placing prominent notices on other machines with infringement potential is a good plan. Consider notices for computers, overhead projectors, VCRs, opaque projectors, CD burners, and cassette recorders.

Local area network resources: Networked software also requires monitoring. License tracking is available through networking software and third party products. A low-tech solution to monitoring license agreements is to use the networking software to control access to networked programs and resources. Set up network logins as the application itself (e.g. "word") and only allow these logins to access the necessary files to run the program. Set the number of simultaneous logins for that login name to the number of licenses you have for the program. You can easily control the number of people who can access a given program because the network software will not allow more people to log in to that account than you have established.

Internet: Since there are no specific guidelines for use of Internet works, interpret fair use item-by-item using the existing guidelines. Include copyright compliance in acceptable use policies, and make information about copyright part of all Internet training. Internet is a danger spot in copyright compliance because so much material is mounted on the Web in violation of copyright. Just because something is on the Web doesn't mean it is free for use, or is mounted with permission.

Managing people

Dealing with the human factor will be the largest problem of copyright compliance. Most teachers will not like a change in copyright enforcement. Some of them have been operating under the "if it's for educational use it's OK" assumption for many years. The person who tells them that their common, convenient practice is a copyright violation is apt to be met with hostility. Help them accept the change by having materials on hand to provide simple record keeping. Offer public domain or royalty-free materials to fill in for infringing uses of protected materials. A few materials with public performance rights are always useful for those stressful times like when a teacher must leave unexpectedly and an aide fills in until a substitute can arrive. Public domain materials or materials with performance rights are also useful for time fillers (waiting for the bus, rainy day recess, etc.) and reward situations (perfect attendance, achievement of academic goals, etc.). The cost of public performance rights pales in comparison to the costs of a lawsuit. Many materials come with public performance rights already. Ask vendors, or see Appendix L for a list of suppliers who offer public performance rights with their wares. Here are some tips on dealing with the human factor in copyright compliance:

Students: Students, in their short excerpts in papers and incorporation of minor images in artwork or collages, haven't been significant copyright risks for schools. New multimedia guidelines and the ability for students to publish widely on the Internet have made student use of copyright protected materials a new area of concern.

The multimedia guidelines in the U.S. require that all multimedia presentations using copyrighted materials adhere to a set of recommendations that include opening screens which notify of copyrighted content, and credit pages listing complete copyright ownership information for each item used under fair use. When students are taught this procedure from an early age, documentation can simply become part of the creative process. Since wording of notices isn't specified in the guidelines, these notices can be put in terms that even 2nd graders can understand. See Appendix E for examples.

Teachers: For many years the teacher has been able to use, without challenge, whatever materials s/he felt necessary or convenient. Disabusing the faculty of these notions is a monumental task. As the instructional leader of a building, the building administrator needs to take a leadership role in guiding the faculty to a new understanding of their obligations regarding copyright. This guidance can be as simple as a directive, "We will abide by all laws that affect our work." A better approach is to encourage faculty to move toward copyright compliance, with the administration taking extra pains to ensure that they model the behaviors they expect from the faculty.

One technique that has worked well for many schools on the road to copyright compliance is to clear all video with the principal. This process, while painful to some, is likely to bring copyright to the forefront of discussion. One elementary school, after a vivid copyright workshop, chose to enforce appropriate use of video as their first step toward copyright compliance. All video shown in classrooms had to be pre-approved by the principal to verify legitimate tie-in to the curriculum of the grade level and subject. At the end of the first school year of compliance, the librarian reported that video usage had declined by 75%! Incidentally, test scores also rose in that building that year, though there had been no changes in curriculum or methodology. While no attempt was made to tie the rise in test scores to the reduction of non-compliant video, consider that if one tallied up all the entertainment and reward video shown in school, and applied that time to curricular instruction, how much content might be covered?

Staff: Most staff involvement with copyrighted material will be in photocopying. With the support of the administration, training the clerical staff on copyright of print material will likely be sufficient to raise awareness of what can and should be copied. Encourage record keeping, especially for multiple copies for classroom use.

Administrators: Getting the attention of the administrator is key to copyright compliance in a school building. Bringing to their attention materials on copyright settlements in neighboring school districts, and those publicized by copyright compliance groups like AIME and SIIA, can go a long way to opening the eyes of a reluctant administrator. Knowing that the building-level administrator is likely to be named in any copyright infringement action can also get an administrator's attention. As the instructional leader in the school, the building level administrator is expected to be aware of all educational uses of materials within his/her purview. Some of the suggestions below, plus those in chapter 14, will help focus the administrator on the severity of the problem in a given building.

Important recommendations in copyright management

Here are some suggestions to get started in a school that is less than enthusiastic about copyright compliance, and which seems bent on shooting the messenger:

- *Suggest to the principal that you track requests in one area for a grading period. A good place to start is with video use. Prepare a report to the administration to see the extent of the problem in this area. Remind them that there are many other areas with similar or potentially worse reports. Another option for tracking is to obtain a copy of the free trial program WRQ Express Inventory, SPA Edition from the Software and Information Industry Association and conduct a software audit of up to 100 building computers. Seeing the results in black and white can sometimes generate significant response.*

- *Prepare a copyright notification slip that will inform teachers and others that a particular use of material (fill in the blank) is likely a copyright infringement. Make the wording helpful and informative, not accusatory. Give copies to the principal.*

- *Encourage, request, insist on a copyright policy for your building and district. Board approved policy gives you a firm footing when trying to raise the standard of copyright compliance.*

- *Educate, educate, educate. Consult with teachers as they plan units, help students document use of other's materials in their work, help administrators consider copyright implications in non-curricular applications. Remember that plagiarism and copyright violation are totally separate and generally unrelated issues.*

Chapter 14

Copyright and Administrators

Whether in charge of a building or district, the school administrator may unexpectedly become embroiled in a legal tangle over the copy machine or the videocassette recorder. While student performance should be the focus, the unwary administrator's attention may have to be diverted to deciphering abstruse details of copyright law. Even worse, administrators who are unprepared may find themselves and their organizations the subject of expensive litigation, costly even if the school is exonerated.

We are in an era characterized by lawsuit. One lawyer, when asked who should be named in a particularly confusing case, is said to have remarked, "Sue 'em all!" Unfortunately, this is often the mindset in copyright litigation. An administrator who is unaware of, or simply chooses to ignore, copyright violations may suddenly find a cease and desist letter on his or her desk. These letters from attorneys are written in a demanding fashion; violations are spelled out, penalties enumerated, and few options are proposed.

Without the backing of a school board policy or building procedures supporting copyright, an administrator is likely to have little maneuvering room when the ominous letter arrives. Most school district attorneys are better prepared to deal with civil rights charges than those involving intellectual property. In fact, most details of the day-to-day operation of a building or district are much more pressing than considering the woes of authors and copyright owners. But the fact remains that an administrator who knowingly or unknowingly allows copyright infringement to occur is likely to be named among the defendants in any legal action.

And the district will pay for his carelessness. Penalties can be stiff. Fines begin at $750 per infringement and rise to $30,000. For "innocent infringers" (those who infringe, but had no reason to think they were infringing), fines are not less than $200. If the infringement is considered willful, penalties can be imposed up to $150,000 per violation per day. In the case of computer software infringements, penalties can be as high as $250,000, and the offense may be considered a felony! Criminal status was added to certain video recordings and distributions in 2005. The administrator need not actually participate in the infringement to be considered responsible, at least in part, for the violation. Some recent court cases may suggest that districts might be found immune to judgment under the 11th amendment (sovereign immunity) but individual administrators and teachers are not extended this protection.

The truth is that most copyright suits are settled out of court. Only a few well-publicized cases have made the trek through the courts to establish the precedents upon which current practice is based. Even when an infringement action is settled out of court, much time is spent, considerable stress is borne, and much money encumbered to resolve the conflict. Copyright watchdog groups use these settled claims as spoils of war to advertise their victories over infringers.

Once the cease and desist letter arrives on the administrator's desk, the die is cast. The best plan is to try to minimize losses because, like it or not, the lawyers usually have the goods; the infringements have most likely occurred.

So how can an administrator minimize exposure to copyright litigation? As with most endeavors, plan, plan, plan. The first and most important step is to have a comprehensive copyright policy. If the district has no policy in place, the building chief should establish a building policy. Such a policy should demand adherence to copyright law and establish a system of checks to ensure the law is followed. It also helps if the administration supports the efforts of the librarian in copyright compliance. Tracking and interpreting the many layers of copyright is no mean feat.

Faculties accustomed to free rein in plucking the fruits of authors' and artists' labors will howl that they are being hamstrung. They will moan that they can't conduct their classes without unrestricted access to the many resources they used in the past. They will most likely blame the messenger for the disturbing news.

Your building librarian is probably the only person on staff who had some level of copyright training while in a preparation program. The professional librarian attempts to balance the needs of teachers and students while staying within the legal requirements. The librarian should not be thrust alone into the role of "copyright police," however. If building and district policy is to abide by the law, the librarian should not be judge and jury in the procedure.

But the librarian must stand fast, and the administration must provide moral and procedural support. Apologies aren't necessary. As educators, we want to model responsible citizenship to our students. Among the behaviors we endorse is adherence to the laws of the city, state, and country. Copyright is federal law. We would certainly advocate paying income taxes, no matter how much we would wish they were no more. Well, copyright laws may be just as confusing, and we may wish that they allowed as many loopholes as the IRS, but we should still accept them as legal and binding.

Once a policy is in place to endorse adherence to copyright, someone will need to be available to explain the implications to teachers who may have long ignored the requirements of the law, either from unfamiliarity with the regulations or intentional oversight. The building librarian is the most likely person to be charged with this task. During their professional training, most librarians have acquired at least a smattering of information about copyright. The library literature is dotted with articles concerned with copyright and day-to-day library practice. Also, the library is the source of most of the materials and equipment involved in potential copyright problems. The librarian must have unqualified and open support in monitoring copyright compliance. After all, the object is to keep the entire school community out of trouble! The librarian must not be allowed to become the "bad guy" or the "fall guy" in matters of copyright.

Unequivocal policies supported vigorously by administrators and the board are essential. It is important that the administrator take a firm stance with staff regarding copyright; expectations should be conveyed to them in no uncertain terms. Educational and informative sessions should be planned to inform the staff annually of their obligations under federal law and district (or building) policy.

Administrators must be ready to counter the "But-we've-always-done-this!" argument. They should establish clear procedures for compliance, especially in the areas of photocopying, computer software, and use of audiovisuals. Documentation of compliance is essential, too, so a "paper trail" will exist in case of challenge. Establish a cooperative and collegial atmosphere. Nurture an atmosphere in which one teacher can freely say to another, "I'm not sure that use is within copyright law. Let's get an impartial opinion."

Administrative support for individual creative efforts of staff will encourage them to create, instead of borrow, intellectual property. Additional suggestions from the viewpoint of a building principal may be found in the article "Read my lips: Copyright" by Robin Pennock in the June 1991 issue of *School Library Journal.*

If building principal or district supervisor is in doubt about the need for administrative involvement and support, a computer software audit may be the one act that will demonstrate the need for copyright compliance. A software audit will give the administrator a list of every computer program installed on every computer in a district or building. Once equipped with the list, the school should document ownership of legal copies of every software program and operating system on the list. Why bother? Because this is exactly what will be required of the school should a representative of a computer software firm appear at the door with a search warrant and federal marshals in tow. A similar exercise could be done with videotapes.

Monitoring compliance is not something the librarian can do alone or without support. Encourage the librarian to bring issues of copyright to the administrative office. Request teachers document use of video with concrete tie-ins to lesson plans and district curriculum. Don't fall for ruses. Demand hard evidence. Is a showing of *The Lion King* really an appropriate curricular video for a unit on mammals? Encourage alternative rewards beyond passive television viewing. Look on the bright side: Copyright compliance can result in better, more creative teaching. Failing to monitor compliance is like leaving the keys in the ignition of a new Corvette with the doors unlocked. You shouldn't be surprised when something unpleasant happens.

Suggestions for administrators

- *Model copyright compliance. Request permission before photocopying copyrighted materials for your faculty. (There is limited fair use for copying for staff, anyway.) Mark the copies as "Reprinted with permission from . . . ."*

- *Be aware of video use in your building. How much video is used? Is it all directly related to instruction? Is it appropriate? Teachers never have enough instructional time. Can students afford to spend an hour and a half watching an entertainment video?*

- *Request teachers document each video performance in their lesson plans. There should be a close correlation between the video and the current lesson and district or state curriculum.*

- *Insist that teachers clear all video use through your office. Develop a form that identifies the teacher, the video, the length of clip being shown, and the purpose of the showing. Teachers are less likely to use time-wasting video if they feel the administrator is aware of what is being shown.*

- *Know your curriculum. If fourth grade studies volcanoes, why is the third grade teacher showing a video on them?*

- *Watch extracurricular activities. The fair use exemption permits limited use of copyrighted materials in classroom situations. That exemption does not permit free use of copyrighted materials for student council dances, cheerleading posters, or video yearbooks.*

- *Look around your building. What type of decorations do you see? Are they bought from school suppliers, original materials created by teachers, or are they copied from greeting cards, cartoons, movie characters, and the like?*

- *Enlist the assistance of those staff members most likely to be aware of copyright violations in the building. Teacher aides know what types of materials are being photocopied. Librarians know what video is being shown and what multimedia is being appropriated. They can assist you with record keeping, but they shouldn't be put into the role of copyright police.*

- *Help teachers find creative, non-video ways to reward students. Reward videos are public performances and require payment of royalties or written exemption from the copyright holder. Games such as checkers, chess, Password,™ and Scrabble™ develop higher order thinking skills that pay off on standardized tests.*

- *Keep accurate purchase records for audiovisual materials and computer software. These records should be retained as long as the materials are in use. The records may be needed if there should ever be a question of legality.*

- *Purchase a performance license for your building to show some non-instructional videos for rewards or as quick fill-ins when events get rained out or teachers are tied up in conferences. Don't use the license as an excuse not to teach.*

- *Assist staff in their efforts to stay copyright compliant. Make sure there are enough copies of computer software (or appropriate licenses) to cover each machine that will use the software. Budget for record-keeping supplies, compliance reminder stickers for equipment, and sufficient consumables.*

- *Keep an upbeat attitude. Long-held habits die hard. Encourage efforts to stay compliant. Commiserate with those who complain that their favorite items are no longer permitted. Look on the bright side: You'll see how creative your teachers can be.*

- *Remember that a good faith effort and an honest accounting can go a long way when someone does slip up. Everyone makes occasional mistakes. Learn from them and go on.*

Chapter 15

Copyright Policies

C opyright policies are the skeleton that keeps your copyright compliance program together. A carefully worded, but not verbose, copyright policy states the expectation of the organization that the law be understood, obeyed and enforced.

Why have one?

Why bother to have a copyright policy? A devil's advocate would say that there is no need for a policy. Why state the obvious? There is no policy requiring compliance with the local building code, is there? It's just common sense. One complies with the building code because it is the law. Doesn't one also comply with copyright because it is the law? Everyone obeys copyright; there's no need for a policy. Besides, who's going to catch a violator?

Well, our devil's advocate is oversimplifying. Do police departments expect all motorists to observe the speed limit because it is the law? Hardly. That's why they purchase and use radar units. Publishers and media producers are of a similar opinion. They know people will attempt to violate their rights under copyright, and they exercise various means to discover and prosecute the offenders. And while an occasional inadvertent slip might be overlooked, widespread or systematic infringement is likely to bring a hailstorm of litigation.

The purpose of a copyright policy is to state the institution's intention to abide by the law. AIME (Association for Information Media and Equipment), the copyright watchdog group, boasts of its successes in redressing copyright infringement. While most of the cases are settled out of court, AIME publishes many of the settlements in its periodic newsletters. The majority of the settlements involve the establishment of an institutional policy regarding copyright as well as comprehensive training and plans for tracking and monitoring copyright compliance. Agreements to discharge key employees or place official letters of reprimand in personnel files are sometimes included in the out-of-court settlements.

Having an institutional copyright compliance policy is one way to beat the producers to the punch. AIME makes a good case with the following statement:

> "AIME takes the position that a copyright policy is important for an educational entity to develop. It helps to avoid confusion on the part of the staff and administrators and takes a definitive position on the importance of knowing the law and obeying it. A copyright policy also has the potential to insulate the agency or institution and administrators from liability if an infringement action were to be instituted because of activities by individuals contrary to the policy and against the law" (Dohra, n.d.).

Q: Our school administration is reconsidering our copyright policy to include electronic formats and Web sites. What should we include?

A: If your current policy is a good one, it will not need updating. The policy shouldn't be medium-specific. It should state that employees will follow the current federal law, and it should outline the consequences for disobeying. If your policy is appropriately written, changes in the law will be covered automatically. However, you will need to train your staff on changes in the law and on the impact of copyright on new technologies.

What should a policy contain?

AIME produces a packet of information on developing an institutional copyright policy. Included in the packet is a small booklet titled *A viewer's guide to copyright law: What every school, college and public library should know.* The primary author of this booklet is Ivan Bender, an attorney specializing in copyright issues. The booklet has an excellent section on development of copyright policy.

Appendix F is an example of a district-wide copyright policy adopted in 1993. Several points in the policy are worth noting:

1. *The policy states the institution's intention to abide by the letter and spirit of the copyright law and the associated Congressional guidelines.*

2. *The policy covers all types of materials including print, nonprint, graphics, and computer software.*

3. *The liability for noncompliance with copyright rests with the individual using the work.*

4. *The district mandates training for all personnel who might need to make copies.*

5. *The person using the materials must be able to produce, on request, copyright justification for its use.*

6. *The district appoints a copyright officer who serves as a point of contact for copyright information both within and without the district. That person will likely track licenses, serve as the registered copyright agent for the school's Web site and will oversee training of all students and teachers in copyright compliance.*

Some authorities recommend additional measures be included in a policy, such as requiring the district to develop a copyright manual for all employees, requiring notices be affixed to all copy-capable equipment, and even reprinting the entire law and guidelines (Vleck, 1987, p. 10; AIME, 1987, p. 7).

Regardless of the wording of the policy, simply having a policy that states institutional intent to obey the law will provide some small measure of protection. However, the more the faculty and staff know about copyright and the management of copyrighted materials, the better protected the organization and the employees are from threat of suit. If an infringement were to occur, the administration that has undertaken a thorough copyright education program could present a credible case that they did not condone the activity and that they had taken vigorous action to prevent infringement. The infringing employee, though, would have a poor chance of claiming "innocent infringement," a defense for infringers who claim they had no knowledge they were infringing, because the institution would have records of staff development in correct application of copyright principles.

A further measure to protect the institution from individual acts of infringement is to have employees sign a statement indicating they have been informed of copyright laws and guidelines and that they will abide by both the institutional policy and the applicable laws. (See Appendix A.) This is similar to the OSHA requirement that employees be informed of hazards of chemicals in the work place. Frequently employees are required to view a training tape or attend a staff development session on a topic for which they are "signed off." Such record-keeping indemnifies the organization from claims of negligence in informing the employees of potential hazards. Copyright infringement is certainly hazardous for both the individual employee and the organization, and having employees sign a compliance agreement or sign in at a staff development session on copyright at the beginning of the school year is not an unbearable burden when tracked at the building level.

The most efficient way to develop a copyright policy is to search out examples of model policies. AIME provides multiple examples of acceptable policies in its copyright policy development kit. A custom-developed copyright policy can be quickly assembled by cutting and pasting the best parts of the samples. Administrators, librarians, television and media people should all have a say in the final wording. Bringing in an outside expert may be the best way to persuade doubters who believe a comprehensive policy isn't necessary. The final draft of the policy should go to the district's legal counsel for approval, because collective bargaining agreements and teacher contracts may affect wording of policies. A spokesperson should be prepared to appear before the board to underscore the importance of the policy and explain the risk of leaving copyright compliance to individual employees. And a plan should be in place to train employees and monitor compliance in libraries, classrooms, and offices.

Works cited

Association for Information Media and Equipment. (1987). *A viewer's guide to copyright law: what every school, college, and public library should know.* Elkader, IA: AIME.

Dohra, A. (n.d.). Copyright information packet. Elkader, IA: AIME.

Vleck, C.W. (1987). *Copyright policy development: a resource book for educators.* Friday Harbor, WA: Copyright Information Services.

Chapter 16

Appendices

Appendix A

Copyright compliance agreement

Middletown School District

Copyright Compliance Agreement

I have been informed of the appropriate uses of instructional media, fair use guidelines, and the copyright compliance policy of the Middletown School District. I, the undersigned, acknowledge that I understand these policies and guidelines and that any uses I may make of instructional materials or audiovisual equipment in a classroom setting will be in accordance with both federal law and said policies and guidelines.

_____

Teacher

_____

Date

_____

Campus

Appendix B

Copyright do's and don'ts for schools

DO make sure that all audiovisual material shown to students is directly related to the curriculum. Be especially aware of film ratings (G, PG, R).

DON'T show films or videos for reinforcement or reward. Encourage teachers to try popcorn and soda parties, games, stickers, or free time. You may rent movies for such performances, paying a minimal public performance fee, from suppliers such as Movie Licensing USA. Video rental stores cannot authorize you to give public performances, nor can you use any copy identified as HOME USE ONLY.

DO ask your faculty to sign a copyright compliance agreement.

DON'T loan VCRs or DVD-Rs with patch cords or dual deck units. Watch for questionable situations: why would a teacher need two recorders except to copy programs?

DO write the record date on all videos you record.

DO write the required erase date on all videos you record. This date will vary with the program. See advertisement of program, flyer from producer, or calculate fair use date.

DON'T copy commercial computer software, except to make an archival (one that isn't used) copy.

DON'T copy cartoon or TV or film characters for decorations, bulletin boards, or handouts. Purchasing clip art, duplicator books, and bulletin board figures is acceptable, but you may not enlarge, modify, or change the medium (e.g., make slides or coloring sheets).

DO keep receipts and purchase orders for all media and computer software. Keep the catalog (or pertinent pages) to verify purchase of public performance rights.

DO require teachers to verify recording date and source for all home-recorded videos. Fair use guidelines say that programs must be used for classroom instruction within 10 days of taping. After that date, the recording may only be used for evaluation for possible purchase. Erase after 45 days.

DO write for permission to retain recordings of useful programs. The worst a copyright holder can do is say no.

DON'T record programs off cable without investigating the recording rights first. Only programs recorded off the air (VHF and UHF channels) can be recorded without express permission. Look for this permission in teacher's guides that the various networks and program producers send out. These guides will also tell you the retention rights (e.g., seven days plus fair use; one year; life of tape/disc). Keep a photocopy of the permission with the recording at all times, and make sure there is a copyright notice on each copy.

DO post a copyright notice on VCRs, DVD-Rs, scanners, computers, overhead projectors, and opaque projectors similar to that on your photocopy machine.

DON'T record a program because you know a teacher will ask for it later. Requests to record programs must come from a teacher in advance and in writing. Also, requests to record programs must come from the "bottom up," i.e., your teachers can ask you to record programs, but your principal may not.

DO remember that the person who pushes the button is also liable. So is the principal who knows copyright is being violated. Notify in writing both the principal and teacher when you are aware of copyright infringement. Keep a copy in your own file.

DO keep a copy of Kidsnet or Access Learning to verify taping rights from the various networks. Kidsnet also lists supporting materials and addresses where inexpensive copies of non-recordable programs can be obtained. Both Kidsnet and Access Learning have online counterparts.

DO encourage teachers to use fast forward. Often only a portion of a video will make as effective a point as an entire film. Also, some producers will allow use of "excerpts" when they will not allow use of an entire program. Write for permission. As of 2005, clearplay DVDs will meet this need.

DON'T create anthologies on tape, disc, or the photocopier. Copying an article, poem, or excerpt is fine, but combining them into a "new work" is not permitted.

DON'T apologize for obeying federal law. If you would like a free copy of the law, visit the Copyright Office Web site for a copy of Circular 92.

Copyright for kids

When you work very hard on a project, you are very proud of yourself. You want your teacher, your classmates and your parents to appreciate the hard work you put into your project. You don't like it when someone takes your work without your permission. It isn't fair. It isn't nice. It isn't OK. It's stealing.

When an author writes a book, or an artist paints a painting, or a photographer creates a photograph, they are also proud of their work. Not only do they want people to appreciate their work, they want to be paid for it. Writing and creating pictures are their jobs, and selling their writing, or painting, or photographs is how they are paid. An author or artist owns a right to decide how their works will be used. This right is called "copyright" and it is part of the laws of the United States. When someone takes the work of an author, an artist, or a photographer without permission, the author, artist or photographer doesn't get paid. It isn't fair. It isn't nice. It isn't OK. It's stealing.

Students must read the works of authors, and look at paintings and photographs in books. They must often use small bits of information from books and pictures to do their schoolwork. Authors and artists understand this. An exception in the law, called "fair use," says that students can use these small pieces in certain ways if the student tells whose work it really is. If you don't tell whose work it is, you are pretending the work is your own. This pretending is called "plagiarism," and it is just like cheating. It's not fair. It's not nice. It isn't OK. It's stealing.

So, how can students use the works of authors and artists to complete schoolwork without breaking the law? Here are some tips:

- Always say where you got the information you use. Tell the author, the book, and the page number.

- Use as little information as you possibly can and still make the same point.

- Don't change the author's words or the artist's pictures without permission.

- Don't make copies of the schoolwork you have that uses materials from other sources.

- Don't forget that everything you write or create is yours to decide how it should be used, except for the parts you borrowed from others.

- If you make a presentation on the computer, there are very clear rules to tell you how much of someone else's work you may use.

- Ask nicely for permission to use more of someone's work. A polite request is often granted.

Appendix D

Useful sources of information

AIME (Association for Information Media and Equipment)
P.O. Box 1173
Clarksdale, MS 38614
601-624-9355
http://www.aime.org

American Society of Composers, Authors & Publishers (ASCAP)
One Lincoln Plaza
New York, NY 10023
212-621-6000
e-mail: info@ascap.com
http://www.ascap.com

Association of American Publishers
71 Fifth Avenue
New York, NY 10003
212-255-0200
http://www.publishers.org/

Bell & Howell Information and Learning
300 N. Zeeb Road
P.O. Box 1346
Ann Arbor, MI 48016-1345
800-521-0600
e-mail: info@umi.com
http://www.umi.com

Broadcast Music, Inc. (BMI)
320 W. 57th Street
New York, NY 10019
212-586-2000
http://www.bmi.com

Business Software Alliance
1150 18th Street, N.W. Suite 700
Washington, D.C. 20036
202-872-5500
http://www.bsa.org

Cable in the Classroom Magazine
1800 N. Beauregard Street, Suite 100
Alexandria, VA 22311
800-743-5355
http://www.ciconline.com/

Cancopy
1 Yonge Street, Suite 1900
Toronto, ON
M5E 1E5
800-893-5777
http://www.cancopy.com/

Copyright Clearance Center
222 Rosewood Drive
Danvers, MA 01923
978-750-8400
http://www.copyright.com

CSS Music (royalty free music)
1948 Riverside Dr.
Los Angeles, CA 90039
(800) HOT-MUSIC
www.cssmusic.com

Discovery Channel School
P.O. Box 970
Oxon Hill, MD 20750-0970
800-321-1832
http://school.discovery.com

Docdel.net (Links to document delivery services)
http://www.docdel.net/Full-Service_Providers.html

Films for the Humanities & Sciences (source of copyright-cleared sound effects)
PO Box 2053
Princeton, NJ
800-257-5126
www.films.com

FTC Publishing Group (source of multimedia sound files)
P.O. Box 1361
Bloomington, IL 61702-1361
888-237-6740
www.ftcpublishing.com

Freemusic4video (Narrator Tracks Music Library)
4701 Industrial Park Road - Suite A
Stevens Point, WI 54481
800-448-6467
www.freemusic4video.com

Fresh Music (royalty free music)
888-211-8576
www.freshmusic.com

Harry Fox Agency (mechanical rights for music)
711 Third Avenue
New York, NY 10017
212-370-5330
http://www.nmpa.org/

Kidsnet
6856 Eastern Avenue N.W., Suite 208
Washington, DC 20012
202-291-1400
202-882-7315 FAX
http://www.kidsnet.org

Kit Parker Films (rental for public performance)
P.O. Box 16022
Monterey, CA 93942-6022
800-538-5838
http://www.kitparker.com

Motion Picture Association of America
15503 Ventura Blvd.
Encino, CA 91436
818-995-6600
http://www.mpaa.org/

Motion Picture Licensing Corporation
5455 Centinela Avenue
Los Angeles, CA 90066-6970
800-462-8855
http://www.mplc.com/

Movie Licensing USA
201 S. Jefferson Ave.
Saint Louis, MO 63103-9954
877-321-1300
http://www.movlic.com/

Music Publishers Association of the U.S.
PMB 246
1562 First Avenue
New York, NY 10028
http://www.mpa.org/

National Music Publishers Association
711 Third Avenue
New York, NY 10017
212-370-5330
http://www.nmpa.org

National Writer's Union
National Office East
113 University Pl. 6th Fl.
New York, NY 10003
212-254-0279
Fax:(212) 254-0673
http://www.nwu.org/

Public Domain Report
P.O. Box 3102
Margate, NJ 08402
800-827-9401
www.pubdomain.com

Punchstock
8517 Excelsior Dr. Ste 200
Madison, WI 53717
800-390-0461
www.punchstock.com

Showpoppers! (royalty free video)
1948 Riverside Dr.
Los Angeles, CA 90039
800-468-6874
www.showpoppers.com

Software and Information Industry Association
1730 M Street, N.W.
Washington, DC 20036
202-452-1600
http://www.siia.net
This group also provides a software inventory management package in either PC or Macintosh formats.

Soundzabound Music Library
PO Box 492199
Atlanta, GA 30349-2199
888-834-1792
www.soundzabound.com

Swank Motion Pictures, Inc

350 Vanderbilt Motor Parkway, Suite 203

Hauppauge, New York 11787-4305

800-876-5577

http://www.swank.com/

United States Copyright Office

Library of Congress

Washington, DC 20559

202-479-0700

202-707-9100 (to order forms and circulars)

Main Web site—**http://www.copyright.gov/**

Circular 1, Copyright basics—**http://www.copyright.gov/circs/circ1.html**

Circular 21, Reproduction of copyrighted works by librarians and educators—

http://www.copyright.gov/circs/circ21.pdf

Copyright law, complete text—**http://www.copyright.gov/title17/**

Appendix E

Copyright warning notices

All interlibrary loan request forms must include the following notice (Code of Federal Regulations, Title 37, Section 201.14). It must be printed within a prominent box on the actual order form. The notice may be on the front of the form, or adjacent to the section requiring the patron's signature. The notice cannot be in type any smaller than that used throughout the form, and in no case may it be smaller than 8-point type. The notice must be clearly apparent, legible, and comprehensible to even a casual viewer of the form. Standard ALA ILL forms available from library supply houses comply with this requirement.

The same notice must be displayed at the place where ILL orders are taken. Such notice must be printed on heavy paper, in type no less than 18 points in size. It must be placed so as to be clearly visible, legible, and comprehensible near the place where ILL orders are accepted.

NOTICE WARNING CONCERNING COPYRIGHT RESTRICTIONS

The copyright law of the United States (Title 17, United States Code) governs the making of photocopies or other reproductions of copyrighted material.

Under certain conditions specified in the law, libraries and archives are authorized to furnish a photocopy or other reproduction. One of these specific conditions is that the photocopy or reproduction is not to be "used for any purpose other than private study, scholarship, or research." If a user makes a request for, or later uses, a photocopy or reproduction for purposes in excess of "fair use," that user may be liable for copyright infringement.

This institution reserves the right to refuse to accept a copying order if, in its judgment, fulfillment of the order would involve violation of copyright law.

Photocopies made by libraries, both for interlibrary loan and for patrons, should be marked with a copy if all information from the original copyright notice, or the copyright page copied and included with the item. If an item has no copyright notice, a notice of possible copyright restrictions must be added. While specific wording isn't detailed in the law, many libraries use wording similar to the following:

NOTICE: This material may be protected by Copyright Law (Title 17 U.S. Code).

The multimedia guidelines specify that a notice must be on the opening slide (not necessarily the title slide) of a work that incorporates copyright protected materials. The wording is not specified in the guidelines though the content of the notice is described. Adults may use a notice similar to this:

WARNING: The following presentation uses copyright protected materials used under the Multimedia guidelines and fair use exemptions of U.S. Copyright law. Further use is prohibited.

Young students must also have a compliant notice on their presentations. A notice that a young student might be able to understand, yet still meeting the intent of the guidelines, would be:

WARNING: I used other people's stuff to make my project. I followed the rules. Please don't copy it.

Software circulated by nonprofit libraries must have the following notice "durably attached" to each package:

Stickers and forms with these notices can be purchased from:

Demco
www.demco.com

Gaylord
www.gaylord.com

Highsmith
www.highsmith.com

Sudanco, Inc.
www.sudanco.com

Appendix F

Sample copyright policy

It is the intent of the XYZ School District, its board of trustees, staff and students, to adhere to the provisions of current copyright laws and Congressional guidelines. Employees and students are to adhere to all provisions of Title 17 of the United States Code, entitled "Copyrights," and other relative federal legislation and guidelines related to the duplication, retention, and use of copyrighted materials.

Specifically:

○ Unlawful copies of copyrighted materials may not be produced on district-owned equipment.

○ Unlawful copies of copyrighted material may not be used with district-owned equipment, within district-owned facilities, or at district-sponsored functions.

○ The legal and insurance protection of the district will not be extended to employees who intentionally and unlawfully copy and use copyrighted materials.

○ Employees who make copies and/or use copyrighted materials in their jobs are expected to be familiar with published provisions regarding fair use and public display, and are further expected to be able to provide their supervisor, upon request, the justification under sections 107 or 110 of USC 17 for materials that have been used or copied.

○ Employees who use copyrighted materials that do not fall within fair use or public display guidelines will be able to substantiate that the materials meet the following tests:

1. The materials have been purchased from an authorized vendor by the individual or the district and a record of the purchase exists.

2. The materials are copies covered by a licensing agreement between the copyright owner and the district or the individual employee, OR;

3. The materials are being previewed or demonstrated by the user to reach a decision about future purchase or licensing and a valid agreement exists that allows for such use.

4. The District will appoint an officer to assist employees in fulfilling their obligations under U.S. Copyright law, and who will maintain records of licenses and permissions.

Appendix G

Release form

MIDDLETOWN SCHOOL DISTRICT PUBLICATION RELEASE FORM

I, the undersigned, having full authority to execute this Release on behalf of myself and on behalf of

_____ _____(child's name) of

_____ (school name) hereby grant permission to

MIDDLETOWN SCHOOL DISTRICT (hereinafter called "MSD") to use the following materials

provided by me or on my child's behalf to MSD, for the purposes identified below:

My or my child's: (initial where appropriate) _____Name _____ Voice _____Likeness

_____ Quotes _____ Papers, articles, poems, or other written material as specified:

_____

_____

_____ Graphics, photographs, or other artwork as specified:

_____

_____

I warrant and represent that the materials submitted under this agreement are owned by and/or are

original to me or my child, and/or I have full authority from the owner of said materials to permit

MSD to use said materials in the manner described below: _____ Newspapers, magazines, other

print publications _____ Television or radio _____ Internet or computer network _____

Presentation for teaching, staff development, or professional conference _____ Retention and use

as exemplars _____ Public display or performance.

I understand that MSD is and shall be the exclusive owner of any and all right, title, and interest,

including copyright, to any and all materials into which the aforementioned items are incorporated,

except as to my preexisting rights in any of the items herein released.

Date: _____

Signature: _____

Name/Relationship: _____

Address: _____

_____

Telephone: _____

Appendix H

Copyright and plagiarism guidelines for students

1. You may make a single photocopy of any material you need to do your schoolwork, or for your own personal research. You may keep the copies you make as long as you like, but you may not sell them, nor may you make copies of your copies.

2. You must respect the copyright of the materials you use. Only the creators, or the persons or companies who own the copyright may make copies of the material, except as noted above. You may not modify or change the material, nor may you perform or display the material except in conjunction with class work.

3. You may use copyrighted material to do your schoolwork, but if you use an author's ideas you must give the author credit, either in the text or in a footnote. If you use an author's words, you must put the words in quotation marks or other indication of direct quotation. Failure to give credit to the author is plagiarism. If you use an extensive amount of a single work, you must obtain permission.

4. Use of copyrighted materials outside of regular class work requires written permission of the copyright holder. This includes graphic material such as cartoon characters on posters or other spirit or decorative matter.

5. You may not copy computer software from the school computers.

6. Information received from the school computers may be used only for regular schoolwork or personal research.

7. The source of any information used in your school work should be acknowledged in the format prescribed by the teacher. Use of another's intellectual work without attribution is plagiarism, as outlined in the Student Code of Conduct.

Appendix I

Significant copyright law section references

(All references are to U.S. Code title 17.)

Moral Rights: 17 United States Code, Section 106-106(a)1

Fair use: 17 United States Code, Section 107

Library copying: 17 United States Code, Section 108

First sale doctrine: 17 United States Code, Section 109(a)

Circulation of computer software: 17 United States Code, Section 109(b)(1)(A) ff

Public display of lawful copies: 17 United States Code, Section 109(c)

Face-to-face teaching exceptions: 17 United States Code, Section 110(1)

Distance learning performances: 17 United States Code, Section 110(2)

Digital audio performances: 17 United States Code, Section 114(d) – (j)

Computer software requirements: 17 United States Code, Section 117

Architectural works: 17 United States Code, Section 120

Special exceptions for the blind and physically disabled: 17 United States Code, Section 121

Duration of copyright: 17 United States Code, Section 302

Certain exemptions for librarians and educators: 17 United States Code, Section 504 (c)

No Electronic Theft: 17 United States Code, Section 506

OSP liability: 17 United States Code, Section 512

Technological protections: 17 United States Code, Section 1201-1205

Appendix J

Bibliography of selected works on copyright

A&M Records, Inc. v. Napster, Inc., 284 F.3d 1091 (C.A.9 (Cal.),2002)

Althouse, J. (1997). *Copyright: the complete guide for music educators.* (2d ed.). Van Nuys, CA: Alfred.

American Library Association. (1982). *Model policy concerning college and university photocopying for classroom research and library reserve use.* Chicago: ALA.

American Library Association. (2004). *Fair use and electronic reserves.* Chicago: ALA. Retrieved January 4, 2005 from http://www.ala.org/ala/washoff/WOissues/copyrightb/fairuseandelectronicreserves/ereservesFU.htm.

American Library Association. (2004). *Guidelines and Procedures for Telefacsimile and Electronic Delivery of Interlibrary Loan Requests and Materials.* Retrieved January 5, 2005 from http://www.ala.org/ala/rusa/rusaprotools/referenceguide/guidelinesprocedures.htm.

American Library Association. (2002). *Video and copyright.* Retrieved January 5, 2005 from http://www.ala.org/Template.cfm?Section=libraryfactsheet&Template=/ContentManagement/ContentDisplay.cfm&ContentID=24635.

Association of Research Libraries. (2002). *Copyright timeline.* Retrieved January 5, 2005 from http://arl.cni.org/info/frn/copy/timeline.html.

Association for Information Media and Equipment. (1990). *Press release.* Elkader, IA: AIME.

Association for Information Media and Equipment. (1987). *A viewer's guide to copyright law what every school, college, and public library should know.* Elkader, IA: AIME.

Band, Jonathan. (2001). *The Digital Millennium Copyright Act. Washington, DC: Association of Research Libraries.* Retrieved June 19, 2004 from http://www.arl.org/info/frn/copy/band.html.

Blair, Julie. (1998). *Pirated software could prove costly to L.A. District. Education Week.* Retrieved June 14, 2004 from http://www.edweek.org/ew/vol-17/43soft.h17.

Barlow, J.P. (1994). *The economy of ideas.* Retrieved January 3, 2005 from http://www.wired.com/wired/archive/2.03/economy.ideas.html.

Bender, I. (1996, Summer). *The Internet—It's not free and never was.* AIME News.

Berman, D. (13 May 1993). *Re: Questionable videotapes. Discussion on liability in the use of copyrighted videotapes.* Message posted to CNI-COPYRIGHT electronic mailing list.

Bielefield, A. & Cheeseman, L. (1999). *Interpreting and negotiating licensing agreements: A guidebook for the library, research, and teaching professions.* New York: Neal-Schuman.

Bielefield, A. & Cheeseman, L. (1997). *Technology and Copyright Law: A Guidebook for the Library, Research and Teaching Professions.* New York: Neal-Schuman.

Bridgeport Music v. Dimension Films, 383 F.3d 390 (6th Cir. 2004).

Business Software Alliance. (24 February 1999). *Five Southern California Organizations Settle Software Copyright Claims.* Retrieved January 5, 2004 from http://www.bsa.org/usa/press/newsreleases/Five-Southern-California-Organizations-Settle-Software-Copyright-Claims.cfm.

Columbia Pictures Industries v. Redd Horne, 749 F.2d 154 (3rd Cir. 1984).

Copyright Office. (1998). Circular R21: *Reproduction of copyrighted works by educators and librarians.* Washington, D.C.: Library of Congress.

Copyright Office. (1999). *Fair Use.* Retrieved on January 7, 2005 from http://www.copyright.gov/fls/fl102.html.

Crews, K. (1998). *Indiana University Online Copyright Tutorial.* Bloomington, Ind: University of Indiana.

Crews, K.D. (2000). *Copyright essentials for librarians and educators.* Chicago: ALA.

Dohra, A. (n.d.). *Copyright information packet.* Elkader, IA, AIME.

Dukelow, R.H. (1992). *The library copyright guide.* Washington, D.C.: Copyright Information Services, Association for Educational Communications & Technology.

Education Software Management: A K-12 Guide to Legal Software Use. (1994). Washington, DC: Software and Information Industry Association.

Eldred v. Ashcroft, 537 U.S. 186 (2003).

Electronic Frontier Foundation. 2004. *How not to get sued by the RIAA for file-sharing.* Retrieved December 30, 2004 from http://www.eff.org/IP/P2P/howto-notgetsued.php

Electronic Privacy Information Center. (2004). *EPIC Archive – Privacy.* Retrieved August 3, 2004 from http://www.epic.org/privacy/.

Ensign, D.J. (1992, Winter). *Fax—a special case: implications of copyright law for facsimile document delivery.* The Bookmark, 50, 125-8.

Family Entertainment and Copyright Act of 2005, Pub. L. No. 109-9, (effective April 27, 2005).

Fishman, S. (2000). *The copyright handbook.* 5th ed. Berkeley, CA: Nolo.

Gasaway, L.N. (2002). *Copyright considerations for electronic reserves. In Managing electronic reserves.* Chicago: ALA. Retrieved January 5, 2004 from http://www.ala.org/ala/ourassociation/publishing/alaeditions/samplers/rosedale_er.pdf.

Goldstein, P. (1998). *Copyright.* (2nd ed.). New York: Aspen Law & Business.

Hoart, H. (1992). Re: *Copyright infringement.* Letter to Report on Education Research subscribers.

Hoffman, G.M. (2001). *Copyright in cyberspace: questions and answers for librarians.* NY: Neal-Schuman.

Hoffman, I. (2002). *The visual artists rights act.* Retrieved June 18, 2004 from http://www.ivanhoffman.com/vara.html.

Individuals with Disabilities Education Improvement Act of 2004, Pub. L. No. 108-446, 118 Stat 2647 (2005).

I.T. Vibe. (1 May 2004). *RIAA sue another 477 music sharers.* Retrieved January 8, 2005 from http://itvibe.com/news/2501/.

Jackson, M.E. (1991). *Library to library: copyright and ILL.* Wilson Library Bulletin. 66(2), 84-7.

Jassin, L.J. & Schechter, S.C. (1998). *The copyright permission and libel handbook.* New York, John Wiley.

Jensen, M.B. (1992, Winter). *I'm not my brother's keeper: Why libraries shouldn't worry too much about what patrons do with library materials at home.* The Bookmark, 50, 150-4.

Kelly v. Arriba Soft Corp., 280 F.3d 937 (9th Cir. 2002).

Kruppenbacher, F. (14 June 1993). Re: CC and copyright. Discussion on the addition of closed captioning to commercial videotapes. Message posted to CNI-COPYRIGHT electronic mailing list. Legal Information Institute. (2004). *LII: Law About ... Trademark.* Retrieved August 3, 2004 from http://www.law.cornell.edu/topics/trademark.html.

Legal Issues & Education Technology: A School Leader's Guide. (1999). Alexandria, VA: National School Boards Association.

Litman, J. (2001). *Digital copyright.* Amherst, NY: Prometheus.

Lutzker, Arnold. (1999). *Memorandum.* Retrieved June 18, 2004 from http://www.arl.org/info/frn/copy/notice.html.

Marshall, P.G. (21 May 1993). Software piracy. *CQ Researcher.* Retrieved April 30, 2005.

Music Publisher's Association. (2004). *Making a Record: Do I Have To Obtain a Mechanical License?* Retrieved on January 8, 2005 from http://www.mpa.org/copyright/you.html#record.

Nimmer, M.B. & Nimmer, D. (1999). *Nimmer on Copyright.* New York: Matthew Bender & Co.

Office of General Counsel, University of Texas System. (2001, November 12). *Fair use guidelines for electronic reserve systems.* Retrieved January 4, 2005 from http://www.utsystem.edu/OGC/IntellectualProperty/rsrvguid.htm.

Office of General Counsel, University of Texas System. (2003, January 30). *Copyright in the library: reserve electronic copies.* Retrieved January 3, 2005 from http://www.utsystem.edu/OGC/IntellectualProperty/l-resele.htm.

Office of General Counsel, University of Texas System. (2004, December 22). *CONFU: the Conference on Fair Use.* Retrieved January 4, 2005 from http://www.utsystem.edu/OGC/IntellectualProperty/confu.htm.

Official fair-use guidelines: complete texts of four official documents arranged for use by educators. (4th ed.). (1985, 1987). Friday Harbor, WA: Copyright Information Services.

Recording Industry Association of America. (2003). *Downloading and uploading.* Retrieved December 30, 2004 from http://www.riaa.com/issues/music/downup.asp.

Recording Industry Association of America. (2002). *RIAA Releases Mid-Year Snapshot of Music Industry.* Retrieved January 7, 2005 from http://www.riaa.com/news/newsletter/082602.asp.

Reed, M.H. (1989). *Videotapes: copyright and licensing considerations for schools and libraries.* Syracuse, NY: ERIC Clearinghouse on Information Resources. (ERIC Document Reproduction Service No. ED 308 855).

Schneider, B. (1992, December). *Practice safe multimedia: wear a copyright. Newmedia.*

Shepherd, C.R. (24 May 1996). Re: Sales of videotapes. Discussion on permissions required for sale of videotapes of school performances. Message posted to CNI-COPYRIGHT electronic mailing list.

Sinofsky, E. (14 June 1993). Re: Closed-caption videotape conversion. Discussion on the addition of closed captioning to commercial videotapes. Message posted to CNI-COPYRIGHT electronic mailing list.

Sivin, J.P. & Bialo, E.R. (1992). *Ethical use of information technologies in education: important issues for America's schools.* Washington, DC: U.S. Department of Justice.

Software and Information Industry Association. (2005). *Educational Copyright Resources.* [online] http://siia.com/piracy/pubs/EducationalCopyright.pdf [accessed 1-3-05].

Stanek, D.J. (1986, March). *"Videotapes, computer programs, and the library,"* Information technology and libraries.

Stim, R. (2000). *Getting permission: How to license & clear copyrighted materials online & off.* Berkeley, CA: Nolo Press.

Talab, R.S. (1999). *Commonsense copyright: a guide for educators and librarians.* Jefferson, NC: McFarland.

UCLA Online Institute for Cyberspace Law and Policy. (2001). *The Digital Millennium Copyright Act.* Retrieved June 18, 2004 from http://www.gseis.ucla.edu/iclp/dmca1.htm.

UCLA Online Institute for Cyberspace Law and Policy. (1998). *The 'No Electronic Theft' Act.* Retrieved June 18, 2004 from http://www.gseis.ucla.edu/iclp/hr2265.html.

United States Department of Justice. (1997). *Criminal Resource Manual 1844 Copyright Law—Preemption of State Law.* Retrieved August 3, 2004 from http://www.usdoj.gov/usao/eousa/foia_reading_room/usam/title9/crm01844.htm.

United States Department of Justice. (1998). *The 'No Electronic Theft' Act.* Retrieved June 18, 2004 from http://www.cybercrime.gov/netsum.htm.

Vleck, C.W. (1987). *Copyright policy development: a resource book for educators.* Friday Harbor, WA: Copyright Information Services.

Appendix K

Important Internet links for copyright information

Agreement on Guidelines for Classroom Copying in Not-For-Profit Educational Institutions with Respect to Books and Periodicals
http://www.musiclibraryassoc.org/Copyright/guidebks.htm

American Library Association. Copyright and fair use.
http://www.ala.org/ala/alcts/divisiongroups/ig/nrm/copyrightfair.htm

Association for Instructional Media and Equipment
http://www.aime.org/

Brad Templeton's "Ten Big Myths about Copyright Explained"
http://www.templetons.com/brad/copymyths.html

Complying with the Digital Millennium Copyright Act
http://www.utsystem.edu/OGC/IntellectualProperty/dmcaisp.htm

Copyright for educators.
http://falcon.jmu.edu/~ramseyil/copy.htm

Copyright for music librarians.
http://www.lib.jmu.edu/org/mla/

Copyright resources for schools and libraries. Wisconsin Dept. of Public Instruction.
http://www.dpi.state.wi.us/dpi/dltcl/lbstat/copyres.html

Copyright Implementation Manual, Groton, CT, Public Schools
http://www.groton.k12.ct.us/mts/cimhp01.htm

Copyright Law in Cyberspace.
http://www.utsystem.edu/OGC/IntellectualProperty/distance.htm

Copyright Notices for Supervised Library Copying: Updated Information for Library Services
http://www.copyright.iupui.edu/supercopying.htm

Copyright Office. Online Service Providers
http://www.copyright.gov/onlinesp/

Copyright timeline
http://arl.cni.org/info/frn/copy/timeline.html

Copyright Web site
http://www.benedict.com

Copyright workshop—Copyright with Cyberbee
http://www.cyberbee.com/copyrt.html

Designation of Copyright Agent, Library of Congress
http://www.copyright.gov/onlinesp/

Fair Use Guidelines For Educational Multimedia
http://www.utsystem.edu/ogc/intellectualproperty/ccmcguid.htm

Guidelines for Educational Uses of Music
http://www.musiclibraryassoc.org/Copyright/guidemus.htm

Guidelines for Off-Air Recordings of Broadcast Programming for Educational Purposes
  http://www.musiclibraryassoc.org/Copyright/guiderec.htm

Information for Today
  http://www.ift.merit.edu

Library and Classroom Use of Copyrighted Videotapes and Computer Software
  http://www.ifla.org/documents/infopol/copyright/ala-1.txt

MARC record guidelines for copyright management information
  http://lcweb.loc.gov/marc/bibliographic/ecbdnot2.html#mrcb540

PBS Teacher Source
  http://www.pbs.org/teachersource/copyright/copyright.shtm

PDInfo – Public domain music
  http://www.pdinfo.com/

Performance Rights for Copyrighted Videorecordings
  http://www.dpi.state.wi.us/dpi/dltcl/lbstat/coplicen.html

Public Domain Report
  http://pubdomain.com

Report on Copyright and Digital Distance Education (U.S. Copyright Office)
  http://www.copyright.gov/disted

Sample off-air videotape label
  http://www.pbs.org/teachersource/copyright/copyright_sample_label.shtm

Stanford University. Copyright and Fair Use Web site
  http://fairuse.stanford.edu/

SupportNet Online – Copyright and fair use
  http://supportnet.merit.edu/webclubs/copyright.html

University of Texas System Crash Course on Copyright
  http://www.utsystem.edu/ogc/intellectualproperty/cprtindx.htm

Use of Music on a Multimedia Web site
  http://www.ivanhoffman.com/music.html

Using Software: A Guide to the Ethical and Legal Use of Software for Members of the Academic Community
  http://www.ifla.org/documents/infopol/copyright/educom.txt

A visit to Copyright Bay
  http://www.stfrancis.edu/cid/copyrightbay/

World Book and Copyright Day – UNESCO
  www.unesco.org/culture/bookday/

Appendix L

Sources of audiovisual works with public performance rights

Source: courses.unt.edu/csimpson/cright/ppr.htm

NOTE: Not all films sold by these producers and distributors may have public performance rights, but all listed companies sell some materials with public performance rights. Some sell the same materials with and without such rights. Order carefully and note price differentials.

actiVision (including Dr. Lee Salk's Super Sitters)
857 W. Webster Ave.
Chicago, IL 60614
773-404-0030
www.activision.com/en_US/home/home.jsp

Agency for Instructional Technology
Box A
1800 North Stonelake Drive
Bloomington, IN 47402-0120
800-457-4509
www.ait.net

AIMS Multimedia (see Discovery Education)
9710 DeSoto Avenue
Chatsworth, CA 91311
800-367-2467
www.aimsmultimedia.com

Allied Video
P. O. Box 702618
Tulsa, OK 74170
800-926-5892
www.allieddvd.com/

Ambrose Video Publishing, Inc.
28 West 44th Street Suite 1115
New York, NY 10036
800-526-4663
www.ambrosevideo.com/

Annenberg/CPB
401 9th Street, NW
Washington, DC 20004-2036
202-879-9648
www.learner.org/

ArtMattan Productions
535 Cathedral Parkway
Suite 14B
New York, NY 10025
www.africanfilm.com

Attainment Company
PO Box 930160
Verona, WI 53593-0160
800-327-4269
www.attainmentcompany.com/

BFA (See Phoenix Films)

Bullfrog Films (all titles except "home video versions")
P.O. Box 149
Oley, PA 19547
800-543-3764
www.bullfrogfilms.com

California Newsreel
149 Ninth Street
San Francisco, CA 94103
415-621-6196
www.newsreel.org

Cambridge Documentary Films, Inc.
P.O. Box 390385
Cambridge, MA 02139-0004
617-484-3993
www.cambridgedocumentaryfilms.org

Cambridge Educational
P.O. Box 931
Monmouth Junction, NJ 08852-0931
888-744-0100
www.cambridgeeducational.com

Carousel Film & Video
250 Fifth Ave., Ste. 204
New York, NY 10001
212-683-1660
www.carouselfilms.com

Chip Taylor Communications (discount, no-rights versions available)
2 East View Drive
Derry, NH 03038
800-876-CHIP (2447)
www.chiptaylor.com/index.htm

Choices Video (see World Almanac Education)

Churchill Films (see Clearvue/EAV)

The Cinema Guild
130 Madison Avenue, 2nd Floor
New York, NY 10019-7038
800-723-5522
www.cinemaguild.com

Classroom Video
4739 University Way, NE, Suite 1606
Seattle, WA 98105
800-665-4121
www.classroomvideo.com

CLEARVUE/eav
6465 North Avondale Avenue
Chicago, Illinois. 60631-1996
800-253-2788
www.clearvue.com/index.html

Contemporary Drama Service (see Meriweather Publishing, Ltd.)
www.contemporarydrama.com

Coronet (see Phoenix Films)

Crystal Productions
800-255-8629
www.crystalproductions.com

CVLI
800-462-8855
For licensing churches for public performances of entertainment video
http://www.cvli.org/cvli/index.cfm

Design Video Communications (See First Light Video)

Discovery Educational
www.discoveryed.com

Disney Educational Productions (see Web site for specific limitations)
3800 W. Alameda Avenue, 16th Floor
Burbank, CA 91505
818-569-5991
http://dep.disney.go.com/educational/index

DK (Dorling Kindersley) Publishing, Inc.
95 Madison Avenue
New York, NY 10016
212-213-4800
www.dk.com

Educational Video Network, Inc.
1401 19th St.
Huntsville, TX 77340
800-762-0060
www.evndirect.com

Ergo Video (for additional fee)
PO Box 2037
Teaneck NJ 07666
201-692-0404
www.jewishvideo.com

Fanlight Productions
196 Washington St, Suite 2
Boston, MA 02131
800-937-4113
www.fanlight.com/

Films for the Humanities and Sciences
PO Box 2053
Princeton, NJ 08543-2053
800-257-5126
www.films.com

Filmwest Associates
300 West Second St.
Carson City, NV 89703
775-883-8090
www.filmwest.com

First Light Video (for non-revenue uses)
2321 Abbot Kinney Blvd.
Venice, CA 90291
800-262-8862
www.firstlightvideo.com/

First Run/Icarus Films
32 Court Street, 21st Floor
Brooklyn, NY 11201
718-488-8900
www.frif.com/

Forest Glen TV Productions (for non-revenue uses in schools and colleges)
P.O. Box 101823
Fort Worth, Texas 76185-1823
817-920-9662
texashistory.com

Goldhil Home Video
137 East Thousand Oaks Blvd. Suite 207
Thousand Oaks, CA 91360
800-250-8760
www.goldhil.com/

GPN (Reading Rainbow and others)
P.O. Box 80669
Lincoln, NE 68501-0669
800-228-4630
gpn.unl.edu/rainbow/
* Note: only for titles bought directly from the producer. Reading Rainbow titles bought from
jobbers do not include public performance rights.

Guidance Associates
100 South Bedford Road, Suite 120
Mount Kisco, NY 10549
800-431-1242
www.guidanceassociates.com

Home Vison (see Public Media)

Icarus Films (see First Run Features)

Insight Media (limited titles)
2162 Broadway
New York, NY 10024-0621
800-233-9910
www.insight-media.com/public_html/IMPage_Main.asp

Instructional Video (all except those marked HUO "home use only")
2219 C Street
Lincoln, NE 68502
800.228.0164
www.insvideo.com/

International Historic Films, Inc. (most titles)
P.O. Box 29035
Chicago, IL 60629 USA
773-927-2900
ihffilm.com/info.html

ITS

P.O. Box 1290

State College, PA 16804

814-359-2410

www.its.itmonline.com

January Productions

210 Sixth Avenue

Hawthorne, NJ 07507

Keep America Beautiful

1010 Washington Boulevard

Stamford, CT 06901

203-323-8987, ext. 19

www.kab.org

Knowledge Unlimited

P.O. Box 52 (800) 356-2303

Madison, WI 53701

608-836-6660

http://thekustore.com/

Landmark Media

3450 Shade Run Dr.

Falls Church, VA 22042

800-342-4226

www.landmarkmedia.com

Learning Seed

330 Telser Road

Lake Zurich, IL 60047

800-634-4941

www.learningseed.com/

Library Video Company (Schlessinger Media video titles only)

7 E. Wynnewood Road

Wynnewood, PA 19096

800-843-3620

www.libraryvideo.com

Library Video Network

320 York Road

Towson, MD 21204

800-441-TAPE

www.lvn.org

Live Oak Media
P.O. Box 652
Pine Plains, NY 12567
800-788-1121
www.liveoakmedia.com

Live Wire Media
273 Ninth St.
San Francisco, CA 94103
800-359-5437
www.livewiremedia.com/

Lucerne Media
37 Ground Pine Road
Morris Plains, NJ 07950
800-341-2293
www.lucernemedia.com

Maypole Studios
18 Bartlett Square
Boston, MA 02130
877-622-5226
www.maypoles.com/mporderformz.htm

Media for the Arts (limited titles)
360 Thames Street, Suite 2N
Newport, Rhode Island 02840
800-554-6008
art-history.com/

Meriwether Publishing, Ltd.
Box 7710
Colorado Springs CO 80933
719-594-4422
www.meriwetherpublishing.com

Motion Picture Licensing Corp.
800-462-8855
For licensing non-public schools, daycare centers, YMCAs, etc.
www.mplc.com

Movie Licensing USA
201 South Jefferson Avenue
St. Louis, MO 63103-2579
877-321-1300
www.movlic.com
For licensing public schools, public libraries, etc.

National Film Board of Canada
350 Fifth Avenue, Suite 4820
New York, NY 10118
800-542-2164
www.nfb.ca
Watch for differing prices on some titles

National Geographic Educational
School Publishing
P.O. Box 10597
Des Moines, IA 50340-0597
800-368-2728
www.nationalgeographic.com/education/
* Note: only for titles bought directly from the producer. National Geographic titles bought from
  jobbers do not include public performance rights.

New Dimension Media
680 North Lake Shore Dr, Suite 900
Chicago, IL 60611
800-288-4456
www.ndmquestar.com

New Day Films
22-D Hollywood Avenue
Hohokus NJ 07423 USA
888-367-9154
www.newday.com

Noodlehead Network
107 Intervale Ave.
Burlington, VT 05401
800-639-5680
www.noodlehead.com/

Partridge Films (see Survival Anglia)

PBS Video (all lines except PBS Home Video)
1320 Braddock Place
Alexandria, VA 22314
800-344-3337
www.pbs.org
* Note: only for titles bought directly from the producer. PBS titles bought from jobbers do not
  include public performance rights.

Phoenix Learning Group (including Phoenix, BFA and Coronet) (most products)
2349 Chaffee Drive
St. Louis, MO 63146
800-221-1274
www.phoenixlearninggroup.com

Princeton Book Company
P.O. Box 831
Hightstown, New Jersey 08520-0831
www.dancehorizons.com/

Pyramid Media, Inc
P.O.Box 1048
Santa Monica, CA 90406
800-421-2304
www.pyramidmedia.com

Questar, Inc.
680 N. Lake Shore Dr., Ste 900
Chicago, IL 60611
312-397-2156
www.questar1.com

Revels, Inc. (videos only)
Department R
80 Mount Auburn Street
Watertown, Massachusetts 02472-3930
617-972-8300
www.revels.org/revels_nationwide/starting_a_revels.htm

Rich-Heape Films, Inc. (limited titles)
5952 Royal Lane, Suite 254-4
Dallas, Texas 75230
888-600-2922
www.richheape.com/

RMi Media Productions
1365 North Winchester Street
Olathe, KS 66061
800-745-5480
www.rmimedia.com/

Schlessinger Media (see Library Video Company)

Scholastic, Inc. (all titles except those marked "Home Use Only")
555 Broadway
New York, NY 10012-3999
800-724-6527
www.scholastic.com

Shopware, Inc.
P.O. Box 921
Monmouth Junction, NJ 08852-0921
304-744-9323
www.shopware-usa.com

Spoken Arts
195 South White Rock Road
Holmes, New York 12531
800-326-4090
www.spokenartsmedia.com

SuperSitters (See actiVision)

Survival Anglia, Ltd. (for a fee, on a very limited basis)
Anglia House
Norwich
Norfolk England NR1 3JG
01603 615151
www.angliatv.co.uk

SVE & Churchill Media
6677 North Northwest Highway
Chicago, IL 60631
800-829-1900
www.svemedia.com

Swank, Inc.
201 S. Jefferson Avenue
St. Louis, Missouri 63103-2579
800-876-5577
www.swank.com
Licensing for individual showings of movies by a limited list of producers, including Disney.

Thinking allowed
2560 9th Street, Suite 123
Berkeley CA 94710
800/999-4415
www.thinkingallowed.com

TMW (Tell Me Why) Media Group (for non-revenue uses)
2321 Abbot Kinney Blvd
Venice, CA 90291
800-262-8862
www.tmwmedia.com/

United Learning (Altschul Group)
1560 Sherman Avenue, Suite 100
Evanston, Illinois 60201
800-323-9084
www.unitedlearning.com

United Wildlife (see Survival Anglia)
University of California Extension
Center for Media and Independent Learning
2000 Center Street, Fourth Floor
Berkeley, CA 94704-1223
510-642-0460
www-cmil.unex.berkeley.edu/media/

Video Aided Instruction
485-34 South Broadway
Hicksville, NY 11801-5071
800-238-1512
www.videoaidedinstruction.com

The Video Project
200 Estates Dr.
Ben Lomond, CA 95005
800-4-PLANET
www.videoproject.org

VisionQuest Video (see TMW Video Group)

Weston Woods (all titles except those marked "Home use only")
143 Main St.
Norwalk, CT 06851
800-243-5020
www.scholastic.com/westonwoods

World Almanac Education
369 S. Doheny Drive
PMB #1105
Beverly Hills, CA 90211
310-358-0885
www.wae.cc/

Appendix M

Database of copyright actions against schools

Available at http://www.school-library.org, Copyright Resources link

Appendix N

Copyright questions and answers: a reproducible brochure.

The following brochure is designed to be reproduced at 115% onto 2 sides of standard 8 1/2" x 11" paper and tri-folded. Reproduction for a single school building is permitted as long as copyright management information remains intact. For reproduction beyond a single building, please contact Linworth Publishing for fees.

Copyright for Educators Responsibilities

cop•y•right \‐,rīt \ n (1735): The exclusive right to reproduce, publish, and sell the matter and form of a literary, musical, or artistic work.

PRINT

What can I copy?

A single copy of a chapter from a book, a newspaper or magazine article, a short story, short essay, or short poem, or a single chart, graph, diagram, drawing, cartoon or picture from a book, periodical, or newspaper may be made for personal or research use, or for use in teaching a class.

Multiple copies for classroom use?

Yes, but copy length is limited: you may copy a whole poem only if it is under 250 words (or a 250 word excerpt from a longer poem); a whole article, story or essay only if it is less than 2500 words (or an excerpt if it is less than 1000 words or 10% of a work, whichever is less); a single chart, graph, diagram, drawing, cartoon, or picture per book or magazine; and only two pages of a picture book (as long as the two pages don't contain more than 10% of the total text of the book).

How many copies may I make?

You may make a single copy of the items listed above if the copy is for personal use, research, or to teach a class. For multiple copies for classroom use you can make only enough copies for each pupil enrolled in the course, i.e., no "extra" copies. You may not copy more than one entire item (or two excerpts) from a single author, or three articles from a single book or periodical volume during one class term (semester or year, depending on the course). You can not have more than nine instances of multiple copying per course during a class term.

AUDIOVISUAL

How can I use a radio or television program in class?

You may record a program as it is broadcast by a local radio or television station; you may, within ten school days of recording the program, use it once with each class for instructional purposes and once again for reinforcement. From the 11th day through the 45th calendar day after the broadcast, it may be used only for evaluation purposes; after that period of time, the recording must be erased unless permission (from the copyright holder) to keep it has been obtained.

Copies of the recording may be made to meet the needs of other teachers, but all copies share the same time restrictions as the original. Unless specific permission is granted (such as with National Geographic specials and some Project Discovery programs) you may not use recordings made from cable-only television channels. See Access Learning magazine for permissions.

I have a VHS video; it would be easier to use on DVD. Can I have it transferred?

To make a copy of an audiovisual work other than one recorded under the off-air taping guidelines (above) requires permission of the copyright holder. Works that are in an obsolete format may be transferred to other formats if that work is not available for sale in an updated format, but to be considered "obsolete" the equipment to play the medium must not be available for purchase at a reasonable price. VHS machines are still available, so you would need permission to make this transfer.

We have a video program that was very expensive to purchase and I'm worried that it might be destroyed by accident. Since it's OK to make a backup of computer software, isn't it OK to make a backup copy of a tape or DVD?

No. In order to make a backup copy of a video program, you must have purchased "archival rights" from the copyright holder or receive written permission prior to making the copy.

May I show rented tapes in class?

Yes—if you rent a tape that applies to your instructional needs and use it in "face-to-face" instruction, and the showing occurs in a classroom or other instructional place, and only teachers and students in the class view the showing. In such a situation, the showing would fall under the AV Fair Use Guidelines.

No—if the tape is to be shown as a reward, enrichment, or entertainment, it cannot be used. Rental stores do not ordinarily purchase the public performance rights required for a reward or entertainment showing to a public group (a class constitutes a public group and therefore doesn't qualify for a Fair Use exemption without meeting the AV guideline requirements.) Many libraries purchase or receive public performance rights, but you should ask.

I wish to remove an objectionable scene from a movie I plan to show. May I edit the scene out?

You aren't required to show an entire video, but you may not edit the program. If you wish to skip the objectionable scene, you can fast forward past it.

Administrative note:

Always use discretion in showing rented videos in your classroom, making certain that you choose only those that are appropriate. Check the ratings regarding language, sex, violence, nudity and morality and if in doubt, don't show it.

Ⓒ

This brochure was reprinted from
Copyright for Schools: A Practical Guide, 4th edition,
by Carol Simpson,
Linworth Publishing, ©2005.

When and how may I use the copies?

You, the teacher, must make the decision to make the copies. (Your principal or supervisor is not allowed to tell you to make copies of copyrighted material.) You must decide to make the copies so close to the time you would need them in class that writing for permission would be unreasonable. (Two weeks would be a reasonable time.) You can only copy the item for one course (all your English I classes, for example.) Each item copied must have a notice of copyright.

This sounds hard! Why don't you just tell me what I can't copy?

You can never copy, in any form, items intended to be consumable. That includes workbook pages, standardized tests, coloring books, answer sheets, test booklets, etc. You also can't make so many different copies that you are, in effect, creating your own textbook. Copying cannot take the place of books, publisher's reprints or magazine subscriptions. You can't charge students for copying above the actual cost of the copies. And **you can't copy the same materials from semester to semester.** In other words, if you copied it last semester, you can't copy it again without getting permission from the copyright owner.

COMPUTER SOFTWARE

What can I copy?

Nothing…. Without the express written permission from the copyright holder. The one exception to this rule is if you have purchased a copy of the software, you may make one backup copy of the original diskettes. This backup copy is only for emergency purposes and it may never be used unless the original copy is somehow destroyed or lost. The software may be copied onto the hard drive of a computer in order to run the program, but it is against the law to maintain simultaneous copies in different hard drives.

How many copies may I make?

Same as above. You may have only one backup copy of a computer program. Unless you have a license or other permission, you may not copy a computer program onto another computer. This includes loading a program into more than one computer by using one diskette intended for a single user.

Computer manuals and documentation are covered in the same manner as computer programs. You **may not** make multiple copies of computer documentation for classes. Copying a computer program intended for a single user onto a network is the same as making multiple copies of the program. It's a no-no. A network license if required to load a computer program onto a network, despite the fact that the program may, indeed, work in a network environment. So don't do it.

How long can I keep it?

As long as you own the program, you may keep a copy of a computer program on your hard drive and a backup copy in addition to the original diskettes or CD. If you should lose the copy on the hard drive, you may reload the program from the original or backup disks. If you sell or transfer the program to another person, you must transfer all diskettes and documentation to the new owner, and you must remove all copies of the program from your computer's hard drive and memory.

When and how may I use it?

Use of a computer program is usually governed by a license agreement, so it depends… some licenses say you may freely make copies, other say you must pay a fee to use the software, or to install the software onto multiple machines. This is a contractual agreement and it supercedes the copyright restrictions.

You **may not** decompile a program and use program instructions in new programs. You may not defeat any form of copy protection built into the program. You **may not** use a single user version of software on a network. You **may not** install a program on more than one computer at a time without express, written permission from the copyright owner. This means that you cannot install the program on your computer at home and your computer at school unless you own two copies of the program or have permission to do so from the copyright owner or the software license. Depending on the program, you may also be limited in what you can do with the output of the program. Some educational licenses restrict what you can do with computer output, or mark the output as educational material. You may not defeat these copy restrictions.

MUSIC

What can I copy?

You may make emergency copies of music for an immediate performance, provided replacement copies have been ordered.

You may copy excerpts (not to exceed 10% of a work) provided they do not constitute a performable unit, and provided you make no more than one copy per student.

You may make a single recording of a copyrighted performance by students for evaluation purposes; it may be retained, but copies of it may not be made.

I have an old record. May I copy it to cassette and use that instead?

If the format of the record is obsolete (78 rpm, for example) and no other version is available, you may transfer the recording to a usable format. If the format is still available (33 1/3 rpm or 45 rpm) the transfer would require permission of the copyright holder. An exception would allow a teacher to make a single copy for the purpose of auditory exercises or examinations. The single copy made for such use may be retained by the teacher.

My students are preparing a presentation for class and want to use parts of popular songs. Is this permissible?

If the presentation is created with multimedia software, the students may use up to 30 seconds of a popular song. If the presentation is anything other than multimedia, such use falls into a gray area. Use by students is permitted if the students instigate the performance themselves (i.e., the students must decide on their own to use a specific song; the teacher may determine the suitability of the material, but may not tell the students to use a specific song.) The music students use should be played from legitimately purchased or borrowed recordings, or recorded off the air.

Appendix O

Copyright infringement reporting form

Copyright Infringement Reporting Form

Middletown School District

MSD has the legal responsibility to abide by copyright laws. Employees of the District shall comply with all provisions of United States Copyright Law. Board Policies outline the District's copyright policy.

Name of Person(s) Allegedly Violating Copyright Laws

_____

_____

_____

Campus _____

Date of Infringement _____

Describe exactly what happened. Be sure to include what items were infringed, where it happened, and how many times it happened. _____

_____

_____

_____

_____

_____

_____

_____

_____

Person making report (optional)_____

Please return this form to the District Copyright Officer

Index

E